THE
GREAT
movie
COMEDIANS

By Leonard Maltin

TV MOVIES
MOVIE COMEDY TEAMS
BEHIND THE CAMERA: THE CINEMATOGRAPHER'S ART
(reissued as The Cinematographer's Art)
THE GREAT MOVIE SHORTS
THE DISNEY FILMS
CAROLE LOMBARD
OUR GANG: THE LIFE AND TIMES OF THE LITTLE RASCALS (with Richard W. Bann)
OF MICE AND MAGIC: A HISTORY OF AMERICAN ANIMATED CARTOONS
THE COMPLETE GUIDE TO HOME VIDEO (with Allan Greenfield)

THE GREAT MOVIE COMEDIANS

Updated Edition
from charlie chaplin to woody allen

BY LEONARD MALTIN

BELL PUBLISHING COMPANY
NEW YORK

© 1978, 1982 by Leonard Maltin

*Published by Bell Publishing Company, distributed by Crown Publishers,
Inc., One Park Avenue, New York, New York 10016.*

Published simultaneously in Canada by General Publishing Company Limited

Library of Congress Cataloging in Publication Data

Maltin, Leonard.
    The great movie comedians—updated edition.

    Includes filmographies and index.
    1. Moving-picture actors and actresses—United
States—Biography. 2. Comedians—United States—
Biography. 3. Comedy films—Catalogs. I. Title.
PN1998.A2M274 1982   791.43′028′0922 [B]   81-6999
ISBN: 0-517-361841   AACR2

H G F E D C B A

BELL EDITION 1982

BOOK DESIGN: SHARI DE MISKEY

Photograph credits and acknowledgments: Columbia Pictures, Samuel
Goldwyn Productions, Metro-Goldwyn-Mayer, Paramount Pictures, Hal
Roach Studios, RKO Radio Pictures, Twentieth Century-Fox, United Artists,
Universal Pictures, Warner Brothers, CBS Television, American-
International Pictures, Cinerama Releasing Corporation, Independent-
International Pictures, Time-Life Films, Academy of Motion Picture
Arts and Sciences, Eddie Brandt's *Saturday Matinee, Movie Star News,*
Museum of Modern Art Film/Stills Archive; with special thanks to
Eddie Brandt, Carol Carey, Mary Corliss, Bob Epstein, Doug McClelland,
Adam Reilly, Sam Sherman, and Jerry Vermilye

CONTENTS

INTRODUCTION

"Through humor, we see in what seems rational, the irrational; in what seems important, the unimportant. It also heightens our sense of survival and preserves our sanity."

—CHARLES CHAPLIN

"A friend once asked me what comedy was. That floored me. What is comedy? I don't know. Does anybody? Can you define it? All I know is that I learned how to get laughs, and that's all I know about it. You have to learn what people will laugh at, then proceed accordingly."

—STAN LAUREL

"In order to laugh at something, it is necessary 1) to know what you are laughing at, 2) to know why *you are laughing, 3) to ask some people why* they *think you are laughing, 4) to jot down a few notes, 5) to laugh. Even then, the thing may not be cleared up for days."*

—ROBERT BENCHLEY

If comedy were a science, it could be explained and defined much more easily. But it is not a science, and the gag is not a mathematical formula. Creating comedy involves instinct as much as anything else, and those who possess that instinct are endowed with a rare and precious gift.

I came to appreciate this more than ever in 1976 when I was given the privilege of presiding over an eight-month Bicentennial Salute to American Film Comedy at the Museum of Modern Art in New York City. Selecting, locating, and writing program notes for some 450 films gave me a unique

Chester Conklin and Ben Turpin revive the Keystone spirit in a
1939 feature film, *Hollywood Cavalcade.*

opportunity to become immersed in the world of comedy for nearly a year.
That experience inspired me to collect my thoughts on some leading comedy
practitioners for this book.

It also caused me to think more seriously about the comedians I admired
and to reach an understanding of why they achieved such lasting success while
others faded away.

I think one answer is uniqueness. Each of the performers in this book
developed an individual style and personality. Others tried to copy them, but
most of the imitators failed, because there was a basic dishonesty in their work.

Most of the comedians who succeeded *deserved* to succeed. They brought
to their performances an inner spark that reached out and established a special
contact with audiences, then as now. People responded to them as individuals
in the context of a funny situation, which is why lesser comics remained in the
second echelon even though they often had funny material. The truly popular
movie comedians had one quality that set them apart from all their cut-rate
colleagues: humanity.

At the same time, it's foolish to dismiss the second-string comics without
so much as a backward glance. One simply has to examine their work in proper
perspective.

Discussing Ben Turpin, the late writer-director Tay Garnett told me, "I
wrote a lot of stories for him, many in collaboration with Frank Capra, Hal
Conklin, or Vernon Smith (the Sennett writers always worked in teams). In this
area, I have some very definite opinions: Ben lacked a great deal of being a
funny man. He was funny only when placed in a ludicrous position—particularly one of grave danger—then, playing it dead seriously (perhaps a bit over-

seriously), which was the only thing he could do.

"Naturally, his material had to be prepared by someone who was familiar with his limitations. For purposes of illustration, take Stan Laurel or Harry Langdon. We used to say of Laurel (for whom I wrote many stories) that all one had to do was to put Stan in a set with a stepladder, turn the crank, and you were a cinch to come up with a beautiful hunk of very funny film. The same thing, in a lesser degree, was true of Harry Langdon. If you put a ladder in the same set with Turpin, he'd probably look at it, then say 'How'n hell ya expect me to act? Get that goddamned thing outa here!'

"I guess what I'm trying to say is that in my opinion, Turpin was not a mental giant."

This is not to say that Turpin's *films* weren't funny—but those laughs were built in by the gagmen and directors, and not the star. Turpin was just one of many silent comics who depended almost entirely on their material; left to their own devices, they were lost.

Turpin had one unique asset, of course: his face, which was just made for silent comedy. His eyes were genuinely and permanently crossed, although for publicity's sake he once had them insured against uncrossing with Lloyd's of London.

As Garnett indicates, the Sennett crew learned how to use Turpin effectively and put him into scores of funny comedy films during the teens and 1920s. His spoofs of romantic movie stars were memorably ludicrous and reached their apotheosis in the delightful feature film *The Shriek of Araby.* This writer has always had a soft spot in his heart for a two-reeler called *The Daredevil,* in which Ben is cast as a Hollywood stunt-double. The logic of this is simply enchanting: How could Ben Turpin *double* for anyone?

By the time talkies arrived in Hollywood, Ben Turpin was something of a movie relic, and he spent the last ten years of his life playing surprise walk-ons and cameos, in such films as *Million Dollar Legs, Hollywood Cavalcade,* Laurel and Hardy's *Saps at Sea,* and Ralph Staub's re-creation of a Sennett slapstick called *Keystone Hotel.* To the end of his days, Turpin's fortune was his face.

Another breezy Sennett comedian fared much better. Billy Bevan was one of the studio's major comedy stars in the 1920s, but he had no personality whatsoever—just a recognizable face and the ability to do physical comedy. His Sennett two-reelers were exceptionally good, brimming with wonderful sight gags, but Bevan really came into his own after leaving shorts and slapstick behind. In the early 1930s he removed his comedy moustache and sought out character roles instead. He became one of the film world's most endearing Cockneys, in such fine films as *Cavalcade, The Lost Patrol,* and *Cluny Brown,* to name a few, even though his accent was in reality Australian.

Bevan's counterpart at the Hal Roach studio was Harry "Snub" Pollard, also an Australian and also fondly remembered for his distinctive makeup (a Kaiser Wilhelm moustache worn upside down) and peppy comedies. Pollard had made his mark as Harold Lloyd's sidekick and stooge during the teens; when Lloyd became a major star on his own, producer Roach promoted Snub to his own starring series. Like Bevan, he benefited from first-rate sight gags, particularly in such little gems as *It's a Gift,* and he also won support from Charley Chase, who directed some of his finest two-reelers in the early 1920s. But when Pollard

Ben Turpin subdues a villain to save the honor of Kathryn McGuire in *The Shriek of Araby*.

Billy Bevan *(right)* with frequent costars Andy Clyde and Madeline Hurlock in the Sennett comedy short *Whispering Whiskers*.

A character portrait of Billy Bevan from the 1946 feature *Cluny Brown*.

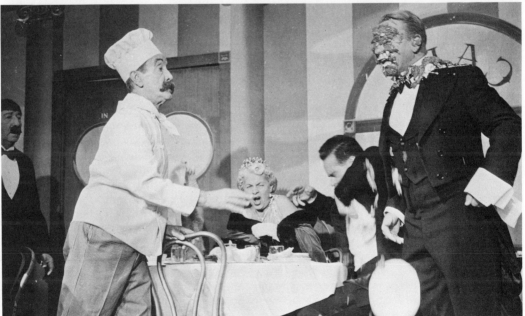

Above

Snub Pollard and Marie Mosquini take time out from an action scene to pose for this still during a Hal Roach comedy of the early 1920s.

Below

Snub Pollard in 1957, looking just about the same, scores a direct target in James Cagney's face for this scene from *Man of a Thousand Faces,* while Hank Mann looks on from extreme left.

left Hal Roach to head his own production unit in 1926, it became apparent that without the Roach staff he was stranded. He plummeted to near-obscurity, surviving in Hollywood for the next thirty years doing bit parts—in everything from Three Stooges shorts to Charles Chaplin's *Limelight.*

Unlike Pollard and Bevan, Larry Semon was a major comedy star for fifteen years. He wrote and directed many of his own films and starred in feature films as well as shorts during the 1920s. Why should he have so little recognition today? Norman Taurog, who directed him in a number of films, offers this reply: "He wasn't funny. That's honest. I loved the man but he wasn't funny. When we made a picture with Larry, he would go to New York and we'd go out and make the picture. When he came back, we fitted him in all the close-ups. That's the truth. Bill Haubor, who used to double for him all the time, was that close to him and that great and could do him that well. We would get as close as a full figure, and I defy anybody to pick it out."

Larry Semon wanted everything BIG. He had big budgets, big sets, and most of all big gags, hence the use of a stunt man. If there was to be a fall through an open window to the sidewalk below, Semon would make the fall twice as long as Sennett might. If there was to be a pie fight, it would have to be on an epic scale, in a bakery with huge vats of cake batter and chocolate involved. But Semon never learned that bigger did not necessarily mean better. His carefully manufactured gags were a little too pat and a bit too awesome at times to be amusing. Most of all, they were cold, just as Semon himself was cold, and his constant use of such stunt men as Bill Haubor kept his comedy at arm's length from the audience.

Undoubtedly Semon's most disappointing endeavor was a feature-length version of *The Wizard of Oz* in 1925, of which Walter Kerr has written, "It is a film that ought to have bankrupted everyone associated with it."

As it happens, Semon's unbridled extravagance did bankrupt him, financially and emotionally. He died in 1928 shortly after completing his first semiserious character role, for Josef von Sternberg, in *Underworld.*

No such pretensions were ever associated with Lupino Lane. He came from a famous theatrical family, which had been prominent in the English theater since the time of King Charles I (the family tradition continues: Lane's niece is Ida Lupino). He was a genius at acrobatic comedy and made this the hub of his two-reel comedies in the 1920s; he took falls and splits that most of his colleagues wouldn't have dared. He also enjoyed slapstick and performed it with unusual zest. Some of his comedies, for example, *Pirates Beware* and *Sword Points,* are dazzling in their comic movement.

But Lane suffered from the same problem that plagued so many of his colleagues: There was nothing tangible or human underneath the surface gags. Even those acrobatics became familiar after a couple of films and started to lose their fresh appeal (there's an eye-popping sequence in *Sword Points* with Lupino leaping in and out of hidden trapdoors in a wall, but this sequence was repeated verbatim just one year later in *Joy Land*).

Lane's stage training brought him immediate success in talkie features, and he was featured in such early musicals as Ernst Lubitsch's *The Love Parade, Show of Shows, Bride of the Regiment,* and *Golden Dawn,* before returning to his native England to resume his career there.

Lane spent most of his time in the 1920s at Educational Pictures studio, which was also home for another talented comic, Lloyd Hamilton. In every sense a comedian's comedian, Hamilton is perhaps the most intriguing and underrated comic from silent comedy's second echelon. He started his career as half of a knockabout team called Ham and Bud, which boasted no particular distinction other than longevity. But as soon as he broke away from Bud Duncan, good things started happening on-screen.

"He had a great, great nose for comedy," says Norman Taurog, who wrote and directed many of Hamilton's films. "He was a funny man. He didn't have to do terrifically broad gags—just a look, and the way he would react. He was a very good story man, also.

"The character was created by Henry Lehrman, Lloyd, a little bit of Jack White, and a little bit of me. I'm the fella who insisted on that walk, as if he always had on tight underwear. If you ever see anybody walk with tight underwear, you know it's very uncomfortable and that's the way he used to walk. Lehrman insisted on the cap, because he said it gave him a boyish look, which was right. Jack White cut off the cutaway coat one day on the set, with a tailor, and made the little short cutaway coat and the baggy pants. Of course, Lloyd discovered his own character. These were things that helped to make the character, but he was responsible for his own character."

Hamilton had a wonderful rubbery face with a fey expression that seemed to express a slight uncertainty of everything around him. His face always told the story and accounted for "reaction" gags that no other comedian could pull off quite so well. The gags and stories in a Hamilton short might be broad and slapsticky, but Hamilton himself was delicate and subtle. He communicated with his audience through "camera looks" and quiet gestures that made the incidents on-screen that much funnier.

Hamilton's character inspired special material from his writers and directors, as Taurog recalls. "One day I happened to look across the street, and a woman who was a pretty good comedienne was eating an artichoke for her lunch, and it struck me kind of funny. So I said to the property man, we're going to work in that restaurant a little later on, get a couple of artichokes, will ya? So he got a couple of artichokes and when we got in there, Lloyd was walking outside on the street. And I had Glenn Cavender, who was a second comic, sitting in the window eating an artichoke. Lloyd, as he came by, stopped and watched this and he was fascinated. And he watched him dip it in the butter and then eat it. He started to go away and looked down and there was a rose on a stem that had been broken off. He picked up the rose and took a petal off and he faked it, pantomimed it, put it in the butter, ate it, and swallowed the rose. And now it was a contest between the two, which developed into a terrific sequence. A very funny sequence. Now, you couldn't do that with anybody else, just a Lloyd Hamilton."

Unfortunately, fate dealt cruel blows to Hamilton—now as well as during his lifetime. In the early talkie era, it seemed as if he might go even further than the domain of two-reel comedies: Featured spots in *Show of Shows* and *Are You There?* with Beatrice Lillie seemed to point the way. But within a year's time he was at Mack Sennett's studio, making a series of woefully unfunny shorts. Financial problems and poor health helped to do him in, and when producer

Larry Semon is about to get what-for from Bull Montana in *Stop, Look, and Listen!*, one of Semon's feature films from 1926.

Lupino Lane is menaced by Wallace Lupino in one of his most famous two-reelers, *Roaming Romeo,* also known as *Bending Her.*

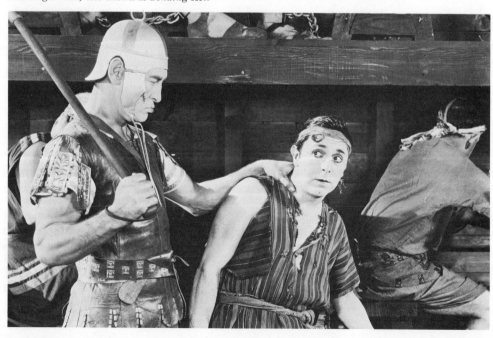

Lupino Lane in a puckish, musical-comedy mood, with Louise Fazenda in the early talkie feature *Bride of the Regiment*.

Louis Lewyn gave him a nonstrenuous bit in one of his all-star Technicolor shorts, *Star Night at Cocoanut Grove* (1935), he looked gaunt and tired. Hamilton died that same year, at the age of forty-eight.

And now the cards are stacked against a reappreciation of Hamilton because so few of his films are available to see. The Educational comedies exist only in isolated prints found in private hands, while his two starring feature films, *His Darker Self* and *A Self-Made Failure* (both produced in 1924), don't seem to exist at all. A two-reel version of *His Darker Self* survives, but it's difficult to judge how the entire film might have looked from this one episode. Even the long-running Ham and Bud series is represented today by only two or three examples, which are hardly enough to judge Hamilton's early work.

So it is that Lloyd Hamilton remains a "minor" comedian in the historical sense, because there is no chance to rescue him from that category without evidence on film. He also seems a talent who never reached his full potential, a unique comic personality who might have had tremendous impact in the right kind of vehicles.

On the whole, in chronicling the careers of movie comedians one finds that the public almost always responded to funny people. Very seldom did great talent go ignored. The problems, when they existed, lay in Hollywood, where

Lloyd Hamilton. in character.

Lloyd Hamilton and Bobby DeVilbiss in an unidentified two-reeler.

the films were made; it was a case of producers, directors, and writers failing to appreciate or exploit comic talent. Film history is full of these tales.

Perhaps no story is more ironic than that of Lucille Ball. Here is a woman universally acclaimed as one of the great comediennes of our time. Yet her comic prowess was stifled and subverted for fifteen years until television gave her a chance to prove herself.

Other comediennes have suffered similar fate, as film makers have grappled with the difficulty of putting women into comedy situations. (This does not include comic actresses, but rather feminine equivalents of the male clowns.) In the silent era, such women as Alice Howell, Dorothy Devore, and Billie Rhodes were well regarded but hampered by lackluster films and no real star buildup. Louise Fazenda, who came closest to inheriting Mabel Normand's throne, opted instead for character roles. Later, Martha Raye and Joan Davis proved their brilliance in spite of their film vehicles and not because of them. The likable Vera Vague had to contend with violence-prone slapstick shorts. It remained for television to give Raye, Davis, and of course Lucy the kind of showcase they deserved.

Black film comedians were caught in the middle of two extremes. In Hollywood there was no chance for them to star in their own films, although supporting roles might be juicy and rewarding, while the starring vehicles they might be offered by companies specializing in films for black audiences were often shoddy and uninspired. Stepin Fetchit came closest to achieving the impossible when Hal Roach signed him for a series of starring two-reelers; but after a "pilot" project with Our Gang called *A Tough Winter,* the idea was dropped. Still, he, Willie Best, and Mantan Moreland managed to get big laughs by working around and through their stereotyped roles and not just languishing in them.

Still, one fact overrides all qualifications and explanations about comedy careers. People have always loved to laugh, and the public never fails to respond to laugh makers who fulfill that desire.

The men and women included in this book enjoyed great success because they earned it. They stayed on top because they remained funny and original. It's no accident that Buster Keaton is still revered, while Larry Semon is of interest only to film students and scholars. The injustices in the field of comedy are few.

This book is not intended as a history. In some cases I felt that a performer's career required discussion, while in others the facts are so well known that it seemed more appropriate to concentrate on the style and substance of that person's comedy. Having had the chance to see so many comedies in such a concentrated period of time, and noting the response of a fresh and receptive audience, I found myself making new and sometimes revised evaluations of people I thought I fully appreciated long ago. I hope the reader will share my enthusiasm for these explorations.

For background material and firsthand observations, I am particularly indebted to Hollywood veterans Edward Bernds, David Butler, George Cukor, Tay Garnett, Harold Schuster, Mel Shavelson, and Norman Taurog. Their generosity has been exceptional. The Taurog and Shavelson interviews were originally conducted under the auspices of the American Academy of Humor, and I am happy to have had the chance to work for Alan King during that organization's lifetime.

I am grateful to Saul J. Turell of Janus Films for permitting me to quote from our recently filmed interview with Hal Roach and to Garry Moore, who many years ago took time out from a TV taping to talk about Buster Keaton and provide valuable insights that have never reached the printed page until now.

For access to films and photographs and assorted other favors, I would like to thank Louis Black, Eddie Brandt, William K. Everson, Herb Graff, Gerald Haber, Ron Haver, Bill Kenly, Douglas Lemza, Sam Sherman, and Jerry Vermilye.

To my wonderful wife, Alice, there aren't enough thanks.

And to my friends and colleagues at the Museum of Modern Art, I will always be grateful for their giving me the opportunity to spend an exciting year working with comedy films. To Adrienne Mancia and Larry Kardish, who made it all possible, and to all the wonderful, dedicated people in the Department of Film, thank you from the bottom of my heart.

Filmographies are included in this book to enhance your enjoyment and enable you to place the essays and photos into a time context.

As basic title listings, these filmographies also include behind-the-scenes credits for those comedians appearing on-screen who doubled as directors, writers, or so on. They exclude, however, casual appearances in such shorts as *Screen Snapshots* and *Hollywood on Parade.* Compilations and documentaries are not included for the same reason.

For the sake of uniformity, films are listed in the order of release, not the order of production.

I am indebted to the scholarship of Louis Black for the Mabel Normand listing, Eileen Bowser for Harold Lloyd, George Geltzer for Charley Chase, Sam Gill for Fatty Arbuckle, Alan Hoffman for Buster Keaton, and Norman Miller for Will Rogers.

Chaplin works his magic—even without his Tramp character—in *Making a Living,* his first starring film. With actor-director Henry Lehrman.

1

CHARLIE CHAPLIN

Charlie Chaplin is the supreme comic artist of our time.

He pioneered the development of film comedy from anarchy to art in just a few short years and created a screen character whose worldwide impact has never been equaled.

Unlike most of his colleagues in the film world, he *knew* he was special. He received international acclaim within months of his film debut and after just one year won not only an enormous salary but complete control of his work. He was an artist who worked at his own pace and in his own style at a time when few other film makers enjoyed those luxuries.

What set Charlie Chaplin apart from all the rest? Why did he become so popular so quickly? Part of the answer can be determined by watching his very first film, *Making a Living,* made in 1914.

Having no established character, Chaplin donned the makeup and costume of a somewhat seedy English gentleman for his screen debut. He plays a would-be dandy down on his luck. The character is really a bounder, but a more delightful rogue could not be imagined. The film is full of subtle touches that run throughout Chaplin's later films and show that much of his comic technique was already intact when he arrived at Mack Sennett's studio.

In one long take, without title-card interruptions, he strikes up a conversation with a man on the street (Henry Lehrman, who also directed the film).

Charlie gets friendly with the passerby and brings himself to confide that he's broke, despite his dapper appearance. The new confidant reluctantly reaches for his pocket to get some money; at this point, Chaplin drops his forlorn facade for an instant to cast an eager, furtive glance at Lehrman's bankroll before returning to his former expression. Then, in a typical Chaplin move, he summons up false pride and refuses Lehrman's money—only to grab for the cash when the agreeable Lehrman starts to take it back!

This wonderful scene is played completely in pantomime, as Chaplin's sighs, shrugs, and grimaces tell the story in hilarious fashion. This was a far cry from the broad gesticulations of Keystone's biggest star, Ford Sterling, who was noted for "telegraphing" his actions before playing each scene. Charlie's more intimate approach to comedy keeps his performance in *Making a Living* fresh and funny after sixty years.

There are other Chaplinesque moments in the film: When he's caught (by two fair damsels) adjusting his clothes, he reacts coyly, laughing and crossing his legs in embarrassment; later, in the midst of a fight with Lehrman, he holds him off at cane's length, just as he would many a later bully.

Chaplin's debut did not go unnoticed, even though his name was not yet known to the press or public. In a now-famous review for *Moving Picture World* an anonymous critic wrote, "The clever actor who takes the role of the . . . sharper . . . is a comedian of the first water. . . ."

Thus, in his first film appearance Charlie Chaplin showed signs of the comic style and stylishness that would quickly cement his reputation. It was his second film *Kid Auto Races at Venice,* that saw him in the earliest version of his Tramp character, and this is when his career began to take off. Until this time, there had been basically two kinds of screen comedians: the broad, grotesque clowns featured by Sennett and other pioneering film companies and the more genteel personalities such as John Bunny and Sidney Drew, whose humor might be called situation comedy. Chaplin was perhaps the first to distill the most appealing qualities of both "types" into his screen character, the Tramp. In his makeup, costume, and attitude, he was common and clownish, but in the nuances of his pantomime and movement, he was clever and distinctive.

Chaplin found himself as popular with the masses, who comprised the largest part of the movie audience, as with the intelligentsia, who disdained the crudities of most motion pictures.

Within several months of his Keystone debut, Chaplin managed to persuade Mack Sennett to let him direct and write his own films, and one can see, in the progression of his thirty-four one- and two-reel shorts during 1914, a growing knowledge of film structure as well as a gradual refinement of his personal comedy technique.

It was difficult for Chaplin to veer away from the Sennett path, however, and cranking out comedy shorts in the roughhouse Keystone atmosphere left little time for reflection on style and purpose. Chaplin's films for Keystone can be as crude and cruel as any of his colleagues' films at times, and Charlie's penchant for throwing bricks and kicking people in the stomach makes it difficult to endear oneself to some of these early comedies.

But even such an undistinguished outing as *Getting Acquainted,* his next-

Charlie's new beat is *Easy Street;* Eric Campbell is his adversary in this classic short.

to-last Keystone, shows great distinction in Chaplin's grasp of comedy film making. The "plot" is pure Sennett: two sets of husbands and wives in a round-robin comedy of errors during an afternoon in the park. Sennett once said that all he needed to make a comedy film was a cop, a pretty girl, and a park bench. Chaplin accepts that challenge and builds a very amusing chain reaction of events that calls on his surefooted knowledge of film construction as well as general comedy know-how. *Getting Acquainted* also benefits from the charm and skill of Mabel Normand as Charlie's vis-à-vis.

When Chaplin left Sennett to set up shop at Essanay studios, he removed himself from one kind of atmosphere and moved toward the artistic isolation that enabled him to create more personal and in some cases more "serious" films. This was a transitional period, with more time to think about each new film and polish his screen character. The Essanay shorts are still rough-edged, but they represent a giant stride from the crudity of his Keystone comedies.

There follows a burst of creativity in 1916 and 1917 when Chaplin made his "golden dozen" two-reelers for the Mutual Company. It's difficult to think of finer comedies than *Easy Street, The Pawnshop, The Cure, The Immigrant, The Rink, The Adventurer, Behind the Screen, The Floorwalker, One A.M., The Vagabond,* and to a lesser degree, *The Count* and *The Fireman.*

Their humor, their warmth, their invention, and their economy are amazing. This final factor should not be dismissed lightly, for it is one of Chaplin's great strengths as a film maker. He strove for a clean narrative line in his films and succeeded with remarkable consistency. Even a feature film like *City Lights* can be described in just a sentence or two. Ironically, Chaplin's classically simple films were created by the most painstaking means, often (in the case of the features) taking years to complete.

Rollie Totheroh, Chaplin's cameraman for nearly forty years, recalled in a 1967 interview, "Pretty near everything prior to *The Great Dictator* was ad lib. He didn't have a script at the time, didn't have a script girl or anything like that, and he never checked whether the scene was in its right place or that continuity was followed. The script would develop as it went along. A lot of times after we saw the dailies the next morning, if it didn't warrant what he thought the expectation was, he'd put in some other sort of a sequence and work on that instead of going through with what he had started out to do. We never had a continuity. He'd have an idea and he'd build up. He had sort of a synopsis laid out in his mind but nothing on paper. He'd talk it over and come in and do a sequence. . . . Sometimes after a set had been torn down, he'd get a new idea and we'd have to reconstruct the whole set exactly as it was before so that he could reshoot some shots for a scene."

Chaplin applied the same techniques—the development of an economical story line and simple but eloquent use of the camera—to his first serious directorial effort, *A Woman of Paris,* in 1923.

The film's costar, Adolphe Menjou, recalled in his autobiography, "At first I had no great faith in the story. To me it was simply a job and a good part. Not until we started shooting did I begin to realize that we were making a novel and exciting picture. It was Chaplin's genius that transformed the very ordinary story. Aside from his own great talent as an actor he had the ability to inspire other actors to perform their best. Within a few days I realized that I was going to learn more about acting from Chaplin than I had ever learned from any director. He had wonderful, unforgettable lines that he kept repeating over and over throughout the picture. 'Don't sell it!' he would say. 'Remember, they're peeking at you.' . . . Another pet line of Chaplin's was, 'Think the scene! I don't care what you do with your hands or your feet. If you think the scene, it will get over.'

"And we had to keep shooting every scene until we *were* thinking it—until we believed it and were playing it with our brains and not just with our hands or our feet or our eyebrows. If I remember correctly, we once did over 200 takes on one scene, and many scenes were shot more than 50 times. There were days when we rehearsed the same little scene time after time and then shot and reshot it until we thought we would go crazy. But Chaplin was satisfied with nothing less than perfection, or as close to it as we could come."

A sophisticated drama with moments of cynical humor, *A Woman of Paris* dazzled most critics in 1923 and reaffirmed Chaplin's genius as a student of, and sly commentator on, human nature. The film was not a success with the general public, and Chaplin returned to his familiar comic Tramp in *The Gold Rush,* but he would never again make a comedy film that didn't also include moments of sentiment or pathos.

These elements had been present in Chaplin films dating back to *The Tramp* of 1915, but the artist himself feels that the first true test came with *The Kid.* He wrote in his autobiography, "Gouverneur Morris, author and short-story writer who had written many scripts for the cinema, often invited me to his house. 'Guvvy,' as we called him, was a charming, sympathetic fellow, and when I told him about *The Kid* and the form it was taking, keying slapstick with sentiment, he said: 'It won't work. The form must be pure, either slapstick or drama; you cannot mix them, otherwise one element of your story will fail.'

"We had quite a dialectical discussion about it. I said that the transition from slapstick to sentiment was a matter of feeling and discretion in arranging sequences. I argued that form happened after one had created it, that if the artist thought of a world and sincerely believed in it, no matter what the admixture was it would be convincing. Of course, I had no grounds for this theory other than intuition. There had been satire, farce, realism, naturalism, melodrama, and fantasy, but raw slapstick and sentiment, the premise of *The Kid,* was something of an innovation."

Chaplin achieved this innovation through the simplest of means. He built his situations on a foundation of reality and created characters so empathic— the orphaned kid played by Jackie Coogan and his devoted guardian, the Tramp —that it was both feasible and logical to go in either direction, toward comedy or toward drama. Even amid the cunningly comic situations that the Kid and the Tramp share (Jackie breaking windows so that glazier Charlie can conveniently happen upon the scene a moment later and find ready work) there is a strong bond between the two that makes the serious scenes—in which orphanage officials want to take Jackie away from Charlie—genuinely upsetting and melodramatically exciting. Of course, it is the artistry of Chaplin and the ingenuous charm of young Jackie Coogan that make this really work.

Some critics were wary of this "new" Chaplin, however. They wanted purer comedy and didn't welcome the infusion of sentiment. But while the debate continued, Chaplin followed his own personal path and created masterworks that have survived the critical squabbles by half a century. With *The Gold Rush* he produced his longest comedy feature film to date and proved to doubters that a great comedy could also be a great film. He artfully interwove a thread of pathos, in Charlie's unrequited love for dance-hall girl Georgia Hale, with a broadly comic tale of the Tramp and his burly partner (Mack Swain) surviving the gold-rush days in the Yukon. He alternated major comedy set pieces—the prospectors' cabin teetering on the edge of a cliff—with moments of delicate and unforgettable pantomime—Charlie gracefully eating the sole of his shoe as if it were an epicurean delight or performing an impromptu dance by sticking forks into two dinner rolls and using them as miniature "feet."

When sound rocked the film industry, just a few years after the release of *The Gold Rush,* Chaplin's colleagues rushed into the production of talking pictures. But Chaplin, who was in the midst of shooting *City Lights,* decided that it should be made silent. After a period of self-debate, he concluded that his character would lose his universal appeal as soon as he spoke—and because Chaplin ran his own studio and controlled his own films, he was able to maintain the courage of his convictions while bucking the trend of the entire film industry.

When the film was finally released in 1931 it was plain to see that sound was about as important to Charlie Chaplin as a pair of roller skates would be to Rin-Tin-Tin. *City Lights* was (and is) such a delightfully funny and ultimately moving film that the lack of dialogue was never felt. In fact, Chaplin composed his own musical score to accompany the picture and added the sound of kazoos to represent voices in the opening scene. Again, Chaplin made a lasting impression by contrasting hilarious comedy sequences (the prizefight-ballet, saving the drunk from drowning, and so on) with the touching story of the Tramp's devotion to a beautiful, blind flower girl. Nowhere was the power of the silent image —and the beauty of Chaplin's work—clearer than in *City Lights'* famous finale, in which the girl, whose sight has been restored through Chaplin's dedication, meets the Tramp face-to-face and realizes for the first time the identity of her benefactor. In his eyes, love, hope, a timid longing, while in hers, mingled emotions of surprise, disillusionment, and understanding. No other screen comedian has ever produced a single moment so memorable.

It was five years before his next film, *Modern Times*, reached the screen, but again Chaplin decided to keep his character silent. This time, however, he added sound sequences and even gave the Tramp a gibberish song to perform. His comic depiction of man vs. machine has remained a striking image with greater relevance in each passing decade, and his crack-up on the assembly line, with its slapstick results, has provided vicarious pleasure for frustrated workers around the world.

Some people found in *Modern Times* a bit too much thought and not enough laughter. By the time of his next film, *The Great Dictator*, it was impossible to ignore the changes in the great man's work. The most obvious was one of philosophy. Chaplin (now Charles, not Charlie) wanted to say more through his films than he felt he could achieve through simple comedy with the Tramp. He was not abandoning comedy—even his blackest film, *Monsieur Verdoux*, has moments of hilarious slapstick—but he was more interested in social comment, satire, and drama as vehicles for his self-expression. At the time of its release, *Monsieur Verdoux* horrified former Chaplin fans. A cynical and uncompromising portrait of a modern-day Bluebeard, it ended with Verdoux walking to the gallows and allowed broad comedy only in Chaplin's brief encounter with the flamboyant Martha Raye. Today one can see that *Verdoux* was ahead of its time; now its black comedy is more impressive, its messages more palatable. But in 1947 it seemed the polar opposite of Chaplin's earlier work.

Other subtler changes were affecting his films as well. Chaplin had maintained his skeleton crew much as it was in the 1920s and continued to use not only the same working methods but the same cinematic approach. His films were designed not to display technical wizardry but merely to showcase Charlie Chaplin. His disregard for detail had been less important—and more easily camouflaged—in silent films. But by the 1940s, his films were beginning to look

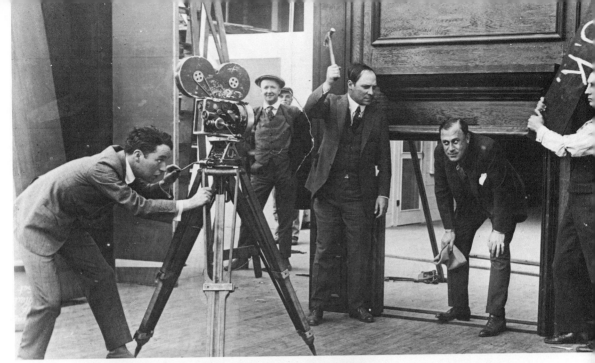

Chaplin visits his colleague Buster Keaton at Keaton's studio and immediately takes up position behind the camera, to fool around. Keaton associate Lou Anger holds the hammer over studio owner Mr. Hochheimer.

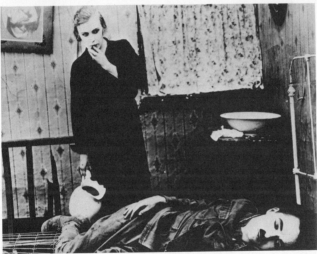

Edna Purviance discovers Charlie asleep in her bed in *Shoulder Arms.*

strangely anachronistic—and disturbingly cheap. Although he shot miles of film and spent thousands of dollars to keep a cast and crew on salary while he deliberated new sequences, he was loath to spend much money on sets or production mounting. His use of shoddy process screens to simulate realistic backgrounds became more appalling with each new film, from *Modern Times* to *A King in New York.*

Chaplin felt that audiences wouldn't care about such trivia while he was on the screen, but he failed to realize that having abandoned the Little Tramp, he now had to work harder to win the public's interest in each new character and story, and that sloppy film making wasn't going to help.

Chaplin's longtime aide Henry Bergman plays a clown with Charlie in *The Circus*.

The picture says it all: Virginia Cherrill and Chaplin in *City Lights*.

Claire Bloom and an older Chaplin
in *Limelight*.

He became more isolated both as an individual and as a film maker during
this period, and this loss of contact is equally apparent in his films. Although
headstrong and arrogant, he had always thrived on a certain amount of feed-
back from his co-workers at the studio, but now he became unapproachable. His
final films show the results of increasing self-indulgence, tolerable only because
Chaplin's indulgences are in themselves fascinating.

A King in New York, doubtless his most self-indulgent film, is still a compelling experience, as Chaplin fires scatter shot in a dozen directions, poking
fun at everything from CinemaScope's wide-screen proportions to the
aftereffects of face-lifts. But its attempts at more serious commentary on humanity and world philosophy are superficial and arrogant, to say the least.

Yet it is the mark of genius that even films with terrible flaws and shortcom-
ings can still retain such extraordinary appeal.

How to sum up the impact of this extraordinary man? Perhaps this will
suffice. In looking back, it seems *The Circus* has always suffered from being
chronologically sandwiched between Chaplin's most admired comedies, *The
Gold Rush* and *City Lights.* It has always been called a "minor Chaplin."

Unseen for many years, it was reissued in the early 1970s to the surprise
and delight of film buffs, historians, and average audiences as well. They found
that while the film may have lacked *The Gold Rush*'s innovations and *City
Lights'* classicism, it had something equally vital to offer: unrestrained hilarity,

Charlie Chaplin's last screen appearance, a bit role in his own film *A Countess from Hong Kong*, with Marlon Brando.

coupled with genuine and deeply moving sentiment.

Moral: A "minor Chaplin" is still leagues ahead of major works by so many others. And what is more, a "major Chaplin" is about as good as any motion picture has a right to be. His art will endure for countless generations to come.

THE FILMS OF CHARLIE CHAPLIN

THE MACK SENNETT SHORTS—1914

Making a Living
Kid Auto Races at Venice
Mabel's Strange Predicament
Between Showers
A Film Johnnie
Tango Tangles
His Favorite Pastime
Cruel, Cruel Love
The Star Boarder
Mabel at the Wheel
Twenty Minutes of Love
Caught in a Cabaret (co-directed by Chaplin and Mabel Normand)
Caught in the Rain (the first film directed by Chaplin; all subsequent films bear his name as director except where noted)
A Busy Day
The Fatal Mallet
Her Friend the Bandit (co-directed by Mabel Normand)
The Knockout (directed by Mack Sennett)
Mabel's Busy Day (co-directed by Mabel Normand)
Mabel's Married Life (co-directed by Mabel Normand)
Laughing Gas
The Property Man
The Face on the Barroom Floor
Recreation
The Masquerader
His New Profession

The Rounders
The New Janitor
Those Love Pangs
Dough and Dynamite
Gentlemen of Nerve
His Musical Career
His Trysting Place
Getting Acquainted
His Prehistoric Past
Tillie's Punctured Romance (this
  pioneer Sennett feature was
  released in November 1914;
  Chaplin took second billing to
  Marie Dressler and did not appear
  as the Tramp)

THE ESSANAY SHORTS (Chaplin
wrote and directed all his subsequent
films)

His New Job—1915
A Night Out—1915
The Champion—1915
In the Park—1915
The Jitney Elopement—1915
The Tramp—1915
By the Sea—1915
Work—1915
A Woman—1915
The Bank—1915
Shanghaied—1915
A Night in the Show—1915
Carmen—1916 (also known as *Charlie
  Chaplin's Burlesque on Carmen*)
Police—1916

THE MUTUAL SHORTS

The Floorwalker—1916
The Fireman—1916
The Vagabond—1916
One A.M.—1916
The Count—1916
The Pawnshop—1916
Behind the Screen—1916
The Rink—1916

Easy Street—1917
The Cure—1917
The Immigrant—1917
The Adventurer—1917

All subsequent films were produced
and owned by Chaplin. Everything
through *The Pilgrim* was released by
First National, and every film
beginning with *A Woman of Paris*
was released by United Artists, of
which Chaplin was part owner and
founder.

A Dog's Life—1918
The Bond—1918
Shoulder Arms—1918
Sunnyside—1919
A Day's Pleasure—1919
The Kid—1921 (Chaplin's first
  starring feature film)
The Idle Class—1921
Pay Day—1922
The Pilgrim—1923 (Chaplin's last
  short subject)
A Woman of Paris—1923 (Chaplin
  produced, directed, and wrote this
  film but did not appear, except for
  a brief walk-on)
The Gold Rush—1925
The Circus—1928
City Lights—1931
Modern Times—1936
The Great Dictator—1940
Monsieur Verdoux—1947
Limelight—1952
A King in New York—1957
A Countess From Hong Kong—1967
  (written and directed by Chaplin,
  who did not star, but again
  appeared in a cameo role)

Chaplin was also featured in a 1918
short called *Triple Trouble,* which
was made up of snips from earlier
Essanay films as well as scenes from
an unfinished project called *Life.*

Keystone Mabel.

Mabel and Ford Sterling in an early
Keystone comedy, *Professor Bean's Removal*.

2

MABEL NORMAND

Mabel Normand was often referred to as "the female Chaplin," and although she was never really in the same league as the multi-talented Charlie, she earned that title with her charm, intelligence, and intuitive comic gift.

Sadly, her career never fulfilled its promise, although her life story would top any fiction Hollywood could ever create, combining romance, comedy, melodrama, and tragedy (a recent attempt to musicalize her life with Mack Sennett stupidly ignored the truth in favor of the authors' silly fabrications).

Mabel was a delicately lovely, dark-haired girl who came from a none-too-successful working-class family. In her early teens she was spotted by illustrator Carl Kleinschmidt and before long she was working regularly as a model for him and such noted colleagues as Charles Dana Gibson and James Montgomery Flagg. Modeling led to movies, at a time when cracking the film "industry" was no great feat.

At the Biograph Studios in New York, Mabel worked for pioneer D. W. Griffith and met one of Griffith's actors and would-be film makers, Mack Sennett. Mabel was attracted to the rough-and-ready Irishman, and they fell in love; several times they planned to marry, but Sennett's devotion to his work, and to extracurricular love affairs, interfered.

Mabel was devoted to Mack, however, and when he got financing to start

13

his own film company, Keystone, she went with him and stayed even when the two were personally estranged.

At Keystone Mabel augmented her acting talent with a willingness to do anything for a laugh, from catching a pie in the face to being dragged through a muddy riverbed. Sennett claimed, in fact, that she threw the very first custard pie. Mabel was an active participant in many of Sennett's "instant films," which were created when the canny producer would hear of some public event that might provide a colorful backdrop for a one-reel comedy, hurry to the scene with cast and cameraman, and improvise comedy action that would later form the basis for a "script." Mabel might be called upon to harass a fireman marching in a civic parade, run in and out of a burning building, or (in a less strenuous endeavor) attend the San Francisco World's Fair.

"For instance," Mack Sennett explained in his autobiography, "we got a tip one day that the city of Los Angeles planned to drain the small lake in Echo Park. When the Water Department boys arrived to unplug the pond, we were there with a camera crew trained on Mabel and a screen lover in a rowboat. The heavy in this comedy, jealous of the boating sweethearts, opens a valve, the water spurts out in a torrent, and the boat sinks swiftly to the muddy bottom of the ex-lake.

"We threw in some trick photography here, which made it appear that the lake was draining at a Niagaran rate and that the rowboat went down faster than McGinty to the bottom of the sea.

"It was taking advantage of situations like this that kept Keystone alive. Audiences were astonished by the apparent expense of such a spectacle—which had cost us nothing."

But inevitably, Mabel Normand grew tired of the frantic pace of Keystone movie making and yearned for a chance to do something more ambitious. Sennett placated her by allowing her to direct some of her own films, and later she collaborated with Charlie Chaplin on the direction of such costarring shorts as *Caught in a Cabaret, Her Friend the Bandit, Mabel's Busy Day,* and *Mabel's Married Life.* He also paid her one of the highest salaries in Keystone history.

It's easy to see why Mabel was dissatisfied with her career at this time. Although she had no theatrical training, she had wonderful instincts and understood the art of acting for the camera. As Richard Griffith once wrote, "Now a child-woman whom strong men hasten to protect, now a most unwomanly spirit of mischief, this comedienne held at her fingertips a repertory of telling gestures which express comedy but suggest a wry knowledge of life."

This talent was often stifled in the repetitious slapstick comedies that Sennett cranked out week after week. A costarring role in the producer's first feature film, *Tillie's Punctured Romance,* gave her a rare opportunity to build a more sustained performance—and also to wear attractive clothes.

Finally, Mack Sennett, who was deeply in love with Mabel, succumbed to her wishes and fashioned a feature-length film especially for her: *Mickey.* He gave her the right to select her director and costars and made sure it was exactly the film she wanted to do. Beset by accidents, delays, and financial problems, it took eight months to film *Mickey* during 1916 and 1917.

"But in the end," Sennett recalled, "we came through with a film that I knew was a handsome and funny production, by far the best thing ever done with Mabel Normand. It gave scope to her whimsical talents for the first time."

Looking at *Mickey* today one still feels that Mabel's potential was not fully realized. She has many fine moments as a mountain girl; the film is beautifully photographed and lit, with choice locations and sets. A tender scene between Mickey and her father is played in silhouette against a window shade, while in a kitchen scene there is a creamy-white cake on the table without so much as a hint of its being hurled in someone's face.

Mickey's story line trods familiar territory: A backward but honest girl bumbles into high society. Then, two thirds of the way through the film, something goes awry, as if Sennett had decided to change course in midstream and turn *Mickey* into a broader, more familiar type of comedy. The story is tossed aside for a series of unrelated and unmotivated vignettes, most of them loaded with action; in one, Mabel disguises herself as a jockey in order to win a crucial horse race. After at least three false endings, *Mickey* comes to a halt, having delivered far less than it promised at the outset.

When the film was completed in 1917, a notice in *Moving Picture World* proclaimed, "Mabel Normand in *Mickey* bids farewell to squash pie comedy to do something more genteel." This may have been the kiss of death, however, because Sennett found himself unable to interest any theater owners in booking the film. Reaction was universally negative. Legend has it that *Mickey* won its first theatrical showing because one Long Island exhibitor needed a last-minute replacement for a canceled film. After this showing, word-of-mouth built *Mickey* into a sensational hit.

But by the time this happened, Mabel Normand had left Sennett to work for Samuel Goldwyn. He delivered the quality productions that Sennett had only talked about, and Mabel became a star of feature films. Unfortunately, virtually all of these films have vanished from film vaults and archives, victims of neglect, and it is impossible to evaluate them except by examining reviews from that time.

The consensus seems clear: Mabel Normand was so well liked by reviewers and audiences that she was welcome even in mediocre vehicles that did not show her off to best advantage. Not all of this was Goldwyn's fault; Mabel was becoming difficult to work with. Mindless of studio discipline, she would show up late, if at all, for shooting, and would capriciously set sail for Europe in the middle of a production!

Because of her unreliability, Sennett was able to convince Goldwyn that he'd be better off without her, and she returned to her home studio for three more feature films. *Molly O'* reportedly exists in an East European archive but is not easily seen today. Of *Suzanna* Robert E. Sherwood, then a film critic, wrote in 1923, "It is the presence of Mabel Normand in the cast which saves it from being just another of those things. You can't imagine this impressive gamin doing anything stupid or dull or obvious on the screen. She has a remarkable flair for impudent comedy."

This leaves *The Extra Girl,* which along with *Mickey* is Mabel Normand's most familiar movie through latter-day revivals and screenings. It repeats the frustrating formula of putting ever-likable Mabel into trite surroundings. The

Mabel relaxes with George Nichols, unidentified cameraman (probably Homer Scott), and director F. Richard Jones on the set of *The Extra Girl*.

Jack Mulhall, Mabel, Anna Hernandez, and George Nichols in *Molly O'*.

Mabel in one of her Goldwyn features, *The Pest,* with James Bradbury.

Anything for a laugh!

Leon Bary and Mabel in *Suzanna.*

Mabel, Ralph Graves, and players in *The Extra Girl*.

comic idea of a small-town girl trying to make good in Hollywood evolves into hokey melodramatics, and its most famous scene has little to do with her buoyant personality: She unwittingly leads a lion through the movie studio on the end of a rope. *The Extra Girl* also reveals the ravages that illness and high living had taken on her appearance; she seems gaunt and a bit forlorn.

There was good reason for this. Mabel was beset by illness and at the height of her partying years had started taking drugs. But the mightiest blow came in 1922 when she was implicated in the scandalous murder of director William Desmond Taylor. Although clearly innocent of the murder and never indicted, her liaison with the murdered man was sufficient fodder for screaming newspaper headlines and boycotts of her newest film, *Molly O'*, by civic groups and women's clubs. The strain showed in Mabel's health and in her subsequent performances. Mabel suffered a setback on New Year's Eve 1923 when her chauffeur wounded a wealthy friend of hers in a late-night scuffle. Again, she was not implicated in the shooting, but the guilt by association hurt her and added to her worries.

After completing *The Extra Girl* she left Sennett for good, at first tired of film making and eager to try her hand on Broadway. When her show flopped, she returned to Hollywood and made several pleasant short subjects for Hal Roach, *The Nickel Hopper, Raggedy Rose*, and *One Hour Married*. Supervising director for the films was F. Richard Jones, who had directed Mabel's biggest successes for Sennett. They were enjoyable and slickly made, with genuinely funny moments, but there was no way to ignore the haggard look of Mabel's face. She could still work wonders with that expressive face, but it just wasn't the same.

After a bout with double pneumonia in January 1927 she recovered sufficiently to resume her active life, partying and seeing friends in Hollywood and New York. But her nurse and companion, Julia Benson, knew that she had tuberculosis. In 1929 she entered a sanitarium and remained for six months. She died on February 23, 1930, just thirty-five years old.

After reading Mack Sennett's evocative autobiography, *King of Comedy,* which is in large part a paean to Mabel Normand, and discovering that everyone she met was enchanted with her, it is all the more difficult to watch the surviving Normand comedies in which her natural gifts are so often suppressed. One longs to find the perfect Mabel Normand film that will reveal this great talent in all its glory, but in all likelihood it doesn't exist.

What does exist are the happy memories of a colorful woman and comic spirit, who left enough pearl-like moments behind on film to confirm her reputation as the premier comedienne of silent films, and the eulogies of such friends as Charlie Chaplin, who wrote not long ago, "She was lighthearted and gay, a good fellow, kind and generous; and everyone adored her."

THE FILMS OF MABEL NORMAND

There are only sketchy records of Normand's earliest film appearances. The following are confirmed screen roles.

VITAGRAPH SHORTS

Over the Garden Wall—1910
Betty Becomes a Maid—1911
Troublesome Secretaries—1911
The Subduing of Mrs. Nag—1911

BIOGRAPH SHORTS (most directed either by D. W. Griffith or Mack Sennett)

The Diving Girl—1911
The Unveiling—1911
The Squaw's Love—1911
Her Awakening—1911
A Victim of Circumstances—1911
Saved From Himself—1911
The Eternal Mother—1912
The Mender of Nets—1912
A Spanish Dilemma—1912
The Engagement Ring—1912
Hot Stuff—1912
The Fickle Spaniard—1912
The Furs—1912

Helen's Marriage—1912
Oh, Those Eyes!—1912
Tomboy Bessie—1912
Katchem Kate—1912
Neighbors—1912
A Dash Through the Clouds—1912
The Tourists—1912
What the Doctor Ordered—1912
Help! Help!—1912
The Interrupted Elopement—1912
The Tragedy of a Dress Suit—1912

THE MACK SENNETT SHORTS

The Water Nymph—1912
The New Neighbor—1912
Pedro's Dilemma—1912
Stolen Glory—1912
Ambitious Butler—1912
The Flirting Husband—1912
The Grocery Clerk's Romance—1912
Cohen at Coney Island—1912
Mabel's Lovers—1912
At It Again—1912

The Deacon's Trouble—1912
A Temperamental Husband—1912
The Rivals—1912
Mr. Fix-It—1912
A Desperate Lover—1912
Brown's Seance—1912
A Family Mix-Up—1912
A Midnight Elopement—1912
Mabel's Adventures—1912
The Duel—1912
Mabel's Stratagem—1912
Saving Mabel's Dad—1913
The Cure That Failed—1913
The Mistaken Masher—1913
The Deacon Outwitted—1913
Just Brown's Luck—1913
The Battle of Who Run—1913
Heinze's Resurrection—1913
Mabel's Heroes—1913
The Professor's Daughter—1913
A Tangled Affair—1913
A Red Hot Romance—1913
A Doctored Affair—1913
The Sleuths at the Floral Parade—
  1913
The Rural Third Degree—1913
A Strong Revenge—1913
Foiling Fickle Father—1913
The Rube and the Baron—1913
At Twelve O'Clock—1913
Her New Beau—1913
Those Good Old Days—1913
Father's Choice—1913
The Ragtime Band—1913
A Little Hero—1913
Mabel's Awful Mistake—1913
Hubby's Job—1913
The Foreman of the Jury—1913
Barney Oldfield's Race for Life—
  1913
Passions, He Had Three—1913
The Hansom Driver—1913
The Speed Queen—1913
The Waiters' Picnic—1913
For the Love of Mabel—1913
The Telltale Light—1913
A Noise From the Deep—1913

Love and Courage—1913
Professor Bean's Removal—1913
The Riot—1913
Baby Day—1913
Mabel's New Hero—1913
Mabel's Dramatic Career—1913
The Gypsy Queen—1913
The Faithful Taxicab—1913
When Dreams Come True—1913
The Bowling Match—1913
The Speed Kings (Teddy Tetzlaff and
  Earl Cooper, Speed Kings)—1913
Love Sickness at Sea—1913
A Muddy Romance—1913
Cohen Saves the Flag—1913
The Gusher—1913
Fatty's Flirtation—1913
Zuzu, The Bank Leader—1913
The Champion—1913
A Misplaced Foot—1914
A Glimpse of Los Angeles—1914
Mabel's Stormy Love Affair—1914
Won in a Closet—1914 (directed by
  Normand)
Mabel's Bare Escape—1914 (directed
  by Normand)
Mabel's Strange Predicament—1914
  (directed by Normand)
Love and Gasoline—1914 (directed
  by Normand)
Mack at It Again—1914
Mabel at the Wheel—1914 (directed
  by Normand)
Where Hazel Met the Villain—1914
Caught in a Cabaret—1914 (directed
  by Normand and Chaplin)
Mabel's Nerve—1914 (directed by
  Normand)
The Alarm—1914
The Fatal Mallet—1914
Her Friend the Bandit—1914
  (directed by Normand and Chaplin)
Mabel's Busy Day—1914 (directed by
  Normand and Chaplin)
Mabel's Married Life—1914 (directed
  by Normand and Chaplin)
Mabel's New Job—1914

Those Country Kids—1914
Mabel's Latest Prank—1914 (directed by Normand)
Mabel's Blunder—1914 (directed by Normand)
Hello Mabel—1914
Gentlemen of Nerve—1914
Lovers' Post Office—1914
His Trysting Place—1914
How Heroes Are Made—1914
Fatty's Jonah Day—1914
Fatty's Wine Party—1914
The Sea Nymphs—1914
Getting Acquainted—1914
Tillie's Punctured Romance—1914 (Mabel costarred with Marie Dressler and Charlie Chaplin in this Sennett feature)
Mabel and Fatty's Wash Day—1915
Mabel and Fatty's Simple Life—1915
Fatty and Mabel at the San Diego Exposition—1915
Mabel, Fatty and the Law—1915
Fatty and Mabel's Married Life—1915
That Little Band of Gold—1915
Wished on Mabel—1915
Mabel and Fatty Viewing the World's Fair at San Francisco—1915
Their Social Splash—1915
Mabel's Wilful Way—1915
Mabel Lost and Won—1915
The Little Teacher—1915
My Valet—1915
Stolen Magic—1915
Fatty and Mabel Adrift—1916
He Did and He Didn't—1916
The Bright Lights—1916

THE FEATURE FILMS

Mickey—Mack Sennett 1917
Dodging a Million—Goldwyn 1918

The Floor Below—Goldwyn 1918
Joan of Plattsburg—Goldwyn 1918
Venus Model—Goldwyn 1918
Back to the Woods—Goldwyn 1918
Peck's Bad Girl—Goldwyn 1918
A Perfect 36—Goldwyn 1918
Sis Hopkins—Goldwyn 1919
The Pest—Goldwyn 1919
When Doctors Disagree—Goldwyn 1919
Upstairs—Goldwyn 1919
Jinx—Goldwyn 1919
Pinto—Goldwyn 1920
The Slim Princess—Goldwyn 1920
What Happened to Rosa?—Goldwyn 1921
Molly O'—Mack Sennett-Associated First National 1921
Oh! Mabel Behave—Photocraft Productions 1922 (apparently filmed by Sennett in 1917 and only released in 1922)·
Head Over Heels—Goldwyn 1922
Suzanna—Mack Sennett-Allied Producers and Distributors 1923
The Extra Girl—Mack Sennett-Associated Exhibitors 1923

THE HAL ROACH SHORTS
(sometimes referred to as features, these were three-reelers, released by Pathé)

Raggedy Rose—1926
The Nickel Hopper—1926
Anything Once—1927
One Hour Married—1927
Should Men Walk Home?—1927

Mabel Normand also appeared in a Goldwyn short called *Stake Uncle Sam to Play Your Hand*, promoting war bonds in 1918.

How they did it: An elaborate studio set that can rock back and forth is flooded for the famous Sennett comedy short *Fatty and Mabel Adrift*, with Arbuckle and Mabel Normand.

3

FATTY ARBUCKLE

It seems tragic that Roscoe "Fatty" Arbuckle should be remembered today for a scandal in his private life and barely recognized for his contribution to screen comedy. To be sure, Arbuckle was never one of the comic giants, except in a physical sense, but his career was more significant than many people realize.

Like John Bunny, Arbuckle had a natural appeal for silent-film audiences because of his girth. At a time when visual trademarks were the cornerstones of most comedy careers, Arbuckle had one of the best: a huge but agile body, plus a winningly cherubic face.

His size and his surprising acrobatic skill made him a "natural" at Mack Sennett's studio, where he worked from 1913 to 1916. He was teamed with Mabel Normand in a series of engaging comedies and starred with virtually everyone else who passed through the Keystone studio, including Charlie Chaplin. By 1915 he was directing his own films.

Although a genteel and gentle man off-screen, Arbuckle took to the Keystone brand of humor with relish and soon made it his own. His sense of comedy was often cruel and crude, but like Chaplin, his taste matured as he gained both comedy and cinema experience.

The informal yet tightly paced one-reelers didn't give Arbuckle much room in which to work, and his first major step forward was a graduation to two-reel comedies in 1915. Most of these early shorts are lost or inaccessible,

Fatty and Keystone Teddy improvise a duet for the still cameraman.

Alice Lake and Arbuckle in *The Hayseed*, one of Arbuckle's Comique shorts.

but some of Arbuckle's 1916 work for Sennett shows him in full command of his powers. *Fatty and Mabel Adrift* is a delightful short with a unique Sennett-like premise: a beach-front house being "launched" out to sea by villains, with Fatty and Mabel waking the next morning to find their beds floating in a roomful of water. But it also contains some directorial "touches" that reveal Roscoe's efforts to combine slapstick with more charm and style: a shot in which he kisses his wife good-night in silhouette and an opening/closing motif for the film that shows Fatty, Mabel, and their pet dog in cupid-like heart cutouts.

Arbuckle experimented even more boldly during a stay on the East Coast, three thousand miles away from the home studio and Sennett's personal supervision. *He Did and He Didn't,* a surprisingly sophisticated comedy involving marital infidelity, is beautifully photographed and cunningly written to involve a deceptive dream sequence.

But several years later, after leaving Sennett and operating independently for producer Joseph M. Schenck, he remarked in an interview, "I endeavor to cater to the masses as well as the classes, not forgetting the kids. Children like the purely physical comedy—the fall and the knockdown—and the more exaggerated the action, the more they laugh. The average person watching a comedy on the screen does not want to be compelled to think—to figure out a piece of business—so that there is always a little hesitancy in dealing with satire and the little subtleties that are enjoyed by the clever people."

Following this principle, when Schenck set up Arbuckle with his own studio and gave him carte blanche to make films as he pleased, Arbuckle es-

Above

Fatty Arbuckle and Buster Keaton in *The Bell Boy*
with Alice Lake.

Below

Fatty, who goes straight in his first feature film, *The
Round-up,* is threatened here by slimy Wallace
Beery.

chewed subtlety in favor of slapstick—if anything, trying to outdo Sennett at his own game! There is a gusto and vitality to Arbuckle's slapstick that is positively overpowering in the films he made for the Comique Film Company.

The first scene of the first Comique film, *The Butcher Boy,* seems to have been choreographed rather than directed; its knockabout comedy, set inside a general store, is galvanizing. The falls, the hurling of pies and sacks of flour, the movement of people and objects within this carefully determined frame, are timed to utter perfection. And the gags are quite funny.

Another highlight of *The Butcher Boy*'s opening moments is the screen debut of Buster Keaton as an unruly customer. Keaton, in New York to begin rehearsals for a show, was introduced to Arbuckle, who invited him to visit the Comique studio in Manhattan. The two became fast friends, and Keaton abandoned his show and his stage career to stay with Arbuckle and learn about film comedy. Theirs was a momentous collaboration.

The critic for the *Morning Telegraph* wrote of *The Butcher Boy,* "Arbuckle will be hard put to it to maintain the quality of his premier release, but if he succeeds, his output will be second to none in the country."

Arbuckle did maintain that level of quality, and his two-reelers helped make him one of the most popular men in movies. Even the weakest of his Comique shorts has energy to spare. When Fatty and Buster perform a knockabout dance in *The Hayseed,* the falls are frantic and the energy of their roughhousing is awesome. If there is to be a rainstorm in *Good Night, Nurse!* it must be the most torrential movie downpour of all time. And when Fatty dons a female disguise, he plays it for all it's worth, even tantalizing Keaton with his flirtatious ways!

Equal partner in this slapstick team was wiry Al St. John, an uninspired comic but an able acrobat, who happened to be Arbuckle's nephew.

Some measure of Arbuckle's enormous popularity can be determined when one considers that Paramount asked him to make feature films in 1919 —before even Chaplin had made that auspicious move. Oddly enough, Arbuckle's first feature was *The Round-up.* As a Paramount ad announced, "Fatty's first full-length drama! And made from the great melodramatic stage success! Will the people eat it up? They will!" In retrospect it may seem strange that a star whose forte was slapstick should have started a feature-film career in a dramatic film, but as William K. Everson has pointed out, "Slapstick comedy was still looked on as something of a poor relation that had no business in 'respectable' full-length features, even though it might be great in shorts."

So, *The Round-up* it was, and although he received top billing, Arbuckle was cast in a supporting role as sheriff Jim Hoover in this stagy drama. His is a fairly serious performance—and quite credible—with only mild comic undertones. His final scene introduces a note of self-pity as he declares, "Nobody loves a fat man."

Paramount's thinking was sound, however. *The Round-up* was a great success, and it enabled Arbuckle to move on to feature-length comedy with confidence. But there would be no cop-chasing park-bench vehicles for Fatty: Paramount purchased such established stage hits as *Brewster's Millions* and stories by Irvin S. Cobb and other *Saturday Evening Post* writers. Sadly, negatives and prints of all these films disintegrated years ago, the lone exception being *Leap Year,* which survives as an extremely pleasant film but little more. Everson writes, "One has the impression all through *Leap Year* of Arbuckle held relentlessly in check, and told to let the situations provide the laughs instead. Yet when he does occasionally take over—as in the series of 'fits' where he makes each fall and grimace a little different—he is quite marvelous."

Ironically, this surviving film was first seen by Americans in the late 1960s, for it was one of two completed films to be withheld from release after the terrible Arbuckle scandal broke in late 1921.

Accused of raping and murdering an "actress" named Virginia Rappe during a San Francisco hotel party, Arbuckle was tried three times and finally exonerated with an unprecedented apology by the jury, but by then it was too late. A verdict had already been reached by the press, and by civic, church, and women's groups around the country for whom this was just one more example of Hollywood debauchery.

While most of Arbuckle's friends and associates in the film capital supported him privately, he was allowed to become a public whipping boy for all of Hollywood's misdemeanors, and his successful career as a screen comic screeched to a halt. An official ban by Will Hays, the newly appointed guardian of film industry morals, kept his films out of distribution, but even after this ban was lifted, the boycott continued.

On September 29, 1923, *Greater Amusements* magazine reported, "Roscoe (Fatty) Arbuckle, erstwhile screen comedian, still is popular with Milwaukee motion picture fans, if demonstrations which greeted him at every performance at Saxe's Strand theater may be taken as a criterion of opinion. The comedian, who appeared at the house recently despite vigorous protests of the city motion picture commission, church organizations and women's clubs, evoked prolonged applause with whistling and stamping of feet demonstrating approval. Business during the week, according to manager E. J. Weisfeldt, was considerably above average. Of the first 6,000 patrons at the theater, only two voted 'no' in the referendum on the question of Arbuckle's proposed return to the screen."

This dichotomy of public opinion plagued Arbuckle for the rest of his life. He found steady work as a comedy director, piloting such stars as Al St. John, Lupino Lane, and Lloyd Hamilton under the pseudonym William Goodrich (his father's name) and working with Buster Keaton without screen credit. (Arbuckle's second wife, Doris Deane, told author David Yallop that he in fact wrote and directed Keaton's classic *Sherlock, Jr.*)

But Arbuckle's return to the screen was many years off. It finally came in 1932 when Sam Sax, who produced Warner Brothers' Vitaphone short subjects in New York, saw Arbuckle in vaudeville and decided it was time for a screen comeback. The first short, *Hey, Pop,* was directed by Joseph Henabery, who had made three of Arbuckle's Paramount features in the early 1920s. Its opening scenes borrowed surefire gags from Fatty's 1916 Sennett short *The Waiters' Ball,* and its plot effectively combined comedy and sentiment. Arbuckle took some characteristically spectacular falls and helped stage a chase scene on Brooklyn streets. Sam Sax even arranged for the short to have a musical score

—unheard of in budget-minded Vitaphone comedies. But most remarkable of all was Arbuckle's ability to recapture the innocence and youthful spirit of his screen characterization after more than a decade in bitter exile away from the camera.

Other Vitaphone shorts ranged from mediocre to excellent, with *In the Dough* standing out for its pie-throwing slapstick and *Buzzin' Around* reteaming Fatty with Al St. John in a delightfully executed sight-gag marathon.

The success of these six shorts led to a feature contract with Warner Brothers. But sadly, the film was never to be. Arbuckle died in his sleep the night after that contract was signed. He was just forty-six.

Roscoe "Fatty" Arbuckle hasn't the reputation of his onetime costar Charlie Chaplin or his longtime friend and partner Buster Keaton. But fate has dealt badly with him. Many of his films are lost or difficult to see, and who is to say what Arbuckle might have accomplished if not for the tragedy that drove him off-screen and ruined his life?

Half a century after that scandal, Fatty Arbuckle still deserves a better break—from film history.

Fatty and Bull Montana in *Crazy to Marry,*
Arbuckle's last feature film released in the
United States.

Arbuckle behind the camera, probably taken at
Educational Pictures.

Fatty in one of his comeback shorts for
Vitaphone, *In the Dough,* with Marc Marion,
Lionel Stander, and a black-faced Shemp
Howard at right.

THE FILMS OF ROSCOE "FATTY" ARBUCKLE

This index includes Arbuckle's acting credits only, from the time he joined the Mack Sennett studio in 1913.

*Fatty and Mabel at the San Diego
   Exposition*—1915
Mabel, Fatty and the Law—1915
Fatty's New Role—1915
Mabel and Fatty's Married Life—
   1915
Fatty's Reckless Fling—1915
Fatty's Chance Acquaintance—1915
Love in Armor—1915
That Little Band of Gold—1915
Fatty's Faithful Fido—1915
When Love Took Wings—1915
Wished on Mabel—1915
*Mabel and Fatty Viewing the World's
   Fair at San Francisco*—1915
Mabel's Wilful Way—1915
Miss Fatty's Seaside Lovers—1915
The Little Teacher—1915
Fatty's Plucky Pup—1915
Fatty's Tintype Tangle—1915
Fickle Fatty's Fall—1915
The Village Scandal—1915
Fatty and the Broadway Stars—1915
Fatty and Mabel Adrift—1916
He Did and He Didn't—1916
The Bright Lights—1916
His Wife's Mistake—1916
The Other Man—1916
The Moonshiners—1916
The Waiters' Ball—1916
A Reckless Romeo—1916
A Creampuff Romance—1916

THE COMIQUE SHORTS (produced
by Joseph M. Schenck for Paramount)

The Butcher Boy—1917
A Reckless Romeo—1917
The Rough House—1917
His Wedding Night—1917
Oh, Doctor!—1917
Coney Island—1917
A Country Hero—1917

Out West—1918
The Bell Boy—1918
Moonshine—1918
Good Night, Nurse!—1918
The Cook—1918
The Sheriff—1918
Camping Out—1918
The Pullman Porter—1919
Love—1919
The Bank Clerk—1919
A Desert Hero—1919
Back Stage—1919
The Hayseed—1919
The Garage—1920

THE FEATURE FILMS (released by
Paramount)

The Round-up—1920
The Life of the Party—1920
Brewster's Millions—1920
The Dollar a Year Man—1921
The Traveling Salesman—1921
Gasoline Gus—1921
Crazy to Marry—1921
Leap Year—1921 (originally released
   in Europe only)
Freight Prepaid—1921 (originally
   released in Europe only)
Hollywood—1923 (guest appearance)

THE "COMEBACK" SHORTS
(released by Vitaphone-Warner
Brothers)

Hey, Pop—1932
Buzzin' Around—1933
How've You Bean?—1933
Close Relations—1933
In the Dough—1933
Tomalio—1933

Arbuckle reportedly does a bit in
Keaton's silent feature *Go West*.

Buster and Joe Roberts in *The Love Nest*.

4
BUSTER KEATON

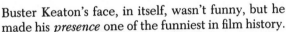

Buster Keaton's face, in itself, wasn't funny, but he made his *presence* one of the funniest in film history.

Buster could create a memorable comic scene just by being there. Example: *The Blacksmith* opens with a quotation from the poem, "Under a spreading chestnut-tree The village smithy stands." Dissolve to Buster, standing motionless in a sparse patch of shade. The camera pans up, and up, and up the trunk of an absurdly tall palm tree, then cuts to a long shot of the entire tableau.

There is no gag here, but it is a sublimely funny moment nonetheless. There is something about Buster Keaton attempting to strike a heroic pose beneath the silliest-looking tree in California that is irresistible.

Buster's stoic face became a mirror for all the absurdities of modern life, and its juxtaposition against a portentous backdrop of any kind was enough to inspire laughter.

As often as not, he would use this as a head start to build even bigger laughs, as in *The Paleface*. An Indian tribe has been cheated by a white plunderer, and the angry chief tells his braves to "kill the first white man that comes in that gate." Of course, we *know* that Buster is going to be the one to appear, and we laugh in anticipation. But he does us one better, for when he strolls through the entrance, he is brandishing a butterfly net! He ambles onto the Indian reservation blissfully unaware of his perilous fate. In fact, when the Indians stalk behind

Above
Keaton, funny without gags, in a momentous moment from *The Frozen North,* with leading lady Bonnie Hill.

Below
Buster woos Kathryn McGuire in *Sherlock, Jr.*

Above
Buster and friend in *The Cameraman.*

Below
Jimmy Durante and Keaton place their votes in *What! No Beer?*

him he thinks they're interested in watching his butterfly-catching technique!

Keaton's is often the comedy of reaction, and he learned this art at an early age. On stage from the time he was three years old, he was billed as "The Human Mop" in his family's vaudeville act, during which his father would toss him around the stage—into the scenery, the wings, and sometimes the orchestra pit. Buster rarely hurt himself in these acrobatic turns, and in fact, he was having a ball. But he soon learned that the audience didn't respond when he seemed to be enjoying himself, and that's when his famous frozen face was born.

Years later his deadpan expression formed the basis of a screen character that countered the Chaplin tradition, for Buster was basically a cold screen personality who earned an audience's laughter without winning its love. If Chaplin was the Universal Everyman, and Harold Lloyd the All-American Boy, then Buster Keaton was the square peg in society's round hole. (His introductory title card to *Go West* reads, "Some people travel through life making friends wherever they go while others—just travel through life.")

Survival is the most important thing in Keaton's films, not happy endings. In fact, two of his films end with images of death: In *Cops* he is apprehended by a legion of policemen in the final shot, and "The End" is chiseled on a tombstone with his porkpie hat perched on top; in *College* he wins the girl, and in a rapid succession of dissolves we see them married, with their children, old and gray, and in their adjacent burial plots.

In order for Buster to survive, he must use his wits. The result is a panoply of gags that equals and often surpasses the finest comedy achievements of all time. Keaton's gags are marvels of invention and execution.

They can be simple or complex, but they share a grace, style, and perfection that is dazzling. They also boast one important asset: honesty. Keaton demanded that his gags look real, no matter how outlandish they might be. The use of stunt men, process screens, miniatures, and photographic mattes, which became commonplace in sound comedies, was abhorrent to Keaton. When he dreamed up the unforgettable gag in *Steamboat Bill, Jr.,* in which the front of a house collapses around him but spares his life because he is standing in perfect position for an open window to pass over his body, Keaton did it for real. "The clearance of that window," he told Rudi Blesh, "was exactly three inches over my head and past each shoulder. And the front of the building—I'm not kidding —weighed two tons. It had to be built heavy and rigid in order not to bend or twist in that wind."

While Buster had a team of expert writers and technicians working with him, there was never any question of who was the guiding genius on the Keaton crew. Director Leo McCarey told Peter Bogdanovich that in the 1920s "all of us tried to steal each other's gagmen, but we had no luck with Keaton because he thought up his best gags himself and we couldn't steal *him!*"

He was silent comedy's Renaissance man: a fine comic actor who also happened to be a superb acrobat, a skilled film director and editor, an inspired gagman, and a brilliant engineer.

Keaton's brilliance could work against him at times, for many of his gags, and sometimes entire films, would be far too subtle for the average audience.

Time hasn't changed this situation: Keaton films rarely induce belly laughs. But they invite, and warrant, careful examination and, as often as not, produce a feeling of awe and wonderment in place of laughter.

In *The Three Ages,* Buster's first starring feature (aside from *The Saphead,* over which he had no control), there is a sequence in which caveman Keaton makes an overture to cavewoman Blanche Payson, a six-foot Amazon type. Her reaction is swift and decisive: She blasts Buster right over a cliff into the river below. But Keaton makes this gag an extraordinary screen moment by cutting from her initial clout to a shot of Buster in close-up as he is knocked backwards over the cliff. In semi-slow motion, he blows her a kiss while falling away from the camera and down to the watery landing. The shot is as startling today as it must have been in 1923.

Keaton made screen history from the moment he walked into camera range. That was in 1917, and it was at the behest of Roscoe "Fatty" Arbuckle, who met Keaton while the young performer was in New York about to start rehearsals for a new show. Arbuckle invited him to drop in at his Manhattan studio where he was about to start his first short, *The Butcher Boy,* for producer Joseph Schenck. Keaton came, saw, and was conquered by the motion-picture medium.

There isn't much of Keaton's personality in the finished short; Arbuckle, as star and director, dominated the film and established its comic motif, a slapstick ballet set inside a general store. But Buster's comic prowess is impossible to overlook. After years of being thrown about the stage in vaudeville, he was able to stage acrobatic falls that outdid even the agile Arbuckle. At one point in *The Butcher Boy,* Buster takes a wild swing with a broom that doesn't connect with its target and sends him spinning like a top. Later in the film, he does a backward fall and spins on his head before coming to rest on the floor. Keaton was made for silent comedy.

In his quest for perfection, Keaton reworked the famous "molasses sequence" from *The Butcher Boy* throughout his career. He performed the skit with Ed Wynn on his TV show in the early 1950s and repeated it on the novelty series *You Asked for It* when a viewer inquired whether it was true that Keaton actually lifted one leg up on a counter and then the other without immediately toppling over. It was true, all right, and Keaton performed the trick as effortlessly as he had thirty-odd years earlier.

Keaton stayed with Arbuckle for several years, interrupted by war duty. Gradually he became more a partner and less a stooge for Fatty, working closely with Arbuckle behind the camera as well as on-screen. Keaton's growing penchant for offbeat gags complemented Arbuckle's fondness for broad slapstick, as in *Moonshine* when Buster falls into a river and Arbuckle blithely hangs him up to dry on a tree branch!

When Arbuckle graduated to feature films, producer Schenck offered Buster a starring series of his own, and a new chapter in screen comedy was written. The Keaton shorts are brimming with incredible ideas that stretch silent comedy to its outermost boundaries. And the gags just never stop. In *The Blacksmith* a boy comes to watch Buster at work, carrying in his hand a helium balloon. Buster is about to dismount the front wheel of a car but doesn't have a jack to keep the car in position. He casually reaches over, takes the boy's balloon, attaches it to the car axle, and the balloon supports the car in place! Then the bratty kid uses a slingshot to burst his balloon, and the car crashes through the floor with devastating results.

In contrast, there is a simple gag in *My Wife's Relations* in which Buster, trying to elude an angry Joe Roberts, is conducting a chase through a hotel, using stairs and an elevator. It's a wonderful moment because we in the audience are just as fooled as Roberts, and it's a gag worth cherishing because it's so disarmingly *simple*.

Even the simplest Keaton gag had to be done just right, however. Keaton was a perfectionist, and he stimulated his close-knit troupe to give him the best they had to offer. When they made the move from short subjects to feature films in 1923, Keaton's crew seemed to flower rather than cringe under the pressure of creating five- to seven-reel comedies. Buster's first feature films—*The Three Ages, Our Hospitality, Sherlock, Jr., The Navigator,* and *Seven Chances*—are unquestionably his best.

"There was one big advantage in those days, when you owned your own studio, and you were the only company in there," Keaton told Kevin Brownlow many years later. "The skeleton of your outfit—that's your technical man, your head cameraman and his assistant, your prop man, your head electrician—these people are all on salary with you for fifty-two weeks of the year. So if I'm sitting in the cutting room, and the picture's been finished, and I want an extra shot, I can do it. If I want to take a sequence out—If I turned to the left in that alley I could drop this whole sequence and pick it up right here—we can get the cameras out that afternoon and go back to the alley and shoot it. Now to do that would cost me the gasoline of the car we owned, and the amount of film we bought from Eastman to put in the camera to take it. Which, when it's all added up, means about two dollars and thirty-nine cents.'

It was this kind of care that enabled such startling gag sequences as those in *Sherlock, Jr.* to be realized. This is the film in which Keaton plays a film projectionist who dreams himself into the action of the picture he's showing but first has trouble coordinating his "real" existence with the happenings on-screen. Backgrounds suddenly change behind him, so that as he's walking along a street he suddenly discovers he's on the edge of a cliff, which then cuts to a jungle scene, and so on and on. The trickery is impossible to detect.

One of Keaton's best-liked films has none of this gimmickry, however, and that is *The General.* This film stands out among all silent comedies because it is solidly constructed and built along the lines of a serious story. Produced on a lavish scale and shot on location in Oregon, *The General* boasts some of the most elaborate trappings ever mounted for a film comedy, including a shot of a train chugging across a burning trestle that collapses under its weight and sends the engine and its cars plummeting into the gorge below.

The General is also brimming with gags, but these comedy sequences are built *into* the story, not added *onto* it. The timing and arrangement of many shots involving moving trains, camera positioning, and the like are flawless. The film is one of Keaton's milestones.

Unfortunately, it wasn't long after *The General* was made that Buster's career took a tragic nose dive. Joseph Schenck sold his contract to M-G-M, which expected Buster to function in their giant-studio atmosphere without his usual crew and its tremendous freedom. His last two silents, *The Cameraman* and *Spite Marriage,* were good comedies but already showed telltale signs of erosion in the Keaton style. They were more conventional, less personal than his earlier films. It was the beginning of the end.

We needn't reiterate the full story of Keaton's decline and fall at M-G-M in the talkie era. But those films of the early 1930s and the later two-reelers he made for Educational and Columbia Pictures had one thing in common: No matter how bad, there are always moments when one can see Keaton's brilliance shine through. Often these moments are fleeting—some of the M-G-M features like *Doughboys,* are execrable, and many of the two-reelers are no better—but it is rare to find a film with Buster Keaton that is completely without merit, simply because he was in it. Time and again he tried to persuade his producers, directors, and writers to let him improve the films by adding his own material and supervising his own gag sequences. As often as not, they refused. What a sad fate for such a gifted artist.

Although Keaton's two-reel comedies of the 1930s and early 1940s were cheaply and quickly made, they afforded him at least the opportunity to return to the milieu that suited him best. Away from the supervisors and experts at M-G-M, he could work in simple surroundings, encore some of the better gags from his silent features, and occasionally experiment with new comedy ideas.

He also won the opportunity to rekindle some of the silent-comedy spirit in Twentieth Century-Fox's feature film *Hollywood Cavalcade,* starring Alice Faye and Don Ameche as prototypes of Mabel Normand and Mack Sennett. Keaton costarred with Faye in a re-creation of a "typical" silent comedy, which was directed by Buster's old friend and associate Mal St. Clair, and which scored a bull's-eye with some genuinely first-rate slapstick and sight gags.

After that feature "comeback" Buster made occasional appearances in films throughout the 1940s, although most were either walk-ons or thankless supporting roles. Exceptions were a plumber sequence in *Forever and a Day* and a pleasingly offbeat role as a whimsical bus driver in *San Diego, I Love You.* Unfortunately, one of Buster's major roles landed on the cutting-room floor: a supporting part in *New Moon* with Nelson Eddy and Jeanette MacDonald.

During the 1940s Keaton also worked as a gagman and comedy troubleshooter at M-G-M. His efforts were usually uncredited, but his tutelage was valuable to such stars as Clark Gable, Judy Garland, Mickey Rooney, and especially Red Skelton.

Buster's reemergence as a performer came about in the early days of television. First he scored with a local show in Los Angeles, which ran from 1949 to 1951. *Life* magazine reported, "One undisputed advantage the citizens of California have over their countrymen is being able to see Buster Keaton on TV. Televised out of Los Angeles, Keaton is reviving the dead-pan pantomime that made him one of the greatest of the silent movie comics. Keaton has not been starred in a movie since 1933, but now at the age of 54 he is taking pratfalls on a bare floor that other comics wouldn't try on a pile of marshmallows. Like Ed Wynn, who first introduced Keaton as a guest star on his own show in December, Keaton is enthusiastic about TV. He feels that it captures some of the movies' early gusto and is just right for spontaneous clowning."

Harvey Korman, Lucille Ball and her old crony Buster Keaton,
doing a TV skit in the 1960s.

Above, left

Buster and Alice Faye re-create a silent comedy for the 1939
feature *Hollywood Cavalcade.*

Below, left

Joyce Compton and Keaton in *The Villain Still Pursued Her.*

Unfortunately, when Keaton tried to capitalize on the success of this live series by committing another series to film, the results were dismal: hackneyed, slow-moving, everything the live shows weren't. And since there was no coaxial cable linking the West and East coasts at the time of his early live broadcasts, the rest of the country was denied the opportunity of "rediscovering" Buster Keaton, a rediscovery that might have made him a major star all over again.

Keaton found regular employment in television, even if there were bittersweet moments. Garry Moore, who had idolized Keaton as a child, hired him to appear on his daytime network show in the early 1950s. "We put him on for two weeks," Moore recalled, "and I said, 'Buster, what are we going to do when we run out of those great routines of yours?' He said, 'Don't worry, I move funny; there are plenty of things we can do.' So after we used up those routines of his, like putting the drunk to bed, we put him on as a comic cameraman. But when you're doing five days a week, you have no time for rehearsal, and that kind of business he did had to be perfectly timed. Like if he was going to turn around and step into a bucket of paste, you have to be able to do it *naturally* —you can't be looking around for the bucket. But with so little rehearsal, it just didn't work out, and we had to let him go. It was so sad—imagine *me* letting Buster Keaton go."

As television grew, it offered fewer opportunities for Buster to work in a free and flexible format. But there were always those magic moments, just as in the films. In the early 1960s Keaton did a series of commercials for New York-based Simon Pure Beer that re-created silent-comedy vignettes and echoed some of his favorite gags (such as the newspaper that opens from a small page to a wallpaper-sized sheet, from *The High Sign*) with remarkable effect.

He did scores of commercials, guest appearances, industrial films, and occasional movies. While filming *The Railrodder,* a comedy travelogue for the National Film Board of Canada, a second crew shot a documentary called *Buster Keaton Rides Again,* which might be subtitled "A Portrait of the Artist as an Old Man." In this fascinating film we see Buster debating the merits of various gags with his director, Gerald Potterton, and sulking when he doesn't get his way. Keaton remained a fighting spirit to the very end.

If it hasn't been made clear already, it must be stated that Keaton was one of the hardest working men who ever lived. No effort, no sacrifice was too great for the sake of his art.

"I asked him how he did all those falls," Garry Moore remembers, "and he said, 'I'll show you.' He opened his jacket and he was all bruised. So that's how he did it—*it hurt*—but you had to care enough not to care."

One of Keaton's last feature films was an American-International Pictures quickie called *Sergeant Deadhead,* which starred Frankie Avalon. The director was a longtime friend whose career also dated back to the silent-film era, Norman Taurog. He tells a story that sums up Keaton to a tee.

"Just before Buster died, he was still funny, still funny. I remember he said to me, 'Hey, Norm, I can get you a surefire belly laugh.' I said, 'How?' He said, 'Let me run with the fire hose. Let me run to the end of it and let me go straight up [in the air] and land down.' I said, 'Buster, at your age, are you out of your mind?' He said, 'I won't hurt myself, Norm, I've done it for years.' I said, 'Go ahead and do it' and he did it. He must have gone six or eight feet in the air and let flap. I'm scared to death to say 'Are you all right, Buster?' so I went halfway in, and Buster said, 'I'm all right!' "

He was all right from the moment he made his film debut in 1917 to the very last time he appeared on-screen. Buster Keaton knew more about film comedy than anyone else in the business.

THE FILMS OF BUSTER KEATON

THE FATTY ARBUCKLE SHORTS
(released by Paramount)

The Butcher Boy—1917
The Rough House—1917
His Wedding Night—1917
Oh, Doctor!—1917
Coney Island—1917
A Country Hero—1917
Out West—1918
The Bell Boy—1918
Moonshine—1918
Good Night, Nurse!—1918
The Cook—1918
Backstage—1919
The Hayseed—1919
The Garage—1920
The Saphead—1920 (Keaton's first
  feature film, produced and released
  by Metro Pictures)

THE KEATON SHORTS (written and
directed by Keaton. Eddie Cline was co-director on all except *The Goat* and *The Blacksmith*, where Mal St. Clair is credited. Keaton received solo credit for his last short, *The Love Nest*. Released by Metro and then— beginning with *The Playhouse*—by First National)

The High Sign—1920, released 1921
One Week—1920
Convict 13—1920
The Scarecrow—1920
Neighbors—1921

The Haunted House—1921
Hard Luck—1921
The Goat—1921
The Playhouse—1921
The Boat—1921
The Paleface—1922
Cops—1922
My Wife's Relations—1922
The Blacksmith—1922
The Frozen North—1922
Daydreams—1922
The Electric House—1922
The Balloonatic—1923
The Love Nest—1923

THE STARRING FEATURE FILMS
(co-directed by Buster Keaton, except for *Sherlock, Jr.*, which he directed himself)

The Three Ages—
  Keaton-Schenck/United Artists
  1923
Our Hospitality—
  Keaton-Schenck/Metro 1923
Sherlock, Jr.—Keaton-Schenck/Metro
  1924
The Navigator—
  Keaton-Schenck/Metro 1924
Seven Chances—
  Keaton-Schenck/Metro 1925
Go West—Keaton-Schenck/M-G-M
  1925
Battling Butler—
  Keaton-Schenck/M-G-M 1926

The General—
  Keaton-Schenck/United Artists
  1926 (the last time Keaton received
  directorial credit on one of his
  films)
College—Keaton-Schenck/United
  Artists 1927
Steamboat Bill, Jr.—
  Keaton-Schenck/United Artists
  1928
The Cameraman—M-G-M 1928
Spite Marriage—M-G-M 1929
Hollywood Revue of 1929—M-G-M
  1929
Free and Easy—M-G-M 1930 (retitled
  Easy Go for television release)
Doughboys—M-G-M 1930
Parlor Bedroom and Bath—M-G-M
  1931
Sidewalks of New York—M-G-M 1931
The Passionate Plumber—M-G-M
  1932
Speak Easily—M-G-M 1932
What! No Beer?—M-G-M 1933

THE EDUCATIONAL PICTURES SHORTS

The Gold Ghost—1934
Allez Oop—1934
Palooka From Paducah—1935
One-Run Elmer—1935
Hayseed Romance—1935
Tars and Stripes—1935
The E-Flat Man—1935
The Timid Young Man—1935
Grand Slam Opera—1936
Three on a Limb—1936
Blue Blazes—1936
The Chemist—1936
Mixed Magic—1936
Jail Bait—1937
Ditto—1937
Love Nest on Wheels—1937

THE COLUMBIA PICTURES SHORTS

Pest From the West—1939

Mooching Through Georgia—1939
Nothing But Pleasure—1940
Pardon My Berth Marks—1940
The Taming of the Snood—1940
The Spook Speaks—1940
His Ex Marks the Spot—1940
So You Won't Squawk—1941
General Nuisance—1941
She's Oil Mine—1941

Miscellaneous Film Appearances

Le Roi des Champs-Élysées—Nero
  Film 1934 (Starring French feature
  film)
*The Invader (An Old Spanish
  Custom)*—British and Continental
  Films 1934 (another starring feature
  film, Buster's last for many years)
Hollywood Cavalcade—Twentieth
  Century-Fox 1939
The Villain Still Pursued Her—RKO
  1940
Li'l Abner—RKO 1940
Forever and a Day—RKO 1943
San Diego, I Love You—Universal
  1944
That's the Spirit—Universal 1945
That Night With You—Universal
  1945
God's Country—Action
  Pictures/Screen Guild 1946
*El Moderno Barba Azul (A Modern
  Bluebird)*—Alsa Films 1947 (a
  starring feature made in Mexico)
Un Duel à Mort—Films Azur 1948
  (French short subject)
The Lovable Cheat—Film Classics
  1949
In the Good Old Summertime—
  M-G-M 1949
You're My Everything—Twentieth
  Century-Fox 1949
Sunset Boulevard—Paramount 1950
Limelight—Chaplin/United Artists
  1952
Paradise for Buster—John Deere and
  Co. 1952 (industrial short)

L'Incantevole Nemica—Orso Film 1953 (cameo role in Italian film)

The Misadventures of Buster Keaton —British Lion 1953 (compilation from Keaton's filmed television series)

Around the World in Eighty Days— United Artists 1956

The Adventures of Huckleberry Finn —M-G-M 1960

Ten Girls Ago—American-Canadian Productions 1962 (unfinished feature)

The Triumph of Lester Snapwell— Eastman Kodak 1962 (industrial film)

It's a Mad, Mad, Mad, Mad World— United Artists 1963

Pajama Party— American-International 1964

Beach Blanket Bingo— American-International 1965

The Railrodder—National Film Board of Canada 1965

How to Stuff a Wild Bikini— American-International 1965

Sergeant Deadhead— American-International 1965

Film—Evergreen Theatre 1965

Buster Keaton Rides Again—National Film Board of Canada 1965

The Scribe—Film-Tele Productions 1966 (industrial film; posthumously released)

A Funny Thing Happened on the Way to the Forum—United Artists 1966 (posthumously released)

Due Marines e un General (War Italian Style)— American-International 1967 (posthumously released)

5
HAROLD LLOYD

Charlie Chaplin was hailed as an artist and a genius within one year of his film debut. Harold Lloyd has seldom if ever been accorded the same recognition, yet in the 1920s his films were more popular than Chaplin's or any other comedian's in America.

Lloyd has been called a workman, a capable gagman, but never an artist. His ability to sublimate his comic ambitions and ideas into a wholly natural characterization—in other words, *to make it look easy*—may have cost him this well-deserved accolade.

There is perhaps some resentment toward Lloyd, as well, because he was so methodical in the preparation of his films, but he was only following a pattern employed by such colleagues as Chaplin and Keaton. Lloyd labored over his feature films for months on end, constantly working to improve sequences and build a stronger plot structure for the gags. When that was done, he tested his films with audiences and then performed further surgery to make them as perfect as possible.

Lloyd's work paid off in the 1920s and continues to yield results whenever his films are shown to modern-day audiences. They are not just funny, they are

Above
Sammy Brooks, Bud Jamison, Harold, and Bebe Daniels in *Ask Father*, one of Lloyd's best short comedies.

Below
Lloyd and Peggy Cartright recall Chaplin's *A Dog's Life* in the short *From Hand to Mouth*.

guaranteed to be funny, because the ingredients for laughter haven't really changed that much in fifty years, and Lloyd's films are audience-proven.

Harold Lloyd's determination to make his films as good as they could be stemmed from his Horatio Alger-type upbringing. A product of the Midwest who caught the acting bug as a youngster, he broke into the movies with the same kind of ambition and optimism he would later portray in his comedies.

But when Lloyd got the chance to star in his own comedy shorts, which were produced by another young man, Hal Roach, whom he had met among the ranks of "extras" at Universal Pictures, it was not as the go-getting All-American Boy but as an ersatz version of Charlie Chaplin's Little Tramp. The first incarnation was called Willie Work, but then Lloyd modified his costume and named the character Lonesome Luke.

The Lonesome Luke films were little more than hand-me-down copies of Chaplin's shorts. They were filmed quickly and cheaply by Hal Roach's fledgling Rolin Film Company, with an able acting troupe that included leading lady Bebe Daniels, sidekick Snub Pollard, and stock heavy Bud Jamison.

The late cinematographer Hal Mohr, who served a brief stint as director on the Lloyd series in 1917, recalled, "The way we worked was, we had a stock company, and they had a little schoolbus; we'd load the stock company in the bus. Harold had a Chandler touring car, and his chauffeur, Gil Pratt, wanted to become a director, so he would co-direct with me. We had no scripts, but we'd get a story idea, and develop the thing, and talk it out. We only had to make nine minutes of film, so we'd get a running gag going. The first picture I made for them was called *The Big Idea,* which opened at the Criterion Theatre the opening week that the theater opened. We'd leave all the interiors until after we'd gotten the exteriors, because the running gags depended entirely on what we did exterior; so then we'd spend a day or two on the interiors, and in one week we'd shoot a film. These were seven-day weeks, of course, not like today. And in the meantime, Harold's other director, Alf Goulding, was preparing, getting his ideas together. So the week that we'd finish, and I'd go into the cutting room to cut the film, Alf was out shooting."

In this fashion Lloyd was able to star in more than 150 one- and two-reel shorts between 1915 and 1919—more films than most performers make in a lifetime!

The Lonesome Lukes are, for the most part, painfully unfunny, and the "pain" is often literal as Lloyd, Pollard, Jamison, and others engage in the kind of casual violence that Chaplin had performed at Keystone. Punching, hitting, and especially kicking are major pursuits, and pie throwing is usually eschewed in favor of hurling bricks or other heavy objects.

Lloyd was never terribly fond of Lonesome Luke, but the character enabled him to launch a starring series with practically no credentials, and it gave him valuable experience. After doing the Luke comedies for two years, he longed to try something different and asked Hal Roach for such a chance. Only Lloyd's growing popularity enabled Roach to persuade his distributor, Pathé, to go along with the idea, provided that he continue producing Lonesome Luke shorts on a regular basis.

So it was that in mid-1917 Harold Lloyd made his screen debut in the "glasses character" that would bring him international renown. But this was no overnight process. At first the contrast between Luke and Harold was minimal; story lines and gags hardly changed at all. But there was one important new factor: Harold was a believable human being, not a caricature like Luke.

Now Harold could pursue Bebe Daniels and audiences could respond. Gradually settings and stories did change to embrace this new, more realistic character whose only trademark was a pair of horn-rimmed glasses—in an era when virtually every screen comic depended on funny costumes or makeup to create a visual impression. At first the Harold Lloyd comedies were one-reel (approximately ten minutes) in length, while the Lonesome Lukes were two reels long. This gave the Luke comedies an opportunity to stretch out and build characterization and stories, while it was the non-Luke films that needed this chance so much more.

Many of Harold's early "glasses" films continued to resemble the earliest park-bench comedies, which seemed to have been invented on the spot. The Chaplin influence remained strong: *Take a Chance* borrowed its convict-clothes chase from *The Adventurer,* while Lloyd's *Pipe the Whiskers* was a cheerful plagiarism of *The Cure.* But with each passing year, experience, bigger budgets, and the greater ambition of both Lloyd and Roach caused the quality of these films to improve.

A 1919 one-reeler called *Ask Father* has just about everything one could ask for in a comedy short. Harold has to obtain the consent of his wealthy girl friend's busy father in order to marry her. Switchboard operator Bebe Daniels keeps setting a pillow in position on the floor of the father's outer office so that Harold will land on it when he's thrown out by two burly guards. But Father has other devices for getting rid of people he doesn't want to see, including a trapdoor and an incredible conveyor-belt mechanism built into the floor. Harold goes so far as to climb the outside of the building to get to the second-floor office, only to be ejected once more. When he finally gets to see Father and obtains his permission, the girl friend tells him she's decided to elope with someone else, and Harold winds up with Bebe instead.

For years it has been thought that *Look Out Below!,* released later in 1919, marked Harold's first building-ledge episode, but *Ask Father* is the probable debut of that gag device. It also typifies the energy and invention that went into some of the more elaborate one-reelers during this period, which alternated with such throwaways as *Off the Trolley* that relied entirely on Lloyd's and Bebe Daniels' winning personalities to carry them along.

Lloyd's graduation to two-reelers in late 1919 allowed him to expand his comic ideas and gave him the first opportunity to think more clearly about his characterization. This was a slow development, which did not reach fruition until his first feature films, but the experiments and growing pains of his two- and three-reel shorts of 1920–21 were more than worthwhile.

From Hand to Mouth opens on a note from Chaplin's *A Dog's Life,* with Harold, a dog, and a little girl scrounging for food, outcasts of life sharing their lot. *Captain Kidd's Kids* involves a bizarre dream sequence in which Harold is held prisoner on a ship run by fetching female pirates—and led by Bebe's battle-ax mother. *His Royal Slyness* spoofs *The Prisoner of Zenda* with Harold taking the place of a lookalike prince.

Some of the shorts, however, show real progress both in Harold's gag style

Above
Mildred Davis and Harold Lloyd in *Doctor Jack*.

Below
Harold is in *Hot Water* with his family, Josephine Crowell, Charles
Stevenson, Jobyna Ralston, and Mickey McBan; Silas D. Wilcox is
the cop.

A typical New York scene, from *Speedy*.

and in his character. *High and Dizzy,* made in 1920, is a conventional comedy, which includes a building-ledge sequence, but by the time of *Never Weaken,* one year later, Harold has learned how to incorporate this "thrill comedy" material into a well-balanced short that utilizes his glasses character to its fullest potential to build a story in which the gags *make sense.*

This notion came to such full flower in *Grandma's Boy* that Hal Roach felt Lloyd had sacrificed comedy in favor of a character study. Lloyd argued that the evolution of his character in this important film *was* the basis for comedy, and the star and producer compromised somewhere between the two extremes. Late in life, Lloyd told Kevin Brownlow that if he had to choose a favorite among his features, it would be *Grandma's Boy.*

In Lloyd's subsequent features, he was careful to think out his characterization and work with his gagmen to see that the story and sight gags grew out of that character. This was, finally, what set Lloyd apart from his talented but undistinguished colleagues in Hollywood who relied on gags alone to make their films funny. Lloyd's character changed from film to film, but whatever the premise, he made sure that he never did anything *out of character* for that particular story.

Lloyd eventually parted company with Hal Roach, for financial reasons and also because Lloyd wanted ownership and control of his films. When he set up his own production company, Lloyd gathered a team of gagman, technicians, and comedy specialists who were on salary year-round, even during lulls between pictures. He had plenty of help to make his films, but as he later remarked, "If anything went wrong and I didn't like it, I had nobody to blame but myself. I had complete control over all my pictures."

Lloyd never released more than two features a year, and after 1924 only one a year, so he was keenly aware of the pressure on him to make each film better than the last. Every time he and his gagmen worked on a film, they tried to devise ways to take the same basic elements and make them funnier, more elaborate than ever before.

The chase is a good example. In *Girl Shy* Harold discovers that the girl he loves is about to marry a conniving bigamist, and he races to rescue her at the church, commandeering a streetcar at one point and switching from one vehicle to another in order to meet his frantic deadline. It's a wonderful climax to this deliberately paced film, but the near-misses of his trolley with passing cars are a bit too regulated, too exact to be entirely convincing.

Lloyd vowed to improve on this chase in *For Heaven's Sake,* but this time it's embellished with a variety of hilarious twists and turnabouts. It's a crowd of pedestrians Harold is egging on, and at one point, turning a corner, the angry mob chases after someone who looks like Harold from the rear, leaving the real Harold behind! Undaunted, Harold hops into a taxi, which easily bypasses the runners; he tells the perplexed "double" to jump inside, and as he does, Harold takes his place and continues the chase!

Harold's character, and the spirit of his comedies, represented everything upbeat and affirmative about America in the 1920s. He was the meek inheriting the earth, an ordinary boy-next-door who survived by his wits, won the girl, and exemplified the ideals that formed the backbone of this country.

Everyone remembers Harold climbing the side of a building and hanging from a clock in *Safety Last,* but it's equally important to recall that the impetus for this action in the film's plot was Harold's desire to make good and impress his girl back home.

When sound came to Hollywood in the late 1920s, it caught Lloyd off guard, and he hastily remade much of his then current production, *Welcome Danger,* to be able to release it as a talkie. But this slow, ponderous production was his first misstep in many years.

Ironically, when Harold returned to familiar ground for his next film, *Feet First,* the reception from critics and audiences was that of a return to "old-fashioned" film making from the silent era.

Thus Mordaunt Hall in *The New York Times* wrote of Lloyd's 1932 *Movie Crazy,* "After the gangster films and those concerned with the more or less serious activities of gossip mongers and crooners, this offering came to those in the packed theater (last night) as a relief, for it made the spectators forget all about the trials and tribulations of the world outside."

As the 1930s wore on, Lloyd's brand of humor became scarce on movie screens, and his films—which came in intervals of two years—were greeted in similar fashion every time. Of *The Milky Way* (1936), Frank S. Nugent wrote in the *Times,* "It's good to have an old-time Harold Lloyd comedy back in town," while the *New Yorker* critic said, "Without any of those mechanical stunts that you find in a Cantor picture or the Marx Brothers' operettas, this Lloyd film manages to sustain a pleasantly soothing humor throughout. It's a comedy of the untoward catastrophes that may befall one of the world's innocents."

There simply wasn't much room for innocence in the 1930s, and more and more Lloyd harked back to a simpler time for moviegoers and critics who appreciated the tranquillity of the 1920s.

After *Professor Beware,* a genial but lackluster film in 1938, Lloyd retired from the screen, without announcement or fanfare. He dabbled in producing at RKO but was generally inactive until the brilliant writer-director Preston Sturges coaxed him back to movies in 1946 with a vehicle tailor-made for him: *The Sin of Harold Diddlebock* (ultimately released as *Mad Wednesday*).

The premise was irresistible: The new film would open with the climax of Lloyd's classic football game from *The Freshman,* in which underdog bench warmer Harold is called into action at the last minute and wins the game. The film would then follow Harold's progress over the next twenty years to show (of all things) that the onetime All-American Hero is now a stoop-shouldered clerk whose life has been one long yawn. Fired from his job after all these years, Harold chances to meet a street straggler name Wormy, who through drink and persuasion changes Harold's personality overnight. He decides to live it up for the first time in twenty years and goes on a mad spree during which he loses track of an entire day and awakens to find that he has somehow purchased a circus! The film even manages to include a brief sequence on a building ledge with Harold and a lion.

Unfortunately, *Mad Wednesday* never quite lives up to its premise. There are individually hilarious scenes and fine performances, but the film lacks a central thrust. The climactic chase on a building ledge, while nostalgic and amusing, also falls short of its goal, particularly in comparison with Lloyd's original daredevil stunts, which were not only hair-raising but credible.

Sturges' biggest mistake was opening his film with a sequence from *The Freshman* so perfect, so funny, that it made everything that followed pale by comparison. *Mad Wednesday* received surprisingly good reviews but failed to score a hit with the public. It was Harold Lloyd's last film appearance.

In later years nothing pleased Harold Lloyd more than showing his films to appreciative audiences, particularly young people. In 1962 he compiled *Harold Lloyd's World of Comedy* and followed it with *Harold Lloyd's Funny Side of Life.*

Harold Lloyd and Hal Roach:
They started together as extras in
the early teens; in 1933 a more
prosperous pair recall the past.

He also prepared some of his full-length features for reissue, and like Chaplin, he refused to stop tampering with them, trying to tighten the editing to conform to modern taste and running them at previews to see where the laughs were strongest.

In 1970, a year before his death, he made several personal appearances with his long-unseen 1927 comedy *The Kid Brother*. He brought it to a cinema class at UCLA made up of young people who had little if any previous exposure to Lloyd's films, who were openly skeptical about the silent film they were about to see. But when the film was over and "The End" flashed on the screen, the class rose at once and gave Lloyd a thunderous standing ovation.

The comedian was obviously moved and could only comment quietly, "I always liked it."

The pride he took in creating film comedy always came through and will keep his films alive for many years to come.

THE FILMS OF HAROLD LLOYD

THE SHORT SUBJECTS (all produced by Hal Roach and released by Pathé)

Just Nuts—1915
Lonesome Luke—1915
Once Every Ten Minutes—1915
    (believed to be a Lloyd film)

Spit-Ball Sadie—1915 (uncertain)
Soaking His Clothes—1915
    (uncertain)
Pressing His Suit—1915 (uncertain)
Terribly Stuck Up—1915 (uncertain)
A Mix-up for Maisie—1915
Some Baby—1915

Harold and Lionel Stander in *Professor, Beware!*

Harold Lloyd's final screen appearance, in *Mad Wednesday (The Sin of Harold Diddlebock)* with Frank Moran, Edgar Kennedy, and Jimmy Conlin.

Fresh From the Farm—1915
   (uncertain)
Giving Them Fits—1915
Bughouse Bellhops—1915
Tinkering With Trouble—1915
   (uncertain)
Great While It Lasted—1915

Ragtime Snap Shots—1915
A Foozle at the Tea Party—1915
Ruses, Rhymes and Roughnecks—
   1915
Peculiar Patients' Pranks—1915
Lonesome Luke, Social Gangster—
   1915

Lonesome Luke Leans to the Literary —1916

Luke Lugs Luggage—1916

Lonesome Luke Lolls in Luxury— 1916

Luke, the Candy Cut-Up—1916

Luke Foils the Villain—1916

Luke and the Rural Roughnecks— 1916

Luke Pipes the Pippens—1916

Lonesome Luke, Circus King—1916

Luke's Double—1916

Them Was the Happy Days—1916

Luke and the Bomb Throwers—1916

Luke's Late Lunchers—1916

Luke Laughs Last—1916

Luke's Fatal Flivver—1916

Luke's Society Mix-Up—1916

Luke's Washful Waiting—1916

Luke Rides Rough-Shod—1916

Luke, Crystal Gazer—1916

Luke's Lost Lamb—1916

Luke Does the Midway—1916

Luke Joins the Navy—1916

Luke and the Mermaids—1916

Luke's Speedy Club Life—1916

Luke and the Bangtails—1916

Luke the Chauffeur—1916

Luke's Preparedness Preparations— 1916

Luke the Gladiator—1916

Luke, Patient Provider—1916

Luke's Newsie Knockout—1916

Luke's Movie Muddle

Luke, Rank Impersonator—1916

Luke's Fireworks Fizzle—1916

Luke Locates the Loot—1916

Luke's Shattered Sleep—1916

Luke's Lost Liberty—1917

Luke's Busy Day—1917

Luke's Trolley Troubles—1917

Lonesome Luke, Lawyer—1917

Luke Wins Ye Ladye Fair—1917

Lonesome Luke's Lively Life—1917

Lonesome Luke on Tin Can Alley— 1917

Lonesome Luke's Honeymoon—1917

Lonesome Luke, Plumber—1917

Stop! Luke! Listen!—1917

Lonesome Luke, Messenger—1917

Lonesome Luke, Mechanic—1917

Lonesome Luke's Wild Women—1917

Over the Fence—1917 (first film with the "glasses character")

Lonesome Luke Loses Patients—1917 (Luke)

Pinched—1917

By the Sad Sea Waves—1917

Birds of a Feather—1917 (Luke)

Bliss—1917

Lonesome Luke in From London to Laramie—1917 (Luke)

The Flirt—1917

Clubs Are Trump—1917 (Luke)

All Aboard—1917

We Never Sleep—1917 (the last Lonesome Luke comedy)

Move On—1917

Bashful—1917

The Tip—1917

The Big Idea—1918

The Lamb—1918

Hit Him Again—1918

Beat It—1918

A Gasoline Wedding—1918

Look Pleasant, Please—1918

Here Come the Girls—1918

Let's Go—1918

On the Jump—1918

Follow the Crowd—1918

Pipe the Whiskers—1918

It's a Wild Life—1918

Hey There—1918

Kicked Out—1918

The Non-Stop Kid—1918

Two-Gun Gussie—1918

Fireman, Save My Child—1918

The City Slicker—1918

Sic 'Em Towser—1918

Somewhere in Turkey—1918

Are Crooks Dishonest?—1918

An Ozark Romance—1918

Kicking the Germ out of Germany— 1918

That's Him—1918
Bride and Gloom—1918
Two Scrambled—1918
Bees in His Bonnet—1918
Swing Your Partners—1918
Why Pick on Me?—1918
Nothing But Trouble—1918
Hear 'Em Rave—1918
Take a Chance—1918
She Loves Me Not—1918
Wanted—$5,000—1919
Going! Going! Gone!—1919
Ask Father—1919
On the Fire—1919
I'm on My Way—1919
Look Out Below!—1919
The Dutiful Dub—1919
Next Aisle Over—1919
A Sammy in Siberia—1919
Just Dropped In—1919
Crack Your Heels—1919
Ring Up the Curtain—1919
Young Mr. Jazz—1919
Si Senor—1919
Before Breakfast—1919
The Marathon—1919
Back to the Woods—1919
Pistols for Breakfast—1919
Swat the Crook—1919
Off the Trolley—1919
Spring Fever—1919
Billy Blazes, Esq.—1919
Just Neighbors—1919
At the Old Stage Door—1919
Never Touched Me—1919
A Jazzed Honeymoon—1919
Count Your Change—1919
Chop Suey & Co.—1919
Heap Big Chief—1919
Don't Shove—1919
Be My Wife—1919
The Rajah—1919
He Leads, Others Follow—1919
Soft Money—1919
Count the Votes—1919
Pay Your Dues—1919
His Only Father—1919

Bumping into Broadway—1919
Captain Kidd's Kids—1919
From Hand to Mouth—1919
His Royal Slyness—1920
Haunted Spooks—1920
An Eastern Westerner—1920
High and Dizzy—1920
Get Out and Get Under—1920
Number Please—1920
Now or Never—1921
Among Those Present—1921
I Do—1921
Never Weaken—1921

THE FEATURE FILMS

A Sailor-Made Man—Hal
    Roach-Associated Exhibitors-Pathé
    1921
Grandma's Boy—Hal
    Roach-Associated Exhibitors 1922
Doctor Jack—Hal Roach-Pathé 1922
Safety Last—Hal Roach-Pathé 1923
Why Worry?—Hal Roach-Pathé 1923
Girl Shy—Lloyd-Pathé 1924
Hot Water—Lloyd-Pathé 1924
The Freshman—Lloyd-Pathé 1925
For Heaven's Sake—Lloyd-Paramount
    1926
The Kid Brother—Lloyd-Paramount
    1927
Speedy—Lloyd-Paramount 1928
Welcome Danger—Lloyd-Paramount
    1929 (Lloyd's first talkie)
Feet First—Lloyd-Paramount 1930
Movie Crazy—Lloyd-Paramount 1932
The Cat's Paw—Lloyd-Fox 1934
The Milky Way—Paramount 1936
Professor, Beware!—Paramount 1938
The Sin of Harold Diddlebock—
    California-United Artists 1946
    (recut and reissued as *Mad
    Wednesday* by RKO in 1950)

Lloyd also released two compilations
of his work, *Harold Lloyd's World of
Comedy* (1962) and *Harold Lloyd's
Funny Side of Life* (1963).

Above
Louise Carver, Jack Cooper, Alberta Vaughn, and Jackie Lucas with Harry
Langdon in the Sennett short *Smile, Please*.

Below
Harry the Innocent, with Arthur Thalasso in *The Strong Man*.

6

HARRY LANGDON

 Of the silent clowns James Agee wrote, "It seemed as if Chaplin could do literally anything, on any instrument in the orchestra. Langdon had one queerly toned, unique little reed. But out of it he could get incredible melodies."

Harry Langdon's career is one of the most curious in the history of film comedy. He was thirty-nine when he signed to make his first film, not for Mack Sennett but for independent producer Sol Lesser. Lesser planned to star Langdon in a feature film for his Principal Pictures Corporation, but the plan never came to fruition, and Lesser apparently sold Langdon's contract to Mack Sennett.

Sennett had seen Langdon in vaudeville, where he had performed a skit called "Johnny's New Car" for nearly twenty years. Langdon's first taste of show business came at age twelve when he ran away from home to join a circus; he eventually developed a vaudeville act and, like so many performers, perfected this routine and played it year in, year out in towns large and small around the country. He wore a clownish makeup in the skit, which involved a breakaway car.

Sennett saw potential in the experienced pantomimist, but others on his staff were skeptical. They didn't know what to do with Langdon. He came to them much as Chaplin had, with no established characterization.

Two of Sennett's writers, Frank Capra and Arthur Ripley, developed an   59 idea for the baby-faced comic, and although there was much room for polishing and revision, this basic concept was ideal. A trade-paper ad proclaimed, "Mack Sennett presents his greatest comedy 'find' since Chaplin," and pretty soon, audiences and critics agreed.

Sennett later wrote of his "find," "Like Charlie Chaplin, you had to let him take his time and go through his motions. His twitters and hesitations built up a ridiculous but sympathetic little character. It was difficult for us at first to know how to use Langdon, accustomed as we were to firing the gags and the falls at the audience as fast as possible, but as new talent arrived, we found ways to screen it and to cope with it. I thought for a while Langdon was as good as Chaplin. Like Charlie, Harry was a slow starter. Even after we learned how to use him—I mean, saw what his essential character was for screen purposes— we had to give him a hundred feet of film or so to play around in, do little bits of business, and introduce himself."

Even with this realization, it was difficult for the Sennett team to work from the point of view of characterization and not gags-for-gags' sake. Such films as *All Night Long, Feet of Mud, Smile, Please,* and *Soldier Man* could have starred anyone on the Sennett lot for all they make of Langdon's fabled screen character. The magic comes in these films' quietest moments, when Harry's pantomime and his screen presence override the action. Such fleeting moments are more meaningful in the long run than the incoherent story lines or elementary gags Capra and Ripley dreamed up.

There's a cherished moment in *The Luck of the Foolish* in which a man prepares to shave in the men's room of a passenger train. The camera takes the mirror's point of view, looking out at Harry as he prepares to share the mirror with this fellow who is standing behind him and poking his head over Harry's shoulder. In a disarmingly simple sequence, Harry drives the poor man crazy, distracting him with his juvenile approach to shaving and his idiosyncratic "finishing touches" that keep the man's eyes on Harry and not himself throughout the episode.

One of Langdon's best Sennett shorts is *Saturday Afternoon,* which successfully combines character and comedy routines into a single entity with complete success. Harry is introduced as "just a crumb from the sponge cake of life," a henpecked husband who goes off for a spree with buddy Vernon Dent and returns home revitalized, hoping to tell off his wife for once and for all. It's a beautiful comedy vignette from start to finish, and director Harry Edwards lets it run on a steady pace without cutting scenes to a pulp and interjecting sight gags where they don't fit.

Like most of Sennett's big stars, Langdon received lucrative offers from other studios, and in 1926 he graduated to feature films at the First National Studio. Langdon took Frank Capra, Arthur Ripley, and Harry Edwards with him, and the films that followed—*The Strong Man, Tramp, Tramp, Tramp,* and *Long Pants*—put him into the front ranks of film comedy. First National declared, "Harry Langdon proves himself to be the World's Greatest Comedian." And a number of critics concurred.

John Grierson wrote, "He wandered pleasantly from picture to picture, braving in perpetual fairy tale, as a child might, the fearful romances of penny banks and Saturday afternoons and colds in the head and women who spoke to him in the street. He survived precipices, tornadoes, and wives, in a fashion which was not so much astonishing as expected, and even by Holy Writ promised to his kind."

In many ways, Langdon reached his zenith with his first feature film, *The Strong Man,* which also marked the directorial debut of Frank Capra. In this film are all the trademarks of Langdon's character as Capra saw it and a perfect showcase for the comedian's unique talents.

Capra told James Agee in the 1940s, "The key to the proper use of Langdon is 'the principle of the brick.' Langdon might be saved by the brick falling on the cop, but it was verboten that he in any way motivate the brick's fall."

There is an obvious example near the beginning of *The Strong Man.* Harry is the much-maligned assistant to Zandow, the strong man, and upon their arrival at New York Harbor, they suffer certain problems in having their passports processed. At one point Zandow whacks Harry on the behind. This causes Harry to lurch forward and hit his head against a trunk. That motion causes another trunk on top to fall off and crash down on Zandow's head.

Harry and Zandow's first encounter is also classic Langdon. It's in the trenches during World War I; Harry is inept with a gun, but he manages to pop Zandow quite successfully with his slingshot. The parallel with David and Goliath is obvious, and by the end of the film Harry's David has not only triumphed over Goliath but performed another miracle of biblical proportions in causing the walls of Jericho (here, a scurrilous saloon) to topple.

There are also some delicious bits of pantomime throughout the film, the most memorable during a stagecoach ride, in which Harry, suffering with a terrible cold, contorts his face in spasms of pain, much to the chagrin of his fellow passengers.

While the foundation of the film is Harry's search for the sweetheart he's corresponded with but never met—a pure and innocent love, with added poignancy because the girl is blind—there is another sequence that reveals an equally important facet of Langdon's screen personality.

Statuesque Gertrude Astor plays a con woman who plants some "hot" money in unsuspecting Harry's coat pocket but can't get it back without arousing his suspicions. So, instead, she tries to seduce him, winning his initial favor by pretending to be his pen-pal sweetheart. In a taxi on the way to her apartment, she makes an amorous advance, and Harry recoils hilariously. He literally cringes at this shocking encounter and wants nothing more than to run away. When the taxi stops, Gertrude pretends to faint, forcing Harry to carry her into her apartment. Once there, she lunges again, and he leads her on a merry chase before being pinned; after an enormous struggle, she kisses him and gets her money. Now she has no further need of this silly pawn, but Harry, while declaring his disdain, reveals in his face that he actually enjoyed the kiss and is sorry to leave!

Langdon is not merely a babe in the woods. He's a unique combination of boy and man, one who knows right from wrong but doesn't mind straying now and then.

If it seems that a lot of time has been spent discussing *The Strong Man,* it

Harry stands alone, in *Tramp, Tramp, Tramp.*

Langdon tries to be Chaplin in his film *Three's a Crowd,* with Gladys McConnell.

Harry with Thelma Todd in his first talkie short, *Hotter Than Hot*.

Langdon in one of his best talkies, *Hallelujah, I'm a Bum*, with Al Jolson.

A talented artist, Harry Langdon caricatures Nancy Carroll on the set of their film *Atlantic Adventure*.

Age has caught up with Harry Langdon in this still from his 1942 short *Carry Harry*, with Dave O'Brien.

is because this one film represents everything great about Harry Langdon. Earlier efforts were filled with promise that was never quite realized; many later films flickered with the reminder of what had been.

After the trio of successful films, Langdon became unmanageable. According to Frank Capra, who directed two of these features, Langdon would scream, "Pathos! I want to do more pathos." Capra would reply, "Harry, the pathos is in your *comedy*. If you deliberately *try* for pathos, it'll be silly, believe me."

Langdon didn't agree and fired Capra, putting himself in the director's chair. If Langdon was naïve about the strengths and weaknesses of his comic character, he was positively inept when it came to film making. *Three's a Crowd* and *The Chaser* are astonishingly clumsy not only in their construction of gags and development of story and character but also in their physical makeup. Matching shots do not match, others are held too long, and so on.

Langdon's career plummeted as quickly as it had soared. The public grew impatient with his films, and by 1928 he was bankrupt. Success had gone to his head, and his unsound business sense had been another crucial failing.

In 1929 Langdon was reduced to making a talkie "comeback" in two-reelers for Hal Roach. But these films only continued his dismal track record. The addition of dialogue changed his character from a sympathetic Everyman to a babyish simpleton, and the Roach studio's uncertainty about sound in 1929 was no help. Worst of all was Langdon's uncooperative attitude: No one could work with him, not even Hal Roach himself.

The producer recalls, "I found out that Harry's friends commented to him on his ability to stretch a scene out longer than any other comedian ... [to] sustain what we call a gag situation. And he got so enthralled by that idea that he could think of nothing else. So when I started to direct him, we would rehearse the scene and we were great. Then I'd say 'Camera' and he'd slow down like a slow-motion picture. And the scene which had run forty seconds would run two minutes before he finally got through.... Well, it took so long that it wasn't funny."

After eight shorts, his contract was terminated and Langdon was considered a has-been. He did not work in 1931 and 1932. Some said he was a broken man.

In 1932 he returned to the screen, starring in cheaply made two-reelers for Educational Pictures, then moving on to Columbia's short-subject unit in 1934, where he worked for the next ten years. These shorts were generally mediocre, but there were flashes of the old Langdon, and they reunited him with such colleagues as Harry Edwards, Arthur Ripley, and costar Vernon Dent. They borrowed freely from earlier successes: The cold-cream compound/limburger-cheese mix-up from *The Strong Man* was repeated in *The Hitchhiker,* produced in 1933, and that film's classic scene, in which Harry carries a woman upstairs step by step, was restaged in *Sue My Lawyer,* in 1938, with a new, more violent twist added by director Jules White. The final sight gag from *Three's a Crowd* topped off *Carry Harry* in 1942.

The main difficulty was re-creating the aura of innocence that was essential to Harry's screen personality. This wasn't easy, especially with advancing age (Langdon turned fifty in 1934). As William K. Everson has pointed out, "Age can be a terrible thing for a comedian ... whose forte is the projection of innocence.... There were certain clowns to whom youth was essential—Stan Laurel, Harry Langdon, Buster Keaton. Once lines began to crease those baby-like features and weight was added to their bodies, they were no longer the believable innocents, but instead old men retreating into infantilism."

One Columbia short that managed to overcome this problem, for the most part, was the delightful *A Doggone Mix-up* in 1938, which depicted Harry's devotion to his unruly dog, but later shorts in the 1940s returned Langdon to the awkwardly stumbling role that ill suited him at this time—and which required a rather obvious stunt man to handle most of the physical gags. He was even teamed with such partners as El Brendel and Una Merkel.

Langdon seemed to fare better during the 1930s in feature films. The charming 1933 *Hallelujah, I'm a Bum* gave him one of his best opportunities as a philosophical wastepaper retriever in Central Park who shares his thoughts with Al Jolson. Even the B-picture *Atlantic Adventure* in 1935 offers some engaging moments with Harry as Snapper, reporter Lloyd Nolan's photographer pal.

In 1938 Langdon returned to Hal Roach studios as a writer for Laurel & Hardy. He contributed to the screenplays of *Block-Heads, Saps at Sea,* and *A Chump at Oxford* (as well as the team's 1939 Boris Morros production, *The*

Flying Deuces)—and even provided the delightful caricatures for *Block-Heads'* opening titles. A mellower man since his first stay at the Roach lot, Langdon was well liked and widely respected. He played a small role in Roach's *There Goes My Heart,* and then found himself costarring with Oliver Hardy in *Zenobia* when Stan Laurel left the studio during a contract dispute. Talk about a Langdon & Hardy team was mostly publicity puff and became a dead issue when Laurel returned to the fold. But Langdon acquitted himself quite nicely in *Zenobia* as the whimsical medicine-show man whose prize elephant takes ill.

In fact, he might have found a whole new career in such amiable character roles, but the 1940s saw him alternating between very standard knockabout shorts at Columbia and equally undistinguished comedy features at Monogram, where he was paired for a time with British comic and writer Charley Rogers.

Langdon died on December 22, 1944, of a cerebral hemorrhage during production of a Republic musical called *Swingin' on a Rainbow.* He was sixty years old.

Frank Capra, who became the preeminent director at Columbia Pictures, dropped in to see his former star one day when he was shooting a scene for one of his two-reel comedies. The sight of this once-great clown awkwardly repeating a gag from *The Strong Man* made him terribly upset.

Mack Sennett wrote, "He was hurt and bewildered at the end and he never understood what had happened to him." Said Capra, "He was the most tragic figure I ever came across in show business."

He was also one of the most individual talents in comedy history.

THE FILMS OF HARRY LANGDON

THE MACK SENNETT SHORTS
(released by Pathé)

Picking Peaches—1924
Smile, Please—1924
Shanghaied Lovers—1924
Flickering Youth—1924
The Cat's Meow—1924
His New Mama—1924
The Luck of the Foolish—1924
All Night Long—1924
The First Hundred Years—1924
Feet of Mud—1924
The Sea Squawk—1924
His First Flame—1925
Plain Clothes—1925
Remember When?—1925
The Hansom Cabman—1925
There He Goes—1925
Boobs in the Woods—1925

His Marriage Wow—1925
Over Here—1925
Sky Scraper—1925
Watch Out—1925
Saturday Afternoon—1926
Fiddlesticks—1926
Soldier Man—1926
Lucky Stars—1926

THE STARRING FEATURE FILMS
(produced by the Harry Langdon
Corporation; released by First
National Pictures)

The Strong Man—1926
Tramp, Tramp, Tramp—1926
Long Pants—1927
Three's a Crowd—1927 (directed by
  Langdon)
The Chaser—1928 (directed by
  Langdon)

Heart Trouble—1928 (directed by
   Langdon)

THE HAL ROACH SOUND SHORTS
(released by M-G-M)

Hotter Than Hot—1929
Sky Boy—1929
Skirt Shy—1929
The Head Guy—1930
The Fighting Parson—1930
The Big Kick—1930
The Shrimp—1930
The King—1930

THE EDUCATIONAL PICTURES SHORTS

The Big Flash—1932
Tired Feet—1933
The Hitchhiker—1933
Knight Duty—1933
Tied for Life—1933
Hooks and Jabs—1933
The Stage Hand—1933 (screenplay by
   Langdon)
Trimmed in Furs—1934

THE PARAMOUNT SHORTS
(produced independently by Arvid E.
Gillstrom)

Marriage Humor—1933
On Ice—1933
Roaming Romeo—1933
Circus Hoodoo—1934
Petting Preferred—1934

THE COLUMBIA PICTURES SHORTS

Counsel on De Fence—1934
Shivers—1934
His Bridal Sweet—1935
The Leather Necker—1935
His Marriage Mix-up—1935
I Don't Remember—1935
A Doggone Mix-up—1938

Sue My Lawyer—1938
Cold Turkey—1940
What Makes Lizzy Dizzy?—1942
Tireman, Spare My Tires—1942
Carry Harry—1942
Piano Mooner—1942
Blitz on the Fritz—1943
Blonde and Groom—1943
Here Comes Mr. Zerk—1943
To Heir Is Human—1944
Defective Detectives—1944
Mopey Dope—1944
Snooper Service—1945

MISCELLANEOUS SHORTS

Sitting Pretty—Jam Handy
   Organization 1940
Goodness! A Ghost—RKO 1940

FEATURE FILM APPEARANCES

A Soldier's Plaything—Warner
   Brothers 1930
See America Thirst—Universal 1930
Hallelujah, I'm a Bum—United
   Artists 1933
My Weakness—Fox 1933
Atlantic Adventure—Columbia 1935
Block Heads—Hal Roach-United
   Artists 1938
He Loved an Actress (original British
   titles: *Stardust; Mad About Money*)
   —Biltmore Pictures 1938
There Goes My Heart—Hal
   Roach-United Artists 1938
Zenobia—Hal Roach-United Artists
   1939
Misbehaving Husbands—PRC 1940
All American Co-Ed—Hal
   Roach-United Artists 1941
Double Trouble—Monogram 1941
House of Errors—PRC 1942
Spotlight Scandals—Monogram 1943
Hot Rhythm—Monogram 1944
Block Busters—Monogram 1944
Swingin' on a Rainbow—Republic
   1945

7
CHARLEY CHASE

Charley Chase is largely neglected in surveys of film comedy. One probable reason is that he worked only in short subjects and never tackled anything particularly ambitious. Another reason is that many people have never stopped to examine his full and colorful career.

Director Tay Garnett recalled, "I knew Charley quite well, working at Roach at the same time he was there, but never had the opportunity to work with him, which I regretted very much, as he was generally regarded as one of the brightest gagmen and story constructionists around at that time. As a comedy director, in his day there was none better."

In 1940, director Leo McCarey remarked, "My association with Charley Chase was one of the most pleasant memories I have in motion pictures. He was a great man, had a keen sense of comedy values, and we were together in fifty pictures at Hal Roach studio. I received credit as director but it was really Chase who did most of the directing. Whatever success I have had or may have, I owe to his help because he taught me all I know."

Above
Charley and Eugenia Gilbert clown with the camera in this publicity still.

Below
Charley's caught between Viola Richard and Anita Garvin in *Never the Dames Shall Meet.*

69

And Hal Roach, who employed Chase for sixteen years, adds, "He was one of the very few comedians who was just as funny off the screen as he was on. Charley was a delight to be with."

Chase's knowledge of comedy was derived from years of solid experience. Born in 1893, he was a professional entertainer while still in his teens, working in burlesque and vaudeville, and even appearing on Broadway. His own act consisted of an Irish monologue, followed by a musical segment in which he sang, danced, and played several instruments. Like so many entertainers who yearned for some relief from the grueling pace of vaudeville, Chase made his way to Hollywood. Reportedly, his first job was at Universal with the Al Christie comedy unit, but by mid-1914 he was working for Mack Sennett.

During his first year at Keystone he appeared in a number of films with Charlie Chaplin, including *The Knockout, The Masquerader, His New Profession, The Rounders, Dough and Dynamite,* and *A Gentlemen of Nerve.* His contribution to these films was negligible, and he had a similarly minor role in Sennett's feature film *Tillie's Punctured Romance.* He also appeared in films with Roscoe Arbuckle, Fritz Schade, and Mae Busch.

But in 1915 Sennett turned Chase's career around by allowing him to co-direct some films with Ford Sterling and Roscoe Arbuckle. "Learning by doing" was the method at Sennett's, and Chase learned quickly; he also adopted the name Charles Parrott behind the camera. His first solo directing effort was *A Dash of Courage,* with Harry Gribbon, Wallace Beery, and Gloria Swanson. Louis Reeves Harrison wrote in *Moving Picture World,* "*A Dash of Courage* contains a dash of new spirit; there is a genuine story involved in pure farce comedy."

Buoyed by this success, Chase left Sennett to write and direct for Fox Pictures' comedy unit, scoring an early hit with a spoof of Theda Bara's *A Fool There Was* called *There's Many a Fool,* with Carmen Phillips as the vamp and Hank Mann as the fool. Over the next few years Chase served directing stints with Billy West, the Chaplin imitator; Mr. and Mrs. Carter DeHaven; and Lloyd Hamilton.

In 1921 Chase joined the still-young Hal Roach studio, which would be his home for the next sixteen years. At first he directed the Snub Pollard comedies and lifted these films out of the routine with his creative approach to sight gags and his knowing use of the camera. In the 1923 *Sold at Auction,* a character knocks Snub out cold, and the camera visualizes Snub's reaction by "melting" into blankness. Moments later when he recovers, the picture reassembles and the action resumes. It's one of the most startling gags in silent films.

If this directorial "touch" had occurred in a feature film, Chase might have been lauded by critics and promoted to more auspicious projects. As it was part of a two-reel comedy, its impact was confined to the close-knit comedy business, where Chase did enjoy the recognition he never really achieved elsewhere.

For a while, he was director-general of the Roach studio, and in this capacity he supervised production of the first Our Gang pictures and personally directed Will Rogers' first Roach short, *Jes' Passin' Through.* He also persuaded Roach to hire his brother to star in a comedy series; this likable comic used the name Paul Parrott and later became Jimmie Parrott before retiring from acting to launch a long and successful directing career at the Roach studio as James

Parrott. This confusion of names, and the similarity of James' and Charley's features, has caused many people to assume that Paul Parrott *was* Charley Chase. This is incorrect.

Still, "Paul" must have had some effect on Charley, for late in 1923 Charley Chase decided to resume his career as a comedian. Hal Roach was happy to oblige and inaugurated this new series in January 1924 with a one-reeler called, appropriately enough, *At First Sight.*

The initial problem for Chase was finding an individual comic personality. The late comedian Billy Gilbert, who was Chase's closest friend, recalled, "I remember one theory he had—he said all comedians should pick another comedian whom they admired, one who was as different physically as possible from themselves and play each scene as they thought he would play it. His model was 'Ham' (Lloyd) Hamilton. He said that when other people saw the end results they could see no resemblance, that he couldn't even see it himself because it came out different. But when he played a scene he always thought, 'How would "Ham" play this?' "

Chase's first screen "character" was called Jimmie Jump, and he resembled a dozen other 1920s screen comics in his breezy but routine manner. Then in April 1924, with nine comedies under his belt, Chase was given a new director, an Irishman with a keen sense of humor who was still feeling his way in the film business. His name was Leo McCarey. The two were perfectly matched: They were young, they loved what they were doing, and what's more, they both were crazy about popular music.

McCarey was not a magician, and he did not resolve the problems of the Chase series right away, but films like *All Wet,* in which Charley maneuvers his car into a water-filled excavation pit and then proceeds to repair it underwater, showed the spark of creativity that existed with this star-director team. When Hal Roach decided to expand the series to two reels in 1925, Chase and McCarey really hit their stride.

A 1925 interview gives ample evidence of the relaxed atmosphere that produced this series of fine films. Although there was a shooting schedule of two weeks per short, McCarey and Chase were known to usually finish ahead of time. As a former director, Chase admitted that he often had ideas of his own that clashed with McCarey's. In such a case, he explained, "We argue a while, stop to play a tune, then do it both ways. We screen each take, see that both are wrong, and ask a neutral referee for advice."

The very first two-reelers Chase made in 1925 cemented his screen personality for the next fifteen years and managed to set him apart from the production-line comics of the day. The first and perhaps most important decision, which had been initiated to some degree in the one-reelers, was to let Chase be himself on screen. He wore no special disguise or costume and in fact was a rather handsome young man. "He could almost be called the matinee idol of the comedians," onetime leading lady Martha Sleeper told George Geltzer many years later, "and I believe it was the secret of his success."

Another vital decision was to eschew slapstick-for-slapstick's sake. While sight gags were an integral part of the Chase films, they always seemed to tie into the plot and have their basis in genuine comic invention.

The Chase character soon came into focus: a dapper, reasonably intelligent

Charley and Thelma Todd in *The Nickel Nurser*.

A stern moment with Spec O'Donnell in *Movie Night*.

but naïve young man who inevitably found himself in some outlandish circumstances through no fault of his own. Throughout his career in two-reel comedies, Chase alternated between films that presented him as a single man with a constant eye for pretty girls and those that portrayed him as a married man under the thumb of his wife. In both silent and sound films, the first formula came off better than the second, perhaps because so many other comics were using the marriage formula and wearing it thin. Nevertheless, Charley always made the most of the genre. Or as Robert Youngson put it in the narration for one of his compilation films, "Charley Chase's life was one long embarrassing moment."

Only Chase could have pulled off the situations in *Mighty Like a Moose* so well. The story concerns a man with a hideous set of buck teeth and his wife (Vivien Oakland) who possesses a grotesque hawk nose. Without telling each other, Charley has his teeth straightened, and Vivien has her nose fixed. The two meet, don't recognize each other, and decide to go out on the town for an evening. When the party they're attending is raided and their picture appears in the morning newspaper, each must face the remorse of having "cheated" on

Above, right
Charley of the Jungle confronts Muriel Evans in
Nature in the Wrong.

Below, right
A perfect mess mars a pretty miss in *The Big Squirt.*

Ann Doran lets Charley have it in *Pie à la Maid*.

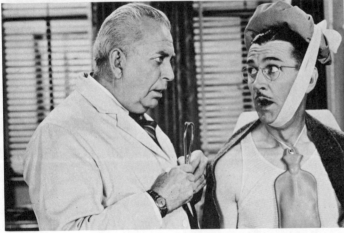

Doctor John Ince gives Charley the bad news in *The Heckler*.

their spouse. It's a superb comedy, which deftly blends sophistication and sight gags and depends as much on *acting* and *personality* to bring it off as any other element. This is where Chase stood out from the crowd of second-echelon comics.

Other Chase gems from the 1920s are numerous: *Innocent Husbands, Bad Boy, His Wooden Wedding, Dog Shy, Crazy Like a Fox, Bromo and Juliet, A One Mama Man, Forgotten Sweeties, Fluttering Hearts, Never the Dames Shall Meet, The Family Group*, and *Movie Night*, to name a few. When Leo McCarey parted company with Chase in 1926 to become supervising director on the Roach lot, he was replaced by Charley's brother, James Parrott, who continued the series' winning streak.

One of Chase's classic silents was directed by yet another comedy hand, that of former propman Fred Guiol. *Limousine Love* is almost as funny described as it is seen (and happily, it can be seen in Robert Youngson's compilation feature *Four Clowns*). Charley is driving to his wedding when his car runs out of gas; he leaves it parked on a desolate road to hike to the nearest filling station. Meanwhile, Viola Richard has a mishap with her car and ends up in a mud puddle. Looking for a place to stay while her clothes dry, she spots Charley's limousine and climbs inside. Charley returns and drives off, not knowing there is a nude girl in his back seat; her clothes are left behind. When he realizes what has happened, Charley is aghast, but hitchhiker Edgar Kennedy lends a helping hand. He tells Charley to drive to his hotel where he will get some clothes for the girl, but when they arrive, it turns out to be the same hotel where Charley's wedding is taking place! The wedding party spots Chase but can't understand why he keeps driving around the block instead of stopping. Finally, one of the guests hops onto Charley's running board to investigate, sees what's happened, and stays on the car, giving a helpless look to the wedding party back on the curb as the car circles the block. Another guest comes to find out what's wrong and also ends up looking helplessly at the guests on the sidewalk, unable to explain. Before long, the entire male population of the guest list is hanging on Charley's car, trying to protect him from an embarrassing discovery. The sight gags that follow as they try to get Viola out of the car and into some clothes without being seen are hilarious.

Again, it's the kind of gag story that belonged to Charley Chase and couldn't have succeeded in lesser hands.

Because situations, stories, and Charley's personality were the major ingredients for Chase's success, he had a much easier transition to talkies than many of his colleagues. What's more, he now had occasion to include songs in his two-reelers, and that he did at the drop of a hat—often performing tunes he'd written himself and sometimes accompanying his vocals on the banjo or guitar.

But Charley was not so confident at first. "He felt uncomfortable in talking pictures," Billy Gilbert recalled. "His great forte was pantomime and a funny way of handling his body. He liked to work with me as I was a 'talking' actor and he could lean on me." Chase's uncertainty was matched by his co-workers at Roach, but after a year of trial and error they settled back into a comfortable groove, and Chase's comedies hit their stride again, although they would seldom reveal the flashes of brilliance that marked so many of his silent shorts.

Chase's obvious rapport with such featured players as Billy Gilbert, Thelma Todd, James Finlayson, and the rest of the Hal Roach stock company gave these talkies an easygoing charm that often surmounted ordinary material—and when the ideas were good, as in such shorts as *Looser Than Loose, The Pip From Pittsburgh, Young Ironsides, Fallen Arches, Another Wild Idea, Nurse to You,* and *The Chases of Pimple Street,* the results were excellent.

Camaraderie on the Hal Roach lot was such that Charley was encouraged to wear several hats and indulge his fondness for writing, directing, and singing just as he pleased. In 1933 he was given a juicy supporting role in Laurel & Hardy's feature film *Sons of the Desert* as an obnoxious conventioneer, and three years later, Stan and Babe returned the favor with a wonderful, unbilled bit in his two-reeler *On the Wrong Trek* as a pair of hitchhikers who "look like a couple of horse thieves" to Charley.

One cannot help but feel that Laurel and Hardy were, in a sense, bidding a fond good-bye to their friend and colleague with that gesture, for 1936 was Chase's last year at the Hal Roach studio.

Economic factors were causing Roach to phase out short subjects, and he tried to promote each of his stars to feature films around this time. Chase filmed a one-hour feature called *Bank Night,* but legal problems with the corporation that sponsored this popular giveaway gimmick forced Roach to withdraw the film after trade screenings and edit the footage down to a conventional two-reel length. The title was also changed to *Neighborhood House.*

Chase's second feature effort for Roach was in a first-rate supporting role with Patsy Kelly in *Kelly the Second.* But apparently the handwriting was on the wall by this time: Charley could not carry a feature film alone, and that meant there was no longer a place for him with Roach.

His onetime cameraman George Stevens wanted to use him as comedy relief in his Fred Astaire musical *A Damsel in Distress,* but Burns and Allen were chosen instead. Another old acquaintance came to his rescue, however: Jules White, head of Columbia Pictures' comedy short subjects, hired Chase as actor-director-writer-producer, just as he had so many other comedy veterans who were now looking for work.

To be unemployed, however briefly, must have been a major blow to Chase. Marital problems had bothered him as well, and he was drinking heavily; his hair went prematurely gray, and he had to dye it black to maintain his comic image. "He was a sweet, sad man who felt among other things that his talent was not fully appreciated," said Billy Gilbert. "He wasn't bitter about it, he just wondered why people didn't rank him with Laurel and Hardy, Keaton, Chaplin, and Lloyd."

Any bitterness was set aside when he went to work for Columbia, however. A thorough professional, he found himself among others who shared his dedication to comedy. Ann Doran, who spent several years at Columbia playing leading ladies and foils for the resident comics, recalls, "It was a joint effort of love. These men liked what they were doing and approached each picture with one idea in mind—make it the best possible. . . . Charley and [director] Del Lord knew what they were doing every minute; they proved ways to open a door, to sit, to put on a hat, to drink a glass of water, to answer a phone. The tiniest thing can make a scene funny. A shrug or a lifted eyebrow at the precise moment can make a scene hilarious. Charley and Del had the same marvelous feeling for timing [as] Jack Benny. It is an inborn sense."

During the next few years, Chase alternated between starring in shorts and directing assignments for such other comedians as Andy Clyde, Tom Kennedy, Smith and Dale, and the Three Stooges. The pace was more regimented than it had been at Roach, but Chase was capable and efficient, and there was always time for a little music between takes. Moe Howard of the Three Stooges recalled, "He played a guitar and sang very well, and we would all harmonize together, real barbershop harmony, with Vernon Dent, who sang a beautiful tenor, and sometimes with Buddy Jamison."

Chase contributed the scripts to many of his Columbia shorts and borrowed liberally from his earlier films. *The Wrong Miss Wright* was a successful remake of his silent *Crazy Like a Fox,* based on a mistaken-identity theme that often served Charley well. *Many Sappy Returns* was a remake of his Roach talkie *Fast Work.*

But some of his best comedies were originals: *Rattling Romeo,* in which Charley purchases a used car that systematically falls apart, and his final short, *The Heckler,* in which he plays a nerve-grating loudmouth whose ability to ruin sports events provides a series of belly-laugh episodes. So good were the Chase scripts that Columbia remade most of them in later years with Billy Gilbert, Andy Clyde, Hugh Herbert, Shemp Howard, Bert Wheeler, and Vera Vague.

Sadly, *The Heckler* was Chase's last film. After completing a season of Columbia shorts he accepted an offer from the Shubert brothers to appear in their play *Worth a Million,* but the show never reached Broadway.

Heavy drinking continued to imperil his health, and on June 30, 1940, he suffered a heart attack and died in Hollywood. He was just forty-six.

Today, the term "situation comedy" connotes a certain brand of television series that floods American home screens. But Charley Chase developed and refined the situation-comedy format in the age of two-reelers as a showcase for pleasing and inventive stories with gags, which also provided a vehicle for his winning personality. He did not dominate the screen the way Chaplin or Keaton did; one did not feel his presence in every frame of film. But Chase was not only a fine comic actor; he was a superb comedy creator, and for this he should not be forgotten.

THE FILMS OF CHARLEY CHASE

Chase worked as a performer for Christie circa 1913 and then joined the Mack Sennett studio. Within two years he stopped performing to become a full-time director and writer, resuming his career as a comedian with his own starring series in 1924. This list chronicles his work from that time onward.

THE SILENT SHORTS (produced by Hal Roach, released by Pathé and then from 1927 on by M-G-M)

At First Sight—1924
One of the Family—1924
Just a Minute—1924
Powder and Smoke—1924
A Perfect Lady—1924
Hard Knocks—1924
Love's Detour—1924
Don't Forget—1924
The Fraidy Cat—1924

Publicity Pays—1924
April Fool—1924
Position Wanted—1924
Young Oldfield—1924
Stolen Goods—1924
Jeffries, Jr.—1924
Why Husbands Go Mad—1924
A Ten Minute Egg—1924
Seeing Nellie Home—1924
Sweet Daddy—1924
Why Men Work—1924
Outdoor Pajamas—1924
Sittin' Pretty—1924

Too Many Mamas—1924
Bungalow Boobs—1924
Accidental Accidents—1924
All Wet—1924
The Poor Fish—1924
The Royal Razz—1924
Hello Baby—1925
Fighting Fluid—1925
The Family Entrance—1925
Plain and Fancy Girls—1925
Should Husbands Be Watched—1925
Hard Boiled—1925
Is Marriage the Bunk?—1925
Bad Boy—1925
Big Red Riding Hood—1925
Looking for Sally—1925
What Price Goofy?—1925
Isn't Life Terrible?—1925
Innocent Husbands—1925
No Father to Guide Him—1925
The Caretaker's Daughter—1925
The Uneasy Three—1925
His Wooden Wedding—1925
Charley, My Boy—1926
Mama Behave—1926
Dog Shy—1926
Mum's the Word—1926
Long Fliv the King—1926
Thundering Fleas—1926 (guest
  appearance)
Mighty Like a Moose—1926
Crazy Like a Fox—1926
Bromo and Juliet—1926
Tell 'Em Nothing—1926
Be Your Age—1926
There Ain't No Santa Claus—1926
Many Scrappy Returns—1927
Are Brunettes Safe?—1927
A One Mama Man—1927
Forgotten Sweeties—1927
Bigger and Better Blondes—1927
Fluttering Hearts—1927
What Women Did for Me—1927
Now I'll Tell One—1927
Assistant Wives—1927
The Sting of Stings—1927
The Lighter That Failed—1927

The Call of the Cuckoos—1927 (guest
  appearance)
The Way of All Pants—1927
Us—1927
Never the Dames Shall Meet—1927
All for Nothing—1928
The Family Group—1928
Aching Youths—1928
Limousine Love—1928
The Fight Pest—1928
Imagine My Embarrassment—1928
Is Everybody Happy?—1928
All Parts—1928
The Booster—1928
Chasing Husbands—1928
Ruby Love—1929
Off to Buffalo—1929
Thin Twins—1929
Movie Night—1929

THE HAL ROACH SOUND SHORTS
(released by M-G-M)

The Big Squawk—1929
Leaping Love—1929
Snappy Sneezer—1929
Crazy Feet—1929
Stepping Out—1929
Great Gobs—1929
The Real McCoy—1930
Whispering Whoopee—1930
All Teed Up—1930
Fifty Million Husbands—1930
Fast Work—1930
Girl Shock—1930
Dollar Dizzy—1930
Looser Than Loose—1930
High C's—1930
Thundering Tenors—1931
The Pip From Pittsburgh—1931
Rough Seas—1931
One of the Smiths—1931
The Panic Is On—1931
Skip the Maloo!—1931
What a Bozo!—1931
Tasty Marriage—1931
The Tabasco Kid—1932

The Nickel Nurser—1932
In Walked Charley—1932
First in War—1932
Young Ironsides—1932
Girl Grief—1932
Now We'll Tell One—1932
Mr. Bride—1932
Fallen Arches—1933
Nature in the Wrong—1933
His Silent Racket—1933
Arabian Tights—1933
Sherman Said It—1933 (Chase
    directed or co-directed this and all
    subsequent Hal Roach shorts under
    the name Charles Parrott)
Midsummer Mush—1933
Luncheon at Twelve—1933
The Cracked Iceman—1934
Four Parts—1934
I'll Take Vanilla—1934
Another Wild Idea—1934
It Happened One Day—1934
Something Simple—1934
You Said a Hatful!—1934
Fate's Fathead—1934
Okay Toots!—1935
Poker at Eight—1935
Southern Exposure—1935
The Four Star Boarder—1935
Nurse to You—1935
Manhattan Monkey Business—1935
Public Ghost No. 1—1935
Life Hesitates at 40—1936
The Count Takes the Count—1936
Vamp Till Ready—1936
On the Wrong Trek—1936
Neighborhood House—1936
    (originally a feature-length film, but
    released in the two-reel format)

THE COLUMBIA PICTURES SHORTS

The Grand Hooter—1937
From Bad to Worse—1937
The Wrong Miss Wright—1937
Calling All Doctors—1937
The Big Squirt—1937
Man Bites Love Bug—1937
Time Out for Trouble—1938
The Mind Needer—1938
Many Sappy Returns—1938
The Nightshirt Bandit—1938
Pie à la Maid—1938 (screenplay by
    Chase)
The Sap Takes a Wrap—1939
    (screenplay by Chase)
The Chump Takes a Bump—1939
Rattling Romeo—1939
Skinny the Moocher—1939
Teacher's Pest—1939
The Awful Goof—1939
The Heckler—1940
South of the Boudoir—1940
His Bridal Fright—1940

FEATURE FILM APPEARANCES

The King of Wild Horses—Hal
    Roach-Pathé 1924
Modern Love—Universal 1929
Sons of the Desert—Hal
    Roach–M-G-M 1933
Kelly the Second—Hal Roach–M-G-M
    1936

Chase also hosted a 1937 M-G-M
short, *Hollywood Party,* not to be
confused with the feature of the same
name.

Raymond Griffith, Gene "Pop" Rogers (*left*), and Mary Thurman in the Sennett comedy *A Scoundrel's Toll*.

8

RAYMOND GRIFFITH

"Raymond Griffith would be the last man in the world to hail himself as the new comedy king," declared a Paramount Pictures advertisement in 1926. "But the truth is, exhibitors and the public are doing it for him. The fact won't be downed that he is a real comedian of a different sort, a new method, a comedian who has already become a box-office draw. Raymond Griffith combines class with humor, good looks with the agility of a Fairbanks."

Today, fifty years later, Raymond Griffith is all but forgotten, except for silent-film buffs and scholars who champion his cause. Eileen Bowser of the Museum of Modern Art feels that "Griffith could shine as brightly as any of [the great comedians]." Walter Kerr goes further, declaring, "Griffith seems to me to occupy a handsome fifth place —after Chaplin, Keaton, Lloyd, and Langdon—in the silent comedy pantheon, a place that is his by right of his refusal to ape his contemporaries and his insistence on following the devious curve of an entirely idiosyncratic eye."

Why should such a fine comedian be so neglected? The main reason is that most of his films are lost, victims of studio neglect. For years Griffith's reputation has rested on one film, *Hands Up!* Happily, this representative work is probably his finest, but it is, nevertheless, difficult to build a strong appreciation for any artist based on one solitary work. In recent years, other Griffith films have turned up, some of them featuring the actor in supporting roles. But even the weakest of these newly discovered silents enhance one's regard for Griffith as

Above

A blasé Griffith with Adolphe Menjou and Gale Henry in
Open All Night.

Opposite page

Edgar Kennedy, player, Betty Compson, and Griffith in
Paths to Paradise.

a unique and fascinating screen comedian; one can only hope that further mining of vaults and archives will prove fruitful.

Griffith came from a theatrical family and received his training on the stage. His comedy training ground was the Mack Sennett studio, where he worked as a performer before turning his attention to writing and directing. As a comedian, he was agile and pleasant, but when he worked behind the scenes he earned a reputation as one of the finest comic minds in Hollywood. In the early 1920s he returned to performing, first in supporting roles and then, as people took notice of his dapper and dryly funny character, in starring vehicles.

Open All Night, produced in 1924, features one of Griffith's scene-stealing supporting performances as the bewilderingly blasé "protégé" of social climber Gale Henry. He is introduced as "the next movie sheik," a running gag that was a topical joke in which Paramount Pictures, having lost its hottest star, Rudolph

Valentino, in a contract dispute, laughed at its own misfortunes. Although *Open All Night*, a sophisticated Lubitsch-like comedy directed by Paul Bern, is quite enjoyable, Griffith walks away with a delicious closing gag that leaves a more powerful impression than anything else in the film: Learning from a newsboy that Valentino has re-signed with Paramount, Griffith nonchalantly changes attitudes and makes a flamboyant gesture, baring his teeth to reveal his new personality: Doug Fairbanks!

Nonchalance is a key to Griffith's screen character. Impeccably groomed and dressed in top hat, white tie, and tails, he is the personification of Cool. In the midst of comic chaos, he never loses his poise.

The film that cemented Griffith's screen character and brought him full-fledged stardom was *Paths to Paradise* in 1926. Betty Compson receives top billing, but there is no doubt that it's Griffith's show all the way. Clarence Badger, a fellow Sennett alumnus, worked with Griffith to create scenes of belly-laugh proportions without ever calling on slapstick. The humor in *Paths to Paradise* stems from sight gags, situations, and a comic sleight of hand that became the cornerstone of Griffith's repertoire. The timing—in the performances, in the direction, and in the editing—is flawless, creating comedy that could only exist on film.

Paths to Paradise was a great hit, and reviewers outdid themselves in praising both Badger and Griffith. *Photoplay* asserted, "Raymond Griffith proves again that he is a real star...." And this time Paramount listened. Griffith graduated to full-fledged stardom in a series of tailor-made comedies.

Hands Up! is as good a feature-length comedy as anyone ever made. As a spy during the Civil War, Griffith enjoys an endless parade of challenges to his ingenuity and unshakable cool—from juggling the affections of two sisters with whom he is in love to distracting a firing squad by hurling plates into the air at which they dutifully fire!

Although he does not normally command great sympathy as a comic figure, we are "with" him all the way in this adventure, sharing the excitement of these escapades and hoping he will always find one more scheme to get himself out of a jam.

Unfortunately, the same characterization does not work as well in the 1926 film *You'd Be Surprised*, the latest Griffith film to be discovered and restored by the American Film Institute. The key to this film's failure is perhaps its cold-bloodedness (Griffith plays a master detective trying to solve a murder) coupled with a problem that director Eddie Sutherland pinpointed later.

As Sutherland told Kevin Brownlow years later, Griffith's "big failing as a comedian was that he didn't know the difference between comedy, travesty, farce, or light comedy. He'd mix it all up. And he would never be the butt of any jokes. Griffith was too vain for this. He would get himself into a problem, and then he'd want to think himself out of it. This worked well for a few pictures, but it wasn't a solid basis."

Still, *You'd Be Surprised* was a big hit in 1926, when it was greeted as a welcome spoof of drawing-room whodunits. Today, as a sought-after Raymond Griffith discovery, it disappoints because of its claustrophobic setting and lack of comic action. In another irony, one is somewhat let down by the lack of wit

Raymond Griffith in his classic *Hands Up!* with Montagu
Love and Mack Swain.

Dorothy Sebastian and Griffith in *You'd Be Surprised*.

Raymond Griffith and an incongruous-looking Louise Fazenda in *The Night Club*.

Three outstanding comic performers, Anita Garvin, Raymond Griffith, and Edgar Kennedy, in *Trent's Last Case,* Griffith's last starring feature.

in the title cards written by Ralph Spence and Robert Benchley. In 1926 these same titles were praised for steering clear of wisecracks!

After *You'd Be Surprised* he made only three more starring features before sound terminated his starring career. The reason was simple: Griffith had injured his vocal cords many years before and could talk in only a hoarse whisper. He did appear in a few talkie short subjects for Paramount-Christie (*The Sleeping Porch* and *Post Mortems*), but they could not override this problem, and his last screen appearance was in *All Quiet on the Western Front* in a silent bit as a dying French soldier.

Griffith did not disappear from Hollywood, however. His reputation behind the camera had not been forgotten, and his friend Darryl F. Zanuck (who once worked with Griffith in Mack Sennett's writing stable) put him to work as production manager, associate producer, and then producer, first at Warner Brothers and then with Zanuck at Twentieth Century-Fox. Among the films with which he was associated are: *Gold Diggers of 1933, The Bowery, The House of Rothschild, Les Misérables, Call of the Wild, Heidi,* and *The Three Musketeers.*

Though seldom heralded during this period, his participation in screen comedy continued. Director Allan Dwan worked with him several times and enjoyed having him as a producer. Dwan told Peter Bogdanovich, "He understood pictures because he'd been in them and knew all the problems. And he was excellent at gags—suggesting bits and stuff during the preparation." On *Heidi*, Dwan said, "We seldom saw him on the set. But he had an effervescent attitude and we were able to get the story to bubble. It could have been a heavy-footed thing, but it turned out all right."

Griffith retired in the 1940s and died in 1957. Only now, some twenty years later, is he starting to come into his own as his silent films are shown once more. The Forgotten Man of silent comedy is finally regaining the recognition he enjoyed in the 1920s, when he created a character and a style of comedy unique in films.

Raymond Griffith's final screen appearance, as a dying French soldier in *All Quiet on the Western Front,* with Lew Ayres.

THE FILMS OF RAYMOND GRIFFITH

Raymond Griffith's early career is difficult to document. He joined Vitagraph in 1914 and then moved on to Kalem and Goldwyn. In 1916 he was hired by Mack Sennett, initially as a comedian (*The Surf Girl, A Scoundrel's Toll, A Royal Rogue*) but then as a writer and director. He stayed with Sennett working behind the camera for six years. In 1922 he resumed an acting career, and this is where our index begins.

The Crossroads of New York—Mack Sennett-Associated First National 1922

Fools First—Marshall Neilan-Associated First National 1922

Minnie—Marshall Neilan-Associated First National 1922

Souls for Sale—Goldwyn 1923 (guest appearance)

The Eternal Three—Goldwyn 1923

Red Lights—Goldwyn 1923

The Day of Faith—Goldwyn 1923

White Tiger—Universal 1923

Nellie, the Beautiful Cloak Model—Goldwyn 1924

The Dawn of a Tomorrow—Paramount 1924

Changing Husbands—Paramount 1924

Lily of the Dust—Paramount 1924

Poisoned Paradise: The Forbidden Story of Monte Carlo—Preferred 1924

Open All Night—Paramount 1924

Miss Bluebeard—Paramount 1925

When Winter Went—Independent Pictures 1925

Forty Winks—Paramount 1925

The Night Club—Paramount 1925 (Griffith's first starring vehicle)

Paths to Paradise—Paramount 1925

Fine Clothes—Louis B. Mayer-First National 1925

A Regular Fellow—Paramount 1925

Hands Up!—Paramount 1926

Wet Paint—Paramount 1926

You'd Be Surprised—Paramount 1926

Wedding Bill—Paramount 1927

Time to Love—Paramount 1927

Trent's Last Case—Fox 1929

Post Mortems—Paramount-Christie 1929 (short subject)

The Sleeping Porch—Paramount-Christie 1929 (short subject)

All Quiet on the Western Front—Universal 1930

Marie and Jane Winton watch Marion Davies'
antics in *The Patsy*.

9

MARIE DRESSLER

It has been said of many great performers that they can make you laugh one moment and cry the next. Often this is wishful thinking, critical extravagance, or press-agentry at work. But in the case of Marie Dressler it is true. She was a supremely gifted comedienne who achieved real screen stardom only when she revealed the humanity behind her broad comic facade.

This is certainly clear in her dramatic roles, but it is even more impressive in the unpretentious slapstick comedies she made with Sennett graduate Polly Moran in the late 1920s and early 1930s, for here, the shallowness of Moran's talent serves to emphasize the depth of Dressler's.

No less dramatic is the saga of Marie Dressler's career. As her friend Will Rogers noted in 1934, "There never was a career—one time big and then clear down, and now up again—like hers."

Early in life she resigned herself to the fact that she was big and had a homely face; she never let it stand in her way, and she was to find many years later that people around the world found beauty in her *character* that was much more important than superficial good looks.

Born in Canada to an itinerant piano teacher and would-be musician, Marie happily left home to seek her fortunes and traveled America in a series of barnstorming theater companies, doing everything from grand opera to comic opera. "She did the most wonderful burlesque opera . . . because she had such a wonderful voice," Will Rogers recalled.

Anxious to succeed, she never stopped, and when one troupe folded, she looked around until she found another job, whether it was in the chorus or in a slightly more exalted speaking part. Eventually she worked with Lillian Russell, Anna Held, Weber and Fields, and other show-business luminaries.

Marie recalled her first taste of stardom in 1896. "*Lady Slavey* was my first big success. I wasn't quite twenty-five when we moved from Washington, where we opened, to the Casino in New York. We played the Casino two years and took the show on the road for two more. It had taken me exactly eleven years to make Broadway. Eleven years of tank towns and hard work and little pay—sometimes no pay at all. But it was worth it all to hang out of a window now and watch my name in electric lights on one of the finest theaters in the country. Even today, out here in Hollywood, surrounded by stars who weren't born then, I can still feel the thrill of those first weeks at the Casino."

During the national tour of *Lady Slavey* a Connecticut woman went to see Miss Dressler backstage, with her strapping son in tow. Her name was Mrs. Sinnott and she wanted advice on how her son could pursue a stage career. Marie Dressler was patient with the naïve young man (who like herself was a transplanted Canadian) and went so far as to give him a letter of introduction to Broadway producer David Belasco.

Some fifteen years later that young-man-made-good brought Marie Dressler to the screen; his name was Mack Sennett, and he was eager to go beyond the one- and two-reel comedies he was making at the Keystone Studio and produce a full-length comedy feature. His backers wouldn't hear of it until he mentioned the name of Marie Dressler, for she was an internationally known stage star whose reputation might carry the film's success.

Stuck for an idea, Sennett and his writers decided to adapt Miss Dressler's stage success *Tillie's Nightmare* into a screenplay, which they called *Tillie's Punctured Romance*. There was trepidation at first on the part of theater owners who weren't yet accustomed to feature films of any kind, let alone comedies, but once *Tillie* found its way into a major theater its success was insured. It became one of the great comedy hits of all time.

It is also one of the most boisterous comedies of all time, combining the bombast of Marie Dressler with the unpolished energy of the entire Sennett crew. There is nothing soft or subtle about the film: In wooing Marie, Charlie Chaplin playfully hurls a brick at her head, and a short time later when Charlie's girl friend, Mabel Normand, first sees him with Dressler (in the middle of the street, dodging traffic), she remarks, "What's this he's got—one of Ringling's elephants?"

Marie presides over much of the film's pandemonium: A farm girl lured to the wicked city by bounder Chaplin, she gets roaring drunk in a restaurant and lumbers about in a series of foolish dances. Later, when she thinks she's inherited a fortune and throws a party in her new mansion, she goes berserk, firing a gun, hurling a cake, and causing general havoc. In the film's climactic chase she's standing at the edge of a pier when the Keystone Kops patrol wagon rides up and slams into her derriere, shoving her off the pier into the water. Bumbling attempts to hoist her out of the drink cause her to be dunked four more times before she reaches safety and has a chance to dry out.

The pants-kicking humor of *Tillie's Punctured Romance* does little to bolster Marie Dressler's reputation as a great comedienne when seen today. What impresses one most is her refreshing uninhibitedness, her ability to throw all caution to the wind in playing a rambunctious character. This must have been electrifying on stage, but of course on film it's a bit *too* broad. Dressler needed direction, and in her first film she wasn't accepting any.

Mack Sennett later wrote, "No matter that this was her first motion picture, she was a great star, this was her story, and she was still inclined to remember me as an awkward boilermaker from Northampton."

Nevertheless, *Tillie's Punctured Romance* was a hit, and while Marie Dressler had no thought of abandoning the stage for a film career, she enjoyed this success and followed it with a pair of so-called sequels, *Tillie's Tomato Surprise* in 1915 and *Tillie Wakes Up* in 1917.

Tillie Wakes Up is significant because it was written for Marie by her friend Frances Marion. Marion had met the star when she was a cub reporter trying to snare an interview; they became good friends and their paths would cross significantly over the years. By 1917 Marion was a successful screenwriter, fashioning original stories for Mary Pickford, Alice Brady, and Clara Kimball Young. Therefore, her script for Dressler is more thoughtful than anything Sennett could have provided. Marie plays a neglected wife who heeds the advice of columnist "Beetrees Flarefacts" to get a Romeo on the side, and Johnny Hines is an unhappy husband who becomes Marie's partner in a daylong "fling" at Coney Island.

Marion doesn't eschew slapstick in her script (as Tillie, Marie gets drunk and decides to rest on a "bed" of peanuts at a vendor's stall, causing the container to collapse under her ample weight), but she offers Dressler her first dramatic screen moments, as a woman whose heart is broken by her callous husband. Perhaps through knowing her offstage, writer Marion realized how sincere and affecting Dressler could be portraying sadness—and what an effective contrast it was to her usual flamboyance.

With minor exceptions she was off-screen for the next ten years. A series of two-reel comedies for the World Film Company in 1917 and 1918 was not well received. During World War I she worked tirelessly to sell Liberty Bonds and to entertain soldiers in army hospitals. She virtually suspended her career "for the duration." When she returned to the New York booking offices after the Armistice, she found herself being called "old-hat" and a "former star."

She continued to work wherever she could and found enormous acceptance in London. But by the mid-1920s her career was on the wane, and after Allan Dwan chanced to offer her a role in his film *The Joy Girl* when he spotted her in a New York restaurant, she told him that he had saved her life: She had planned to jump out a window that very night, a victim of utter despair.

At this point, a mutual friend alerted Frances Marion, who was now a contract writer at M-G-M in California, that Marie was idle. Marion immediately set to work on a script called *The Callahans and the Murphys*, which she

Marie Dressler makes a formidable screen debut in
Tillie's Punctured Romance, with Mabel Normand,
Charlie Chaplin, and Edgar Kennedy.

Dressler as Marthy, the waterfront hag, with
Greta Garbo in *Anna Christie.*

George K. Arthur, Polly Moran, Jack Benny, and Bessie Love share a laugh with the well-dressed Marie during a break in the filming of *Chasing Rainbows* at M-G-M in 1929.

Roscoe Ates seems unimpressed with Marie and Polly Moran's campaign poster in *Politics*.

Polly Moran pleads with bank president Marie in *Prosperity*.

brought to producer Irving Thalberg with the suggestion that he cast Polly Moran and Marie Dressler in the leads. Moran was already on the Metro roster; Thalberg banked on Dressler's longtime stardom and dismissed the notion that she was "washed up."

Marie Dressler returned to Hollywood to play this tailor-made role as the matriarch of a raucous Irish clan who's constantly at odds with her equally boisterous pal, Polly. Somehow their relationship survives the rockiest disruptions, usually caused by selfish, status-seeking Polly. Sentiment and slapstick were the main ingredients of this film; as Marie and Polly toast their children's impending marriage, they get progressively drunker and wind up pouring beer down each other's blouses!

The Callahans and the Murphys seemed a surefire hit, but the Irish population throughout America picketed the film and caused M-G-M great embarrassment. The studio had never anticipated such response and quietly withdrew the picture from circulation—and with it, Marie Dressler's latest bid for stardom.

She did not, at this point, rest idle, as some histories have indicated. She was featured with Polly Moran in an adaptation of the comic strip *Bringing Up Father,* which *Photoplay* magazine aptly labeled "rolling-pin humor." Then she costarred with Marion Davies in *The Patsy,* a sidesplitting comedy directed by King Vidor in which she played Davies' domineering mother. It was energetic, physical comedy, and there were times when it seemed Dressler might actually flatten Miss Davies in the commotion.

In 1929 she free-lanced, winning undistinguished roles in such films as *The Vagabond Lover* with Rudy Vallee and a two-reel talkie short called *Dangerous Females* with Polly Moran, in which the veteran comediennes did their best to contend with a microphone and very weak material.

Then came *Anna Christie.*

Frances Marion was handed the task of adapting Eugene O'Neill's play as Greta Garbo's first talking picture. As she worked on the screenplay for M-G-M, she realized that the role of Marthy, a waterfront hag, was made for Marie Dressler, and as she had done three years earlier, she went to Irving Thalberg and persuaded him to give her a chance.

"To placate her," Marie later recalled, "they agreed to test me as Marthy. They were serene in the confidence that even Frances would see that I was through. To everybody's surprise, except Frances Marion's, the test came out favorably. And when the picture was shown, it was an enormous success."

After seeing the finished picture, Greta Garbo drove to Marie Dressler's home to give her a large bouquet of flowers in appreciation of her outstanding performance.

It was indeed a triumph. For this agreeably meaty role, Dressler dared to unleash her inhibitions just as she would for comedy, but this time to portray a pitiful old rag-mop of a woman. Her performance made people sit up and take notice—and that included the top brass at M-G-M. Because of this they were receptive to Frances Marion's next proposal.

While observing Marie during the filming of *Anna Christie,* Marion started writing another screenplay expressly for her—and for another recent M-G-M

Marie and Wallace Beery in *Tugboat Annie.*

recruit, Wallace Beery. The result was *Min and Bill,* a film that gave Dressler the opportunity to employ the full range of her talent, from low comedy to heart-tug drama.

"Hitherto, in working up a role, I had first to get my teeth in it, so to speak, and then sort of roll it over and put gravy on it before it was really mine," Marie Dressler wrote. "This time, the part had everything when it was handed to me."

Teaming Beery and Dressler was an inspiration; their weather-beaten faces revealed the sorrows and joys of a lifetime and lent credibility to both their clowning and their sentiment. At the Academy Award ceremony in 1931, Marie Dressler was named Best Actress of the Year for *Min and Bill.* She was sixty years old, and in her words, it was "a crown for all the years of suffering and hardship that had gone before."

It was also the beginning of a brief but distinguished career in which she was one of America's most beloved stars. (She ranked Number One in the *Motion Picture Herald*'s tally of box-office champions for 1932 and 1933.) From this point on she was under contract to M-G-M and every one of her roles was designed specifically for her.

George Cukor, who directed her in *Dinner at Eight,* has these observations: "Her personality was overwhelming—and very human. During rehearsals she did the usual 'takems' and generally broad playing. That troubled me for a time, but I realized that the audience accepted Marie Dressler without question. They found her endearing and amusing; she was a law unto herself. She had her own kind of distinction and could achieve the effect that we needed without altering her way of acting. So I left it at that, and she had a great success in the picture."

In contrast to her own ambitious vehicles, M-G-M continued to costar Marie with Polly Moran in their lightweight formula comedies. But Marie kept the formula from going stale. Stubborn Polly would usually catapult the two of them into a dilemma or cause Marie to look bad in the eyes of her family or friends; it would then be up to Marie or some timely deus ex machina to provide a happy ending. Meanwhile, Polly's comeuppance would be in the form of slapstick indignities—a cake in the face, a plunge in a mud bath, and so on. She supplied the low laughs, while Marie provided the heart in such films as *Caught Short, Reducing, Politics,* and *Prosperity.*

Not that Marie was above such foolishness—in *Caught Short,* first Polly's Murphy bed falls on top of her, and later, when Polly encourages her to try it out, the bed folds up into the wall with Marie inside!

But the powers at M-G-M didn't want to tamper with success, and they soon realized that the public enjoyed Marie Dressler in her seriocomic roles more than they did in the Polly Moran outings. The success of *Emma,* a beautiful and all-but-forgotten film, proved them right. (In fact, when Frank Capra prepared to make *Lady for a Day,* the Damon Runyon story, at Columbia in 1933, he felt there was only one actress who could play Apple Annie, and that was Marie. But M-G-M wouldn't consider loaning her out, and Capra had to settle for May Robson, who was wonderful, and whose film career then went into high gear just as Marie's had with *Min and Bill.*) *Christopher Bean* and *Tugboat Annie* were surefire Dressler vehicles, filmed under an ever-darkening cloud—Marie's fragile health.

"She worked like a Trojan, to the limit of her health," wrote Mervyn LeRoy, who directed *Tugboat Annie.* "Marie's three-hour-a-day schedule seriously hampered the picture, but I knew that if it was to be finished at all, it would have to be done to accommodate her pace. When she went home at night, I couldn't help wondering whether she would be able to make it to the studio again in the morning. She was in constant pain, and the pain mirrored itself on her face, on her bearing, but never on her professionalism when the camera was rolling. She never lost her skill."

Louis B. Mayer, the despotic head of M-G-M, had especially warm feelings toward Marie Dressler and saw that she was given the best of care in her final days. For a time he even kept the word from her that she was dying of cancer and had his publicity chief plant items in the trade and fan magazines about upcoming projects for her.

She died on July 28, 1934.

Some small idea of her impact can be measured from the laughter that still resounds at frequent showings of the 1933 classic *Dinner at Eight* when Marie and Jean Harlow exchange the film's memorable closing lines. Strolling toward the dining room, Jean Harlow attempts to make conversation, saying that she's read somewhere that machines are going to replace all human beings. Dressler, who has been listening politely while walking forward, suddenly trips herself in an outrageous physical reaction to the remark that only she could have gotten away with, then stops and eyes the alluring Harlow before replying, "That's something *you'll* never have to worry about!"

The statement could have applied to Marie Dressler just as well, for the years have proven it to be true: She was irreplaceable.

THE FILMS OF MARIE DRESSLER

THE SILENT FILMS

Tillie's Punctured Romance—Mack
  Sennett 1914
Tillie's Tomato Surprise—Lubin 1915
Tillie Wakes Up—Peerless-World
  1917
The Scrub Lady—Dressler 1917
  (short subject)
The Agonies of Agnes—Dressler 1918
  (short subject)
Cross Red Nurse—Dressler 1918
  (short subject)
Fired—Dressler 1918 (short subject)
The Callahans and the Murphys—
  M-G-M 1927
The Joy Girl—Fox 1927
Breakfast at Sunrise—First National
  1927
The Patsy—M-G-M 1928
Bringing Up Father—M-G-M 1928
The Divine Lady—First National
  1929

THE SOUND FILMS

The Hollywood Revue of 1929—
  M-G-M 1929
Dangerous Females—
  Paramount-Christie 1929 (short
  subject)
The Vagabond Lover—RKO 1929
Chasing Rainbows—M-G-M 1930
Anna Christie—M-G-M 1930
The Girl Said No—M-G-M 1930
One Romantic Night—
  Schenck-United Artists 1930
Let Us Be Gay—M-G-M 1930
Min and Bill—M-G-M 1930
Reducing—M-G-M 1931
Politics—M-G-M 1931
Emma—M-G-M 1932
Prosperity—M-G-M 1932
Tugboat Annie—M-G-M 1933
Christopher Bean—M-G-M 1933
Dinner at Eight—M-G-M 1934

Marie Dressler also reportedly starred in some short subjects filmed in Europe during the early 1920s. She appeared with many other M-G-M stars in a 1932 short called *Jackie Cooper's Christmas.*

Opposite page
Billie Burke and Marie Dressler in *Dinner at Eight.*

Stan and Ollie battle it out with James Finlayson in their classic *Big Business*.

10
LAUREL & HARDY

 Chaplin commanded more attention; Keaton inspired a sense of awe and wonderment; but it's doubtful that anyone ever generated more laughter, or more love, than Laurel & Hardy.

Chaplin's Tramp is in many ways a hostile character. Keaton is more passive, but he battles just as strongly against the problems of "civilization." On the other hand, Laurel & Hardy have no grudge with society. When catastrophes occur, they blame themselves; if fortune smiles, they count it as good luck.

"They are perhaps the Civil Servants of comedy," John Grierson wrote in the 1930s. "There is no wonder the life they lead goes to the heart of the multitude."

That accounts for empathy and enjoyment, but the love so many feel for Stan and Ollie derives from their warm screen personalities—or, in a word, their charisma. Despite their many fights and violent slapstick outbursts, one always feels that these are two lovable men who have no meanness in them.

These qualities evolved during the first years that Stan Laurel and Oliver "Babe" Hardy worked together, although popular success came to them immediately. The appeal of a fat-and-skinny team to audiences was as surefire as it seemed to the Hal Roach staff in 1927. Rough outlines of their characters were also apparent from the start, for Hardy had been playing comic heavies and overblown characters, while Laurel had always been cast as a simpleton of one sort or another.

It remained for this sketchy idea to be refined. In the earliest Laurel & Hardy films, Hardy is a gruff character and Laurel the patsy. If they had remained in this two-dimensional mold, it's possible that Laurel & Hardy would have petered out after several years and never been heard from again. But whether by chance, by design, or by virtue of the fact that the two men were not coarse or cruel in real life, a humanity began to grow in their characterizations.

There is another important factor to consider, and that is Stan's and Babe's superb comic-acting talent. They created characters who were so utterly believable that it was difficult to picture them being any different off-screen. This credibility was supported by the men's decision to use their real names on-screen, enabling people around the world to feel as if they actually knew Stan Laurel and Oliver Hardy.

That their voices were so pleasing and enhanced their characters' appeal was a tremendous stroke of luck, but it also had something to do with the kind of screen personalities they were. Chaplin's and Keaton's personas were so stylized and so deeply rooted in the silent world they created that almost any kind of voice would have been jarring to audiences. Laurel and Hardy faced no such barriers. Their characters and the world they inhabited were the same in talkies as they were in silent films, so their natural speaking voices blended in perfectly. Of course, being consummate comedians, they learned to use their voices comically just as they had their faces and their bodies.

As to Laurel & Hardy's comedy style, this too evolved over a span of several years.

Oliver Hardy didn't have much comic style because he'd never been a solo comedian. Most of his career had found him playing opposite someone else, usually as villain or foil. In fact, he had twice before been part of a fat-and-skinny team: with Billy Ruge in the "Plump and Runt" series for Vim Comedies in 1916 and with Bobby Ray in a pair of 1925 comedies called *Stick Around* and *Hop to It* (the slapdash, superficial qualities of these films would be reprised when Snub Pollard and Marvin Loback teamed up in the late 1920s as a sort of road-company L&H).

Hardy had several long-running stints as a stock-company "heavy" with such comics as Jimmy Aubrey, Billy West (the Chaplin imitator), and Larry Semon, before lighting at the Hal Roach studio in 1925. These roles offered little in the way of variety but gave Hardy broad experience in the comedy field. Everyone who worked with him during this time agrees that he was one of the best comic heavies in the business. Once he settled at Roach, however, his roles became more colorful as he shuttled among the studio's various series. Here, for the first time, he was allowed to be *funny*, a luxury he was denied when playing alongside such egocentric stars as Semon.

Stan Laurel was always a clown, but his brand of comedy during the 1920s was more freewheeling and loose-limbed than the style he adopted for his work with Hardy. Stan specialized in playing wide-eyed, goofy types who reacted nervously to calamitous comedy situations. In *The Pest,* after visiting with pretty Vera Reynolds, he can't leave her house because a large neighborhood

Laurel and Hardy as they really were—quite a contrast from their screen personalities.

The boys with Billy Gilbert at the end of a pie-throwing scene deleted from *Pack Up Your Troubles*.

Above
Billy Gilbert again, giving Stan and Ollie his opinion of *The Music Box* in their Academy Award-winning short.

Below
Classic expressions, as seen in *Their First Mistake*.

Above
Laurel, Hardy, and friend in *Babes in Toyland*.

Above, right
The team's final screen appearance, in *Atoll K*.

Left
Laurel & Hardy as zoot-suited hucksters in one of their 1940s features, *Jitterbugs*.

dog "hounds" him at both the front and side entrance and won't let him out. Allowing for typical comic license in a script of this kind, Stan dons a giant dog costume, hoping that the pooch will let him pass. It does, but then the city dogcatcher gives chase. While the situations are in themselves quite funny, *The Pest* relies heavily on Stan's agility and comic know-how to make them come alive. He looked funny, he moved funny, and even in the most ragged and clumsy shorts of the 1920s, he *was* funny.

When Stan joined the Hal Roach company in 1923, a trade ad proclaimed: "A new comedy face, sure to be famous, is peeking above the horizon. . . . His manner, his style and his methods are his own. The name 'Stan Laurel' is going to mean a lot more a year from today than it does now."

But Stan did not become a major comedy star. In fact, after a year's absence he returned to Roach in 1925 not as a performer but in the capacity of writer and director. By this time, Stan's knowledge of comedy was much admired throughout the business. He directed Mabel Normand, Theda Bara, Clyde Cook, and James Finlayson during his stint behind the camera, but chance and providence brought him back to the screen in 1926 where he truly belonged.

"Stan Laurel was one of the great mimes of our time," Marcel Marceau has written, and it would have been criminal for him to spend the rest of his life creating comedy films without appearing in them as well.

If anyone doubts Stan's incredible gifts, there is a scene in the silent short *Wrong Again* that might serve as a "convincer." Walking around the home of a wealthy man, Stan and Ollie confront odd and flamboyant objects d'art. The owner is upstairs taking a bath, which Stan can't understand, since it isn't Saturday night. But Ollie explains that these rich people are a little bit "twisted" and illustrates the term by twisting his upturned hand around in a half circle. Stan nods but doesn't really comprehend.

A short time later, Ollie bumps into a Venus-type statue, knocking it off its pedestal onto the floor, where it breaks into three sections. He hurriedly reassembles the bust and walks away, unaware that he has pieced the statue together so that the torso is backward, with the figure's derriere positioned directly below its chest!

Stan ambles along, sees the statue, and in about a minute's time runs an incredible gamut of reactions and expressions in a tour de force of pantomimed comedy. Initially there is a double take as he passes the statue the first time, then realizes what he's seen in a delayed reaction. His first impulse is to smile, much as a little boy would. Then he looks at the statue again, and this time registers shock. Then he examines the piece one more time and comes to a third reaction: total blankness. Now he stands back to survey this sight as thoroughly as possible. He stares at it again, and finally he smiles with the light of recognition. Delighted that he has solved the puzzle of this startling sight, he raises his hand and turns it around in a reprise of Ollie's gesture—"twisted!"

That film was a special favorite of its director Leo McCarey, who, shortly before he died, recalled it fondly in an interview with Peter Bogdanovich. McCarey, who was a principal architect of the Laurel & Hardy style, also responded to Bogdanovich's comment about the pacing of their films by explaining, "At that time, comics had a tendency to do too much. With Laurel and

Hardy we introduced nearly the opposite. We tried to direct them so that they showed nothing, expressed nothing, and the audience, waiting for the opposite, laughed because we remained serious. For example, one day Babe was playing the part of a maître d' coming in to serve a cake [in *From Soup to Nuts*]. He steps through a doorway, falls and finds himself on the floor, his head buried in the cake. I shouted, 'Don't move! Just don't move! Stay like that.' Hardy stayed still, stretched out, furious, his head in the cake—you could only see his back. And for a minute and a half, the audience couldn't stop laughing."

McCarey's memory tended to distort details, but the principle he describes is true and formed the cornerstone of Laurel & Hardy's unique approach to slapstick.

While it's possible to find antecedents to many gags and stories in earlier comedies, there is no precedent for the Laurel & Hardy process dubbed "reciprocal destruction" by John McCabe. Here, for the first time, slapstick gags were given pace and purpose. In the classic confrontation between the boys and Jimmy Finlayson in *Big Business*, they wreak havoc on one another and on their respective possessions—Fin's house and the boys' car—but they do so in orderly, ritualistic fashion, one step at a time. The adversary stands by while his "opponent" goes about his business, waiting for the conclusion of each particular action before expressing outrage and annoyance.

This was the basis for some of Laurel & Hardy's most memorable comedies, including *The Battle of the Century*, in which for the first time there was a raison d'être for every pie hurled in a victim's face. The juxtaposition of slapstick farce and stone-faced logic was irresistible and worked wonders every time Stan and Ollie used this routine.

This all relates back to the team's fundamental basis in reality, their ability to bring outrageous exaggeration to basically credible situations and characters. Ollie's pompous behavior and insistence on good manners provide another example. He has an uncanny knack for summoning these social amenities when they will do him the least good—whether introducing himself with a flourish to a bullnecked sea captain or grabbing a glass of water away from Stan in the final scene of *Brats* with the admonition "*You* might spill it!," as he opens a door to their kids' bathroom and topples backward in the flood of water that gushes out.

Because their comedies were basically down-to-earth, Stan Laurel loved to play outlandish tricks with the camera from time to time, as if to tease the audience and remind them that it was still a movie. British critic and film maker Basil Wright particularly admired one such gag in *Way Out West*, and wrote in his original review of the film, "Hardy, divested of all but decent covering in the search for the locket, departs into an inner room and gets dressed in the twinkling of an eye. Film technique, children, can do these things—ask Aunt Eisenstein—but Laurel, unguarded innocent, enquires, 'How did you get dressed so quickly?' 'Never you mind,' replies Hardy, sublimely summing up the history of the Avant Garde movement in three pregnant words."

There were also those disarming moments when, with little or no warning, Laurel & Hardy would break into song, sometimes accompanied by dance routines. There is no point in trying to analyze the unaffected charm of such sequences; they succeed not because Stan and Babe are immensely talented singers and dancers but because they are wholly engaging personalities and present these little interludes with such pleasure and lack of pretension. Clearly, they love what they're doing.

Love is the key word in Laurel & Hardy's films: love of comedy and a love of humanity, with all its flaws and peccadilloes. Laurel and Hardy took the most basic brand of slapstick and elevated it to a new level of artistry in their work, and because of the care that went into those comedies, the world has responded to them with love ever since.

THE FILMS OF LAUREL & HARDY

This index does not include Stan Laurel and Oliver Hardy's extensive work before they teamed together. All of Laurel & Hardy's shorts were produced by Hal Roach (with the exception of their first, actually a Stan Laurel short in which Oliver Hardy appeared) and released by Pathé, then M-G-M.

THE SILENT SHORTS

Lucky Dog—G. M. Anderson-Metro 1917
45 Minutes From Hollywood—1926
Duck Soup—1927
Slipping Wives—1927
Love 'Em and Weep—1927
Why Girls Love Sailors—1927
With Love and Hisses—1927
Sugar Daddies—1927
Sailors Beware—1927
The Second Hundred Years—1927
Call of the Cuckoos—1927 (guest appearance)
Hats Off—1927
Do Detectives Think?—1927
Putting Pants on Philip—1927
The Battle of the Century—1927
Leave 'Em Laughing—1928
Flying Elephants—1928
The Finishing Touch—1928
From Soup to Nuts—1928
You're Darn Tootin'—1928
Their Purple Moment—1928
Should Married Men Go Home?—1928
Early to Bed—1928
Two Tars—1928

Habeas Corpus—1928
We Faw Down—1928
Liberty—1929
Wrong Again—1929
That's My Wife—1929
Big Business—1929
Double Whoopee—1929
Bacon Grabbers—1929
Angora Love—1929

THE SOUND SHORTS

Unaccustomed as We Are—1929
Berth Marks—1929
Men O'War—1929
Perfect Day—1929
They Go Boom—1929
The Hoose-Gow—1929
Night Owls—1930
Blotto—1930
Brats—1930
Below Zero—1930
Hog Wild—1930
The Laurel-Hardy Murder Case—1930
Another Fine Mess—1930
Be Big—1931
Chickens Come Home—1931

Laughing Gravy—1931
Our Wife—1931
Come Clean—1931
One Good Turn—1931
Beau Hunks—1931
Helpmates—1932
Any Old Port—1932
The Music Box—1932 (their only
  Academy Award winner)
The Chimp—1932
County Hospital—1932
Scram—1932
Their First Mistake—1932
Towed in a Hole—1932
Twice Two—1933
Me and My Pal—1933
The Midnight Patrol—1933
Busy Bodies—1933
Dirty Work—1933
Oliver the Eighth—1934
Going Bye Bye—1934
Them Thar Hills—1934
The Live Ghost—1934
Tit for Tat—1935
The Fixer Uppers—1935
Thicker Than Water—1935

THE FEATURE FILMS

The Hollywood Revue of 1929—
  M-G-M 1929 (guest appearance)
The Rogue Song—M-G-M 1930
  (supporting roles)
Pardon Us—Hal Roach–M-G-M 1931
  (first starring feature)
Pack Up Your Troubles—Hal
  Roach–M-G-M 1932
The Devil's Brother (Fra Diavolo)—
  Hal Roach–M-G-M 1933
Sons of the Desert—Hal
  Roach-M-G-M 1933

Hollywood Party—M-G-M 1934
  (guest appearance)
Babes in Toyland—Hal
  Roach–M-G-M 1934
Bonnie Scotland—Hal Roach–M-G-M
  1935
The Bohemian Girl—Hal
  Roach–M-G-M 1936
Our Relations—Hal Roach–M-G-M
  1936
Way Out West—Hal Roach–M-G-M
  1937
Pick a Star—Hal Roach–M-G-M 1937
  (guest appearance)
Swiss Miss—Hal Roach–M-G-M 1938
Block-Heads—Hal Roach–M-G-M
  1938
The Flying Deuces—Boris
  Morros–RKO 1939
A Chump at Oxford—Hal
  Roach-United Artists 1940
Saps at Sea—Hal Roach-United
  Artists 1940
Great Guns—Twentieth Century-Fox
  1941
A-Haunting We Will Go—Twentieth
  Century-Fox 1942
Air Raid Wardens—M-G-M 1943
Jitterbugs—Twentieth Century-Fox
  1943
The Dancing Masters—Twentieth
  Century-Fox 1943
The Big Noise—Twentieth
  Century-Fox 1944
The Bullfighters—Twentieth
  Century-Fox 1945
Nothing But Trouble—M-G-M 1945
Atoll K—Les Films Sirius/Fortezza
  Films 1951 (also known as *Robinson
  Crusoeland* and *Utopia*)

Laurel & Hardy also made guest appearances in three Hal Roach talkie shorts: *On the Loose* with Thelma Todd and ZaSu Pitts; *Wild Poses* with Our Gang; and *On the Wrong Trek* with Charley Chase, as well as appearing in *The Stolen Jools,* a benefit all-star short of 1931, and *The Tree in a Test Tube,* a government wartime short of 1943 which was filmed in color.

Above
Will Rogers on the Hal Roach lot in the early 1920s with his first director, Charley Chase.

Below
William Orlamond and Rogers, in costume to do a short scene for the leading man in *Doubling for Romeo*.

11

WILL ROGERS

With characteristic modesty, Will Rogers called himself the worst actor on the screen. Moviegoers of the 1930s repudiated that charge by making Will the nation's leading box-office star. (Of his fan mail he commented, "It's a sign of better times. More people have money to throw away on postage stamps.") Yet the word "actor" seems a poor description of the man, even though he starred in more than sixty films.

Will Rogers was a personality—so magnetic and engaging that plot, characterization, and other screen elements were forced to take a back seat when he appeared. His films were, for the most part, tailor-made to suit that personality, and because of this, Rogers was able to believe in his own character and project certain emotions with a sincerity and impact lacking in many more studied "performances."

This was also the case in silent films, where Will got his first taste of film making, but there he was at a disadvantage, since dialogue was his forte. In silents, he was "forced to act," to use his description, and although the homespun roles he was given suited him well, they began to wear thin as the Goldwyn company hammered the formula into the ground.

Even so, the few silent features that still exist are quite charming. Skillfully directed by Clarence Badger with an eye toward believability and a well-rounded story, the scenarios were based on originals by such authors as Rex Beach, Ben Ames Williams, and Irvin S. Cobb.

Richard Griffith described the elements that contributed to the success of the 1919 feature *Jubilo:* "a carefully developed story-line, a consistent effort to make plot stem from character, and to give the characters themselves individuality. . . . Rogers' own personality was at that time being rapidly developed by the newspapers into a sort of national stereotype as the Homespun Philosopher, but he gives the character of Jubilo highly individual shadings which may startle those who know him only in his public role."

One of his funniest silent outings was the unusual *Doubling for Romeo,* in which cowboy Will ventures to Hollywood in order to learn about lovemaking and please his hometown sweetheart. The film is a felicitous collaboration of the talents of Rogers, playwright Elmer Rice, scenarist Bernard McConville, director Clarence Badger (a former Sennett man), and William Shakespeare.

The Hollywood segment of *Doubling for Romeo* is hilarious; both topical and timeless gags are used (in the former category, a film is being made at the studio called *Why Live With Your Husband?* kidding the popular De Mille pictures of that era whose titles were not too dissimilar).

The Shakespearean segment is equally amusing, if less boisterous. Will falls asleep while reading *Romeo and Juliet* and envisions himself back in Shakespeare's time enacting that story. While the death scene is handled surprisingly straight, the rest of this sequence combines broad burlesque with Rogers' own humor. A title card has Romeo declaring of his love Juliet, "She speakeath, yet like a politician she sayeth nothing."

A child actor in *Doubling for Romeo* is played by Rogers' real-life son, Jimmy, who had a brief screen career of his own in the 1940s.

Unfortunately, many of Rogers' other silent features no longer exist. One, included by Gary Carey in his book *Lost Films,* is particularly intriguing. Written and directed by James Cruze, *One Glorious Day* has a whimsical spirit taking over meek professor Rogers' body and transforming him into a new man to the extent that he licks a gang of sordid politicians and builds up the courage to tell Lila Lee that he loves her. (This film had begun production in late 1921 under the title *The Melancholy Spirit* with Roscoe "Fatty" Arbuckle in the lead, but the scandal that broke in late 1921 caused Paramount to drop Arbuckle and start from scratch with Rogers.)

Unfortunately, by the time *One Glorious Day* was released in 1922, Rogers' popularity with movie audiences was on the wane. An attempt to produce his own short subjects (including the delightful two-reeler *The Ropin' Fool,* which features Rogers' astounding rope tricks) brought the star nothing but headaches and financial ruin.

At this time he accepted an offer from Hal Roach to star in a series of two-reel comedies, most of which are easily accessible today. They vary in quality, some of them succeeding in capturing Rogers' spirit and others remaining conventional comedies in which he just happens to star.

Rogers himself was unhappy with the films. "All I do is run around barns and lose my pants," he complained. "I've lost my pants in every big scene." He persuaded Roach to let an old friend, Rob Wagner, collaborate with him on one short spoofing *The Covered Wagon.* They called their version *Two Wagons, Both Covered.* He and Wagner worked out the whole film ahead of time, calling it "the first complete working script the Roach lot ever had." A preview audi-

Will Rogers as Tom Mix in the Hal Roach short *Uncensored Movies.*

Will is charmed by Fifi D'Orsay in his first talkie, *They Had to See Paris.*

ence gave the film an overwhelming reaction, but the Roach staff still wanted to make films their way. Will gave up and announced, "I'll walk through this stuff until my contract's ended."

The highlight of his stay at Roach's was a series of shorts he did spoofing popular screen stars. His outrageous exaggerations of William S. Hart, Tom Mix, Rudolph Valentino, Douglas Fairbanks, and Ford Sterling made *Uncensored Movies* and *Big Moments from Little Pictures* a delight.

When the Roach contract expired in 1924, Will returned to the stage and made only occasional forays into the film world over the next few years. While appearing nightly in London, he agreed to work during the daytime in a feature for Herbert Wilcox called *Tip Toes,* a silent film based on a Gershwin musical show and costarring Dorothy Gish.

While traveling through Europe, he engaged in the filming of humorous one-reel travelogues for an independent producer named Clarence Stearns Clancy, with such titles as *Hunting for Germans in Berlin with Will Rogers* and *Hiking Through Holland with Will Rogers.* It was not the first time he had participated in offbeat short subjects; at the beginning of the decade, his witticisms were being used as title cards in a short-lived gag newsreel called *The Illiterate Digest.* The travelogues were pure Rogers, since he appeared on-screen as well as contributing the card titles (in *Prowling Around France* a sample title read, "These are the Tuileries, the world's most beautiful gardens.

That thing spouting out is a fountain. If a thing was spouting at home, it would be a Senator.").

With the coming of sound, Fox executive Winfield Sheehan decided that the time had come to give Rogers another try in Hollywood. He signed Will to a one-picture deal, bought an ideal story by Homer Croy, and gave the project to one of the studio's top directors, Frank Borzage. The resulting film, *They Had to See Paris,* was a notable success, and the studio immediately signed the star to a long-term contract.

They Had to See Paris is still one of Will Rogers' greatest films. It became the prototype for a good many of his vehicles, but not every follow-up had the freshness of this one or Borzage's master touch. The film casts Will as the owner of an automobile repair shop in Claremore, Oklahoma (his real-life hometown), happily married and the father of a teen-age son and daughter. He owns part interest in a local oil well, which suddenly pays off and makes him a millionaire. He is unaffected by this good fortune, but his wife starts getting ambitious and decides that the family should spend a year in France.

Things start going wrong as soon as they arrive. The wife, determined to crash society, subsequently tries to keep her homespun husband in the background so he won't embarrass her. The daughter is wooed by a suave gigolo, and the son goes off on his own to live with a young girl in the Latin Quarter.

The social-climbing wife becomes increasingly unbearable, buying her friendships and criticizing Rogers when he won't go along with her schemes. She finally tells him she never wants to see him again, and heartbroken, he leaves. He is cheered up by a vivacious chanteuse (Fifi D'Orsay), whom he had met earlier, and he uses her to lure his family back by pretending that he's fallen in love with her. This, at last, brings his family to its senses, and together they return home for a happy ending, having learned that they can't pretend to be something they aren't.

They Had to See Paris is an exceptional film because so much of it rings true. The viewer finds himself actually caring about the people on-screen and becoming involved in their problems. Borzage later said that Rogers' great quality "was his own ability to make audiences forget that he was a comedian. This quality of his was very apparent in the scenes where Rogers was called upon to portray the simple, human emotions that touch the very soul of mankind. The sincerity and conviction with which he did them is what might be expected of a great tragedian. Audiences forget Rogers the wisecracker and think of him as a human being torn with emotion."

Part of the joy of the film is watching Rogers with Fifi D'Orsay; their scenes have a completely natural, unrehearsed quality about them. One can feel the rapport between the two, which was duplicated when they were reteamed in *Young as You Feel* several years later.

At the end of *They Had to See Paris,* with the family reunited, the action stops dead in its tracks while Will makes a series of observations about family life—this, too, apparently having been done ad lib. He concludes that parents meddle too much in their children's lives. "If parents just keep their children out of jail, they've fulfilled their obligation," he concludes.

Thus began a prolific film career for Will Rogers. He never returned to the stage. The balance of his films run the gamut from paper-thin plot lines, which merely provide him with backdrops for his humor, to intricate scripts that give him little chance to be himself. Best of all are those films that perfectly integrate the two elements of story and Rogers—such films as *Ambassador Bill, A Connecticut Yankee in King Arthur's Court, Doctor Bull,* and most of his later vehicles.

It is interesting to study a group of Rogers films together, for they reveal many interesting points. Most noticeable is the fact that he never did retakes; sequences with fluffed lines, hesitations, and quizzical looks among the players remain intact in the finished films. Yet this is a part of their charm, knowing that they are not simply cut-and-dried studio products. Another factor is Rogers' insistence that certain players be cast in the films, mostly old friends like Irene Rich, Stepin Fetchit (with whom he'd worked in vaudeville), Fifi D'Orsay, and Irvin S. Cobb. The camaraderie that seems to exist on-screen is not artificial but quite genuine.

Rochelle Hudson, who played the ingenue in four Rogers films, once recalled a typical incident on *Life Begins at Forty* when Rogers made an attempt to please his director. "Uncle Bill stubbed his tongue on a scene twelve times and then, on the thirteenth try when he got it perfectly, I just stood there with my mouth open, staring at him and unable to say a word. 'Well,' he drawled, with a sly grin, 'I guess I sort of gave you a precedent to go by, didn't I?' "

Most interesting of all is the way different directors worked with Rogers. His unwillingness to learn lines or repeat scenes was legendary, but directors had to learn to live with it. Some of them knew how to overcome these obstacles and maintain some semblance of pacing and coherence in the films. Others simply couldn't, and they allowed Rogers to take his time and amble through scenes with no regard for timing at all. "He was easy to direct if he liked you," David Butler contends. "And he liked me—we did seven pictures together."

So This Is London, directed by John Blystone, might have been a very pleasant bit of fluff, but every scene goes on too long, stretching the film to an undue ninety minutes. The courtroom climax of Henry King's *Lightnin'* is destroyed by Rogers' ill-timed hesitancy.

Yet no movie with Will Rogers is a total failure, simply because he is there, projecting that lovable personality and offering sage comments on the American way of life. Many of his small-town offerings are particularly pungent today, as Rogers takes his stand against big business, mechanization, and hypocrisy. While unloading a sack of groceries in *Life Begins at Forty* he expresses wonder at canned goods and says that the American emblem shouldn't be an eagle but a can opener. In *Handy Andy* when a fast-talking promoter wants to buy out his personal one-man pharmacy and make it part of a chain, Rogers tells him that "chain stores are about as friendly as chain gangs." He brings this same feeling to Mark Twain's *Connecticut Yankee,* an unusual adaptation of the book that sticks to Twain for the first half or so and then goes off on its own.

Will brings various twentieth-century production ideas to King Arthur's court, such as an armor-wash, operated on the same principle as a gas station (an attendant checks the customer's "oil" to see if the armor is squeaking). His greatest gift to the court is the invention of the bathtub. When the king asks

Joel McCrea restrains Will from
scrapping with Jason Robards,
Sr., in *Lightnin'*.

Above, right

Rochelle Hudson sides with
Rogers against a small-town
snoop in *Doctor Bull*.

Below, right

Will and Stepin Fetchit in
Judge Priest.

Myrna Loy works her charms
on a laconic Rogers in *A
Connecticut Yankee in King
Arthur's Court*.

if people will want it, Will explains that they will advertise; advertising, he says, is where you make people believe that they must have something they've managed to do without all of their lives.

In many of his films, Rogers plays an iconoclast, wiser than the so-called leaders in the town (usually played by Berton Churchill and/or Charles Middleton) but too honest to be accepted by them. This is the theme of two films that probably rate as his best, *Dr. Bull* and *Judge Priest,* both directed by John Ford. Americana at its finest, in *Dr. Bull* Rogers is cast as a small-town doctor whose "antiquated" methods make him suspect to the medical community and whose "radical" ideas, such as inoculation, win him disfavor among the townspeople. In *Judge Priest* his basic fairness and refusal to be swayed by rumors and overblown rhetoric (by Senator Berton Churchill) put him in an uncomfortable position at election time.

In these films, filled with rural stereotypes (which inevitably have their basis in reality), Rogers portrays not just a man but an ideal. He is everything we aspire to be—kind, fair, temperate, witty, above all human—and although he encounters opposition throughout the conflict at hand, he always emerges victorious. It is easy to see why this characterization was so popular with audiences; it is one of the reasons that Rogers' films are still so compelling.

Although many of his films fit into a formula pattern, they also serve to display Rogers' versatility. He obviously loved to sing and did so in a surprisingly high-pitched tenor voice. Incidental songs were interspersed throughout his films, most notably in *Doubting Thomas,* in which he tries to show up his stagestruck wife by "going Hollywood" himself and imitating Bing Crosby, and in one of *Judge Priest's* most enchanting scenes, in which he exchanges impromptu lyrics with Hattie McDaniel.

Another film, *In Old Kentucky,* even gives him an opportunity to dance. The film features the incomparable Bill "Bojangles" Robinson, and in one scene Will is thrown into jail. Robinson comes to visit him and takes his place in the cell while Will, in blackface, tries to escape. On his way out, the sheriff asks him to dance, and forced to keep up the masquerade, he does an elaborate and amazingly good tap routine. Apparently, Will kept his eyes open while working in the *Ziegfeld Follies.*

Co-workers adored Will Rogers as much as the public. Because he shunned retakes, his films were often completed under schedule; every time, Will would pay whatever salary was due the crew for the time they would have worked. Because he took his work so casually, he was always trying to boost his fellow players' stock, urging directors to "give" scenes to other actors or deliberately underplaying to make someone else look good.

He worked especially fast in 1935 to complete three pictures back to back in order to take an extended vacation. When the last one was completed, he bid his friends and colleagues good-bye and took off with Wiley Post for Alaska, where he died in a plane crash on August 15, 1935.

Although Will Rogers' humor was frequently topical, it endures today, in his writings and speeches as well as in his films, because he touched on the very heart of things. Because human nature has not changed, Rogers' wit has remained fresh. His films are a delight because they are a living vehicle for his ideas and ideals; they deserve to be shown again and again to remind us that in a world filled with trouble and hatred there is still room for such a good man.

THE FILMS OF WILL ROGERS

THE SILENT FEATURE FILMS

Laughing Bill Hyde—Goldwyn 1918
Almost a Husband—Goldwyn 1919
Jubilo—Goldwyn 1919
Water, Water Everywhere—Goldwyn 1920
The Strange Boarder—Goldwyn 1920
Jes' Call Me Jim—Goldwyn 1920
Scratch My Back—Goldwyn 1920
Cupid the Cowpuncher—Goldwyn 1920
Honest Hutch—Goldwyn 1920
Guile of Women—Goldwyn 1921
Boys Will Be Boys—Goldwyn 1921
An Unwilling Hero—Goldwyn 1921
Doubling for Romeo—Goldwyn 1921
A Poor Relation—Goldwyn 1921
One Glorious Day—Paramount 1922

The Headless Horseman—
Clancy/Hodkinson 1922
Hollywood—Paramount 1923 (guest
appearance)
Tip Toes—Paramount 1927 (produced
in England)
A Texas Steer—First National 1927

THE SILENT SHORTS

The Ropin' Fool—Rogers-Pathé 1922
Fruits of Faith—Rogers-Pathé 1922
Hustlin' Hank—Hal Roach-Pathé
1923
Jes' Passin' Through—Hal
Roach-Pathé 1923
Two Wagons, Both Covered—Hal
Roach-Pathé 1924
Uncensored Movies—Hal Roach-Pathé
1924
The Cake Eater—Hal Roach-Pathé
1924
The Cowboy Sheik—Hal Roach-Pathé
1924
Big Moments From Little Pictures—
Hal Roach-Pathé 1924
Going to Congress—Hal Roach-Pathé
1924
Don't Park There!—Hal Roach-Pathé
1924
A Truthful Liar—Hal Roach-Pathé
1924
Gee Whiz, Genevieve—Hal
Roach-Pathé 1924
Our Congressman—Hal Roach-Pathé
1924
High-Brow Stuff—Hal Roach-Pathé
1924
With Will Rogers in Dublin—C. S.
Clancy-Pathé 1927
*Hiking Through Holland With Will
Rogers*—Clancy-Pathé 1927
With Will Rogers in Paris—
Clancy-Pathé 1927
*Roaming the Emerald Isle With Will
Rogers*—Clancy-Pathé 1927

*Hunting for Germans in Berlin With
Will Rogers*—Clancy-Pathé 1927
*Through Switzerland and Bavaria
With Will Rogers*—Clancy-Pathé
1927
With Will Rogers in London—
Clancy-Pathé 1927
*Prowling Around France With Will
Rogers*—Clancy-Pathé 1927
*Winging 'Round Europe With Will
Rogers*—Clancy-Pathé 1927
Exploring England With Will Rogers
—Clancy-Pathé 1927
*Reeling Down the Rhine With Will
Rogers*—Clancy-Pathé 1928
*Over the Bounding Blue With Will
Rogers*—Clancy-Pathé 1928

THE SOUND FEATURE FILMS (all
released by Fox)

They Had to See Paris—1929
Happy Days—1930 (guest
appearance)
So This Is London—1930
Lightnin'—1930
*A Connecticut Yankee in King
Arthur's Court*—1931
Young as You Feel—1931
Ambassador Bill—1931
Business and Pleasure—1931
Down to Earth—1932
Too Busy to Work—1932
State Fair—1933
Doctor Bull—1933
Mr. Skitch—1933
David Harum—1934
Handy Andy—1934
Judge Priest—1934
The County Chairman—1935
Life Begins at Forty—1935
Doubting Thomas—1935
Steamboat Round the Bend—1935
(released posthumously)
In Old Kentucky—1935 (released
posthumously)

Above
Joe E. suits up in *Fireman, Save My Child,* with Guy Kibbee, George Meeker, and Ben Hendricks, Jr.
Below
Allen "Farina" Hoskins coaches Joe at Catalina in *You Said a Mouthful.*

12

JOE E. BROWN

Most of the stage comedians who came to Hollywood in the 1930s were either musical-comedy performers or "talking" comics. Of these, only Joe E. Brown developed a screen personality reminiscent of the silent clowns—and significantly, his popularity endured far longer than many of his stage colleagues.

Brown projected likability, innocence, and American stick-to-itiveness in his frequent role as an outcast or underdog. These had been key ingredients in the success of the silent clowns, and they helped endear Joe E. Brown to movie audiences in the talkie era who begged for some relief from the constant chatter and wisecrack dialogue that Hollywood supplied. He was a special favorite of children, and as the 1930s wore on, his major audience became rooted in small towns.

Small-town theater owners expressed their feelings—and the feelings of their patrons—in a regular column for the industry magazine *Motion Picture Herald*. These comments reflect an immediate and authentic record of mass-audience response to Joe E. Brown's comedies, particularly during the Depression era.

Frank J. Ujka, manager of the Grand Theatre in Larimore, North Dakota, wrote of *The Tenderfoot*, "Just the kind of a production my patrons will break away from their radios for, and I wish I could get more of them. My patrons want something to laugh at, something that will make them forget their troubles, and when Joe opens his mouth, it's the start of one big laugh."

Of *Son of a Sailor,* Mrs. R. D. Carter from the Faithfax Theatre in Kilmar-nock, Virginia, wrote, "Very satisfactory both in way of entertainment and business. All of Joe E. Brown's pictures are bright and happy. People want something to laugh at and forget their troubles, so this is why a Brown picture is sure for a good crowd."

Perhaps Brown's appeal also had something to do with sincerity. Although a thorough show-business professional since the age of ten, he was from a small town himself (Holgate, Ohio) and had worked hard for many years to achieve success. He wasn't so very different from the people whom he was trying to entertain; they knew this and responded to it. When people praised Joe E. Brown's clean, wholesome approach to comedy, they also knew that this was the way he conducted himself in private life as well. He was married to the same woman since 1915, a devoted family man who was active in many civic orga-nizations.

Brown happily claimed that he was perhaps the only youngster in show business who ran away from home to join the circus with his family's blessings. At age ten his enthusiasm and youthful skill won him a position with an acrobatic act (The Five Marvelous Ashtons) that toured various circuses and vaudeville theaters. For a poor boy who'd never seen the inside of a circus tent or theater before, it was a heady experience, and it provided him with a lifetime of colorful anecdotes.

He also learned the meaning of discipline during these early years. His body endured great physical punishment as he perfected a variety of acrobatic routines, and Joe's willingness to "take it" stayed with him for the rest of his career. Director Mervyn LeRoy writes in his book *Take One,* "I remember once, in a picture we did called *Local Boy Makes Good* . . . he was required to dive into the back lot lake. He surveyed the lake quickly, then backed off and was ready to plunge in. 'Watch out, Joe,' I said. 'That lake is a lot shallower than it looks.' 'Okay, Mervyn. I'll take it shallow.' He dove in, but with a trajectory such that he didn't go too deeply into the water. Still, when he came up, his face was covered with blood from where he had scraped the bottom. I passed out —I never could stand the sight of blood—but he just mopped it off and got ready for the next shot. He was a wonder."

Joe's transition from acrobat to comedian was hardly unique. Like Clark and McCullough, who were tumblers, Will Rogers, who twirled a rope, and W. C. Fields, who juggled, he began sprinkling comedy into his acrobatic turn in vaudeville and burlesque and came to rely more on comedy as his confidence grew.

By the time he made his Broadway debut in *Jim Jam Jems* in 1920 he was a seasoned performer, and with each successive show he grew more skilled and more popular. Most of his shows were revues, which featured Joe in a handful of comedy skits that he often helped devise. Performing these routines night after night, on Broadway and on the road, gave him not only self-assurance but a knowledge of timing and audience reaction that was invaluable. He had no running character from one show to the next, but he usually appeared as an amiable goof whose comedy depended as much on reaction as it did on action.

To a theater audience his wide mouth wasn't the main attraction; it was his energetic personality and his handling of his body, both in acrobatic comedy and in eccentric dancing.

Who would have predicted that Joe's entrée into motion pictures would be a series of overripe melodramas and backstage tearjerkers? Joe was playing in Los Angeles when an agent got him his first film offers at the FBO Studio, and he happily accepted these roles even though they all but abandoned his comic background. One 1928 outing called *The Circus Kid* cast him as a lion tamer who is gored to death by one of his wild animals! Said *Photoplay* magazine of this gem, "You can sleep through it."

It was only when Warner Brothers offered him comedy roles in some of their Broadway adaptations (*Sally, Hold Everything, Top Speed*) that Joe E. Brown began to register with movie audiences. In time-honored musical-comedy tradition, these films cast Joe as the "comedy lead," which meant that his scenes alternated with those of the "romantic leads," who carried the supposed stories along. After serving his movie apprenticeship in these often thankless parts, Warner Brothers decided that he had earned the right to star in his own comedy vehicles and set to work building Joe E. into a star.

A surprising number of these early films were remakes of late silent efforts, most of them in turn based on Broadway shows. *Local Boy Makes Good* was a remake of *The Poor Nut; The Tenderfoot,* a remake of *The Butter and Egg Man;* and *Going Wild,* a remake of *The Aviator,* which had been filmed just one year earlier with Edward Everett Horton. Each one was dusted off and rewritten to suit Joe E.'s emerging character as a Harold Lloyd Milquetoast type.

Many of his comedies revolved around sports, not only because they provided a natural excuse for physical comedy, but because they took advantage of Brown's athletic skill and versatility. In real life he was a rabid sports fan whose contract with Warner Brothers insisted that they sponsor a baseball team with him as "captain." Over the years Joe's films involved him in baseball, football, swimming, bicycling, polo, wrestling, boxing, and track.

In *Local Boy Makes Good* he's a timid, bookish botany student who pines over photos of a local beauty-contest winner (Dorothy Lee). He writes her love letters and sighs, "If I just had the nerve to mail her one of these . . . ." Unbeknownst to him, one of his letters *does* get mailed, and college queen Dorothy writes back that she's coming to visit his campus to see him compete in his track meet.

Now Joe must make good his boasts of track-and-field stardom, and he gamely wanders onto the field during team practice. When he hurls a javelin and nearly spears the team's star runner (Eddie Nugent), the angry Nugent takes after him and Joe runs for his life—revealing an incredible sprint that takes the coach by surprise! Joe is drafted for the team, but complications set in as he's threatened by a bully from the rival team and torn in his emotions between vampish Dorothy Lee and down-to-earth Marjorie (Ruth Hall), who works with him at the campus bookstore. For the climactic race, Marjorie sends Joe onto the field with a dizzying kiss and a dash of rubbing alcohol in his

Joe leaves the romance to Johnny Mack Brown and Jean Muir in *Son of a Sailor*.

Joe E. Brown tackles Shakespeare—and a turkey leg—in *A Midsummer Night's Dream*, with Hugh Herbert and Frank McHugh.

Joe shows off a new invention to a skeptical Carol Hughes in *Earthworm Tractors*.

Costarred with Judy Canova in *Chatterbox*.

drinking water. The result is a hilarious dash in which Joe becomes so cocky that he runs ahead of his chief rival and faces backward to taunt him while he continues to run forward!

This story seems to owe a lot to Harold Lloyd but was originally written as a play by Elliott and J. C. Nugent and then spruced up for Brown by three scenarists, including former silent-comedy star Raymond Griffith. This worm-turning story became the prototype for many Joe E. Brown vehicles, although an equal number capitalized on some of the same plot points, while casting Joe as a high-spirited braggart. Among these were two of his most successful films, *Elmer the Great* and *Alibi Ike*.

Of the two, *Elmer* was Brown's favorite, because the central character, Elmer Kane, was based on a real-life baseball personality, "big Ed Walsh," as observed by sportswriter Ring Lardner. The comic aspects of this back-patting pitcher were most enjoyable, although the perfunctory "plot" owed something to Joe's baseball picture of the previous year, *Fireman, Save My Child* (in which the plot gimmick was a fire-extinguishing bomb Joe invented in the shape of a baseball). *Alibi Ike* is arguably the better picture, because its plot is less familiar. Joe is Francis X. Farrell, a supremely confident bush-league pitcher who joins the Chicago Cubs and proves his mettle, but can't do anything, on the field or off, without making excuses for it, hence the nickname Alibi Ike. The film wastes no time getting started—Joe makes his entrance in a car that crashes through a stadium fence onto the field—and it moves briskly through the baseball season, and the love season as well, with Olivia de Havilland as Joe's romantic interest. Story conflict emerges as racketeer Paul Harvey tries to get Joe to throw a series of games through gangsterish intimidation.

Exceptional entries like *Alibi Ike* captured attention even from movie-goers who weren't confirmed Joe E. Brown fans. But mixed into Joe's yearly schedule of three films for Warners was a smattering of special and offbeat efforts: *A Very Honorable Guy* cast Joe in the unlikely role of a Damon Runyon gambler whose luck turns on him. For this one it looked as if Joe's luck had turned as well, and even the star made disparaging remarks about the finished product. *Circus Clown,* which had the natural comedy of a circus setting, was bogged down by a dramatic story line; its chief value was its locale, which allowed Joe to work in a circus setting and perform some of his old stunts. This same kind of nostalgia gave *Bright Lights* its brightest moments as Joe harked back to his vaudeville routine in a tired retelling of a backstage tale that was all too familiar to director Busby Berkeley.

But 1935 brought the most unusual departure of all for Joe E. Brown: a role in Warner Brothers' ambitious production of Shakespeare's *A Midsummer Night's Dream.* The film was directed by the celebrated Max Reinhardt (along with another German émigré, William Dieterle).

Brown recalled in his autobiography, "I met the great Reinhardt and I liked him right away. He was an artist, you could sense that immediately. His accent was pretty bad, but I understood him. He said he wanted me to play the part of Flute. I said I didn't know much about Shakespeare. He waved that aside. The first time he saw me, he said, was in the Vendome Restaurant. He had never met me but he recognized me and nodded. 'Und den Brown nodded to me und schmiled—und ven he schmiled Brown faded oudt and Flute faded in.' That was his way of telling me I was a perfect Flute.

"It was the one and only role I ever signed to play without first understanding the part. Had I known more about Shakespeare I would not have attempted it. If you know your Shakespeare you know the role is that of an addlepated fellow who is forced to play a female role in the amateur show being strenuously put on to celebrate the marriage of the Duke of Athens. . . . I was outraged, scared, and obviously wrong as a female impersonator. But that's why Reinhardt put me in it. My look of shame and guilt was just what the role required. Reinhardt insisted that I play it straight."

While the film received mixed reaction, many agreed that of the Warners contract players pressed into Shakespearean service, Joe E. Brown came off exceptionally well. He was named among the Top Ten Moneymaking Stars for both 1935 and 1936, after a three-year absence from the list.

Just one year later, Brown left Warner Brothers to make his films for independent producer David Loew. "It was bad advice and a disastrous move," he said later. "None of the independent pictures were up to the standards set at Warners." Most of these Loew productions looked—and were—cheap, and some of them had scripts to match. There were occasional exceptions, such as the pleasant *Riding on Air,* but Joe's best post-Warner vehicle by far was *The Gladiator,* a snappy, surefire comedy about a trod-upon weakling who's given a Samson serum by his professor friend that turns him into a strong man deluxe! Highlight of the film is a wrestling match with 327-pound Man Mountain Dean (which incidentally sent Brown to the hospital for a double-hernia operation), but the essence of the film's success is Joe's credibility in the role of an underdog who comes out on top.

The shoddiness of these Loew productions diminished Joe's popularity, as well as his standing in the motion-picture business. At this point it was difficult to sell his films as major attractions, and by the end of the decade a Joe E. Brown picture was strictly "B" material.

Ironically, his fortunes improved when, several years later, Joe went to

In the role of Captain Andy, with
Kathryn Grayson and Howard Keel in
Show Boat

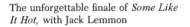

The unforgettable finale of *Some Like
It Hot,* with Jack Lemmon

work for Hollywood's principal B-movie factory, Republic Pictures. Republic
had no pretensions about art, but when that studio made a B it was fast paced
and efficient. The studio had little background in comedy but found itself with
a major attraction in hillbilly comedienne Judy Canova and decided to team her
with Joe E. Brown in a pair of entertaining films, *Joan of the Ozarks* and
Chatterbox.

Joe fared well enough to rate a solo vehicle one year later, and *Casanova
in Burlesque* was the result: a minor but very likable film about a Shakespearean
professor who moonlights during the summer as a burlesque star. The title
number, which opens the film, gives Joe the opportunity to do some of his
delightful eccentric dancing.

With the exception of supporting roles and guest shots, this brought an end
to Joe E. Brown's starring career in film comedy. During World War II he
worked tirelessly to entertain American troops—a mission doubly dear to him
after his son Don was killed during a training flight in the early days of the war.

He enjoyed a triumphant return to the stage in the road company of Mary
Chase's irresistible comedy *Harvey,* which he played for several years in cities
around the globe. Then in 1947 he returned to the screen in a poignant drama
called *The Tender Years.* Its director, Harold Schuster, recalls, "When I was
assigned to the film after having read the script I was told they were thinking
about Joe E. Brown for the lead, and had sent a script on to him in Chicago

where he was doing *Harvey*. They sent me back to Chicago to see the play, and to talk to Brown. After spending some time with him I felt he would be great in the part. He was rather hesitant at first as his reputation had been built on broad comedy. He did want to do another picture, however; we became simpatico, enjoyed each other's company, and before I left for the coast he was ready and willing.

"I got to like him immensely and enjoyed being in his company. We worked well together, and lived near each other; on some weekends we'd meet to talk over the next week's work. He was a most serious and dedicated performer, and very sincere in everything he undertook."

Although a minor film, Joe E. Brown gave it 100 percent, playing a minister in a small town during the 1880s who becomes interested in the plight of some mistreated dogs through his son's love for a boxer.

His next film appearance was as Captain Andy in the 1951 remake of *Show Boat* (which he subsequently played in theater revivals around the country), and then it was five years before a cameo part brought him back to movies in *Around the World in Eighty Days*. In 1959 he was back again, but this time it was no cameo role. It was a plum part in Billy Wilder's classic *Some Like It Hot*, as Osgood Fielding, a softheaded millionaire vacationing in Miami who falls in love with female-disguised Jack Lemmon—and won't take no for an answer. Brown projected the ideal combination of roguishness and imbecility in his characterization, which provided an essential cog in the wheel of farce that Billy Wilder created so brilliantly. He also won latter-day screen immortality with his utterance of the script's famous closing line, after Jack Lemmon finally confesses that he's not a woman. "Well," says Joe E. (still undaunted), "nobody's perfect!"

Brown was sixty-six when he filmed *Some Like It Hot*, but he looked fit and youthful. Although his screen career ended for the most part in the 1940s, he never wanted for work; he toured strawhat theaters, hosted a radio quiz show, acted as TV announcer for baseball broadcasts, and made guest appearances on various television shows through the 1960s, as well as one final film, *The Comedy of Terrors*. He starred in a pilot film for Hal Roach, Jr., which cast him as a homespun proprietor of a general store, and returned to that studio several years later to costar with Buster Keaton in a Screen Directors Playhouse show called "The Silent Partner." He and baseball-buddy Keaton later costarred in episodes of *Route 66* and *The Greatest Show on Earth* in the 1960s.

Throughout his long career, Joe E. Brown made countless friends and fans. His face became associated with happiness, and late in life he appeared in a series of TV commercials for various products in which he didn't speak a word. He didn't have to. His face radiated warmth and joy, and the sponsors knew that this could only enhance the "image" of their products.

Other comedians in film history have been cleverer, more skillful, more artistic. But none could match Joe E. Brown for establishing such immediate and enduring rapport with his audience. He called his autobiography *Laughter Is a Wonderful Thing*, and he spoke from long experience.

THE FILMS OF JOE E. BROWN

Joe E. Brown in Don't Be Jealous—
Vitaphone 1928 (short subject)
The Circus Kid—FBO 1928
Hit of the Show—FBO 1928
Take Me Home—Paramount 1928
Molly and Me—Tiffany-Stahl 1929
My Lady's Past—Tiffany-Stahl 1929
On With the Show—Warner Brothers
1929
Painted Faces—Tiffany-Stahl 1929
Sally—Warner Brothers 1929
Going Wild—Warner Brothers 1930
Hold Everything—Warner Brothers
1930
The Lottery Bride—Schenck/United
Artists 1930
Maybe It's Love—Warner Brothers
1930
Song of the West—Warner Brothers
1930
Top Speed—Warner Brothers 1930
Sit Tight—Warner Brothers 1931
Broad Minded—Warner Brothers
1931
Local Boy Makes Good—Warner
Brothers 1931
Fireman, Save My Child—Warner
Brothers 1932
The Tenderfoot—Warner Brothers
1932
You said a Mouthful—Warner
Brothers 1932
Elmer the Great—Warner Brothers
1933
Son of a Sailor—Warner Brothers
1933
A Very Honorable Guy—Warner
Brothers 1934
Circus Clown—Warner Brothers 1934
Six Day Bike Rider—Warner
Brothers 1934
Alibi Ike—Warner Brothers 1935
Bright Lights—Warner Brothers 1935

A Midsummer Night's Dream—
Warner Brothers 1935
Sons O' Guns—Warner Brothers
1936
Earthworm Tractors—Warner
Brothers 1936
Polo Joe—Warner Brothers 1936
When's Your Birthday?—David
Loew-RKO 1937
Riding on Air—David Loew-RKO
1937
Fit for a King—David Loew-RKO
1937
Wide Open Faces—David
Loew-Columbia 1938
The Gladiator—David
Loew-Columbia 1938
Flirting With Fate—David
Loew-M-G-M 1938
$1,000 a Touchdown—Paramount
1939
Beware, Spooks!—Columbia 1939
So You Won't Talk—Columbia 1940
Shut My Big Mouth—Columbia 1942
Joan of the Ozarks—Republic 1942
Chatterbox—Republic 1943
Casanova in Burlesque—Republic 1944
Pin-Up Girl—Twentieth Century-Fox
1944
Hollywood Canteen—Warner Brothers 1944
The Tender Years—
Alperson-Twentieth Century-Fox
1947
Show Boat—M-G-M 1951
Around the World in 80 Days—
United Artists 1956
Some Like It Hot—United
Artists-Mirisch 1959
It's a Mad, Mad, Mad World—United
Artists 1963
The Comedy of Terrors—
American-International 1963

The Marx Brothers at the height of their powers.

13

THE MARX BROTHERS

Fellow vaudevillian W. C. Fields called the Marx Brothers "the one act I could never follow." They pulverized audiences and left the theater a shambles.

"We were four young guys, full of hell," Zeppo has explained.

When they brought their shenanigans to Broadway, they were forced to submit to a script and direction, but during the nightly grind they found ample opportunity to ad-lib and create the kind of mayhem that had brought them fame in vaudeville. (One night during the run of *The Cocoanuts,* Margaret Dumont saw that the brothers had strayed from the script and were improvising an endless series of routines that obliterated her cue. Finally she decided to make her entrance, come what may. Groucho spotted her and, in a bold attempt to return to the script, declared, "Ah, Mrs. Rittenhouse. Won't you— lie down?")

When the talkie revolution hit the film industry, the Marx Brothers were signed by Paramount Pictures, first to re-create their stage successes *The Cocoanuts* and *Animal Crackers* and then to "go Hollywood" and star in a series of original comedies. In so doing they necessarily diluted some of their spontaneous antics but managed nonetheless to create the closest thing to comic anarchy the screen has ever known.

Everything about the Marx Brothers was "different." While they came from the stage, they were not just "talking" performers. Their bizarre appearance had as much to do with their comedy as anything else—and, of course, Harpo relied chiefly on pantomime. Most teams had a straight man, but in this case there were three comics and one straight man, Zeppo, whose position was made so ludicrously unimportant in the scripts and comedy routines that his very presence became something of a joke. The Marx Brothers took nothing seriously—except perhaps their music—but even this was far from sacrosanct. How many people besides Chico would risk undermining a musical performance by allowing Groucho to stride up to the camera just before a song and declare to the audience, "Listen, I have to stay here, but why don't you folks go out to the lobby for a smoke until this thing blows over?"

Even the Marx Brothers' personalities are slightly unreal. Groucho's canniness and Chico's stupidity are well established, but at a given moment these roles can be reversed! Consider the audacity of Chico taking Groucho to the cleaner's by selling him racetrack tips while singing the praises of tootsie-frootsie ice cream. We don't believe it for a minute—and neither does Groucho —but it doesn't seem to matter. The farce of the situation and the expertise of the players make it irresistible.

The brothers' talents were uniquely well matched. The complemented each other perfectly and never intruded upon one another's territory.

Groucho, of course, was the master of verbal humor. A witty man himself, he was aided and abetted by some of the finest comedy writers of all time. But before long, sharp observers noticed that Groucho could get laughs simply on his *delivery* of a line, whether it was funny or not. He could also take an obvious joke and make it glisten. Remember Groucho's courtroom defense of Chico in *Duck Soup?* "Chicolini may look like an idiot, and he may act like an idiot, but don't let that fool you—he really *is* an idiot!" Picture anyone else getting a laugh with that line.

Chico, on the other hand, recites wheezy jokes and puns with a beguiling innocence that contrasts beautifully with Groucho's wise-guy attitude. When he sits down at the piano in *Cocoanuts* and Margaret Dumont asks him, "What is the first number?" he calls out affirmatively, "Number one!" It is, to Chico, the obvious response and not a joke at all.

This is perhaps the key to Chico's humor: utter sincerity in his outlandish character and dialogue. Chico's Italian heritage is about as authentic as a three-dollar bill, but he never lets down his guard (although his wife was known to reprimand him during screenings of his films, "Chico, your accent is slipping").

When he deals with Groucho, he is not playing at word games. He has no stinging repartee as Groucho does when their conversation becomes tangled up in punnish misunderstandings. He seems to genuinely believe that the logical retort to the use of the word "viaduct" is "All right, why a duck?"

Chico is also the perfect "middle man" for the Marx trio because he is totally opportunistic. He goes whichever way the wind is blowing, whether it be toward helping Groucho or teaming with Harpo to undo his endeavors.

Harpo is perhaps the most "special" of the Marx Brothers. Along with Groucho, he developed a comic presence that induced immediate response. Harpo striding onstage, or on-screen, decked out in his famliar costume, beaming his impish smile, was always enough to get an audience primed for laughter.

Harpo's disarming blend of wide-eyed innocence and wild-eyed lechery is unique among movie clowns and offers him distinctive comic opportunities. On the one hand, he can disrupt a customs inspection with childish glee in *Monkey Business* and provide a wish fulfillment for all of us in his defiance of decorum. Then he can turn around and honk his horn in recognition of a beautiful blonde, giving chase and fulfilling a different kind of vicarious experience for male members of the audience.

Deflating dignity and puncturing pomposity are the stock-in-trade of the Marx Brothers and the principal reason they have retained their appeal for so many years. If anything, their socially destructive humor is more in vogue today than it was in the 1930s, and the threadbare construction of their films is perfectly attuned to the television era.

Those threadbare films are part of *The Rise and Fall of the Marx Brothers in Movies,* an informal survey that goes like this:

In 1929 the Marx Brothers made their film debut in a screen adaptation of their hit show *The Cocoanuts.* It was filmed in Paramount's Astoria studio on Long Island during the day, while the comics played in *Animal Crackers* on Broadway at night. They subsequently filmed *Animal Crackers* in Astoria as well.

These first two films are hopelessly stage-bound, not only in cinematic terms but in their musical-comedy plotting, which has the Marxes trading screen time with sappy romantic leads no one could possibly care about. But this was standard operating procedure at the time, and audiences accustomed to musical shows expected to have their comedy counterbalanced by a "serious" subplot. This of course did not make their comedy any less amusing—it just restricted them from spreading their wings and overtaking the films as their aggressive characterizations would indicate was natural behavior.

At least one critic saw the potential in store after watching *The Cocoanuts* and *Animal Crackers.* He was John Grierson, the brilliant critic and film maker, who wrote in 1930, the Marx Brothers "are great clowns, and may yet, like Grock, Chaplin, and the Fratellini, become historical ones. If, that is to say, the commercial cinema permits them to polish their roles, and refine the Idea that is in them. It is, I admit, a good deal to ask of an institution which has destroyed Langdon and cast away Raymond Griffith. What rare and noble clowns those two might have been!"

With typical perception, Grierson realized not only the Marx Brothers' capabilities but also the likelihood that they would not be able to achieve those heights. Yet, in 1931, Paramount beckoned the Marx Brothers to Hollywood and allowed them to run free in a trio of pure comedies that placed no restrictions on their enormous talents. Grierson responded in kind and wrote of *Monkey Business,* "There is a story somewhere of a gangster feud and an ocean romance, but since it is the job of a Marx Brother to destroy all such evidence of social equilibrium, you will catch only passing glimpses of either. The rest is anarchy."

As wonderful as these films seem today, some critics and moviegoers found

Above

Louis Sorin observes Harpo and Chico in *Animal Crackers.*

Below

Groucho lights up, Harpo eats a banana during the football game in *Horse Feathers.*

Chico and Groucho improvise
at the piano during a break in
filming *Duck Soup*.

Director Sam Wood films
Chico, Harpo, and Groucho in
A Night at the Opera.

them unpleasant and longed for the more orderly world of *The Cocoanuts* with its musical banalities. The unrelieved assault of Marxian comedy was simply too much for some people.

This negative reaction reached its zenith with *Duck Soup*, which today is considered the brothers' masterpiece of insanity. Many right-thinkers laughed themselves silly in 1933—but a larger number didn't, and Paramount had second thoughts about renewing the team's contract. Just at this time Chico happened to play bridge with M-G-M's production chief, Irving Thalberg, who mentioned the possibility of working together. Chico jumped at the idea and persuaded his brothers to go along.

Harpo later wrote, "Our trouble, Irving said, was that we were a big-time act using small-time material. We belonged in 'A' pictures, not in hodgepodge, patchwork jobs. Our movies should have believable plots, love stories, big casts, production numbers. We were afraid this would take us out of our element, but Thalberg said, 'Don't worry about a thing. You get me the laughs and I'll get you the story.'"

Thalberg made good on his promise and, in his quest for perfection, had the brothers take *A Night at the Opera* on the road as a stage attraction in order to test its weaknesses and strengths before committing it to film. "Thalberg was so right," Harpo recounted. "Some of the writers' favorite bits didn't get a snicker. They were cut. On the other hand, stuff that we ad-libbed on stage, as in the 'stateroom scene,' went into the shooting script." The scene as written wasn't getting big laughs until Groucho, Harpo, and Chico started to embellish it and build it into the comedy classic it became.

A Night at the Opera was a tremendous hit and an excellent film. Marx Brothers purists prefer the Paramount films, which reduce the music and romance elements to a minimum, but it must be admitted that those films, hilarious as they are, suffer from awkward pacing and flabby film making. They do nothing to enhance the Marx Brothers' comedy; one is merely grateful that they don't interfere with it.

A Night at the Opera is a different story. It has the luster of an M-G-M super-production. The balance between the Marx Brothers and their able supporting cast is perfect. One never feels cheated during the musical numbers or brief "plot" scenes because they are not taking away from the comedy; instead, they are helping it by providing a showcase, supplying a foundation on which the comedy can rest.

Unfortunately, the Marx Brothers were never to know this perfection again. As critic Cecilia Ager wrote some years later, "The Marx Brothers have never been in a picture as wonderful as they are."

A Day at the Races was only a notch below *A Night at the Opera*. Its comedy sequences were as good as any the brothers had ever performed in, and again, they were audienced-tested. But the film was not as cohesive as *Opera* and its musical numbers *did* intrude on the Marx Brothers' world.

The Marxes moved to RKO for an adaptation of the stage comedy *Room Service*, which served them well, despite its claustrophobic settings and set pieces. But back at M-G-M things went from bad to worse. Groucho had always

Harpo in a scene deleted from
A Day at the Races.

Harpo and Chico in another
scene deleted from *A Day at
the Races*.

The screen's classic couple: Groucho and Margaret Dumont.

blamed this decline on the death of Irving Thalberg during the production of *A Day at the Races*, and he has said many times that with the producer's demise his enthusiasm for making movies diminished considerably.

M-G-M was never a studio for broad comedy, and while Thalberg had found the right combination once, his unillustrious successors piloted the Marx Brothers right down the drain with increasingly shoddy scripts and musical romance subplots that threatened to elevate *The Cocoanuts* to new standards of excellence by comparison. After *At the Circus, Go West,* and *The Big Store,* the Marx Brothers called it quits.

They were lured back one more time, in 1946, by producer David Loew, and the promise of financial participation, in *A Night in Casablanca.* No classic, to be sure, it nevertheless did restore some of the spirit lost in the last M-G-M films and at least provided some honestly amusing moments. *Love Happy,* which was made three years later, had even less to offer, but by this time the mere opportunity of seeing the brothers on film was rewarding enough to carry a second-rate film.

The Marx Brothers never made another film together. Writer-director Billy Wilder wanted to reteam the trio, but the idea never took root. Even a pilot for a television series, *Deputy Seraph*, never got completed (although some footage exists). A fleeting reunion at the end of a TV half-hour called *The Incredible Jewel Robbery* brought the Marxes together before the public one final time. It was our loss.

Others have attempted satire, black humor, pantomine, rapid-fire dialogue comedy, and pure nonsense on the screen, and some have succeeded in those individual goals. But no one has ever matched the consistent and persistent lunacy of the Marx Brothers as an *entity,* a comedy team capable of pulling these elements together as part of their continuing comic personality.

Different people wrote for the Marx Brothers and provided them with material, but they remained their own best comedy resource. A line spoken by Groucho became his and his alone. Chico's dumbfounded dialect comedy would have suited no else. And Harpo's pantomime had a unique personality behind every gesture and movement. These individual identities sprang from the brothers' distinctive personalities off-screen. Groucho was without formal education, but he became a literate man. His wit was fueled by his love of words and wordplay. Chico, a lifelong gambler and womanizer not terribly unlike the carefree character he portrayed, had a solid business head that steered the Marx Brothers for many years. Harpo was by all accounts a warm and loving person; said Groucho, "He was a nice man in the fullest sense of the word," and this too came through in his endearing silent character.

Comedy can be manufactured, as television has proved. But great comic personalities cannot. The Marx Brothers' comedy was unique because the Marx Brothers were unique. Their contribution to film may be small in quantity, and dotted with disappointments and compromises, but its brightest moments shine with a comic perfection that will glow forever.

THE FILMS OF THE MARX BROTHERS

THE FOUR MARX BROTHERS

Humor Risk (silent film, never completed)
The Cocoanuts—Paramount 1929 (based on their Broadway show)
Animal Crackers—Paramount 1930 (based on their Broadway show)
Monkey Business—Paramount 1931 (their first original screenplay)
Horse Feathers—Paramount 1932
Duck Soup—Paramount 1933

THE THREE MARX BROTHERS

A Night at the Opera—M-G-M 1935
A Day at the Races—M-G-M 1937
Room Service—RKO 1938
At the Circus—M-G-M 1939

Go West—M-G-M 1940
The Big Store—M-G-M 1941
A Night in Casablanca—David Loew/UA 1946
Love Happy—Lester Cowan/UA 1949
The Story of Mankind—Warner Brothers 1957 (Groucho as Peter Minuit, Harpo as Sir Isaac Newton, Chico as a monk in separate sequences)
The Incredible Jewel Robbery—Revue/Universal 1959 (episode of General Electric Theatre television series with Harpo and Chico; Groucho makes an unbilled guest appearance in the final scene)

Harpo, Chico, and especially Groucho made additional solo appearances in other feature films and short subjects over the years.

Above
Fields with his clip-on moustache in *Running Wild*, with
Mary Brian.

Below
Fields and Gracie Allen in *International House*.

14

W. C. FIELDS

W. C. Fields off-screen is one of the great enigmas of the twentieth century. But there is no mystery about W. C. Fields on-screen: He was one of the funniest men who ever lived.

Stories are legion about Fields' dislike of babies, dogs, religion, water, and rehearsing. Some of them are true, many are not. Once Fields became well known through movies that established his comic character, he was the first to capitalize on that notoriety by spreading apocryphal publicity stories. The printed record is not much help. The stories by Fields' longtime friends and drinking cronies refute those told by his family, which in turn contradict the stories of his longtime companion Carlotta Monti.

But it is easy to misunderstand Fields even when the facts are presented clearly. Example: Fields' clashes with directors are well documented (Mitchell Leisen said, "He was the most obstinate, ornery son of a bitch I ever tried to work with") and his battles with colleagues onstage to prevent scene-stealing were awesome (the story of his batting Ed Wynn on the head with a pool cue and knocking him out cold when Wynn was distracting an audience is irrefutably true).

However, Fields was an extremely loyal and considerate man in many ways. He had great regard for many fellow comedians and especially looked out for the supporting players he liked, making sure they would be hired for his films. Grady Sutton recalls, "I worked with him in a two-reeler at Mack Sennett's, and I guess that was the first time I met him. That was *The Pharmacist,* and from then on he would ask for me, or write a part especially for me. He'd say, 'Grady's got to do it.' I remember when he did *The Bank Dick* they wanted someone else, I don't know who it was, but the powers-that-be wanted this other guy. Fields said, "No, I want Grady. I like to work with him; I like the way he reacts to me.' And they said no, we want so-and-so. He said, 'All right, then, get yourself another Fields.' They had to hire me, but I didn't work out there for three years or so, they were so mad at me. But he was a wonderful man, so wonderful."

George Cukor, an important director who might have expected a tough time from Fields on *David Copperfield,* told Gavin Lambert, "He was charming to work with, his suggestions and ad libs were always in character. There was a scene in which he had to sit at a desk writing, and he asked me if he could have a cup of tea on the desk. When he got agitated, he dipped his pen into the teacup instead of the inkwell. Another time he was sitting on a high stool and asked for a wastepaper basket so he would get his feet stuck in it."

This brings up another major Fields paradox. Stories abound concerning the comedian's dislike for rehearsals and insistence on ad-libbing, but there is an equal volume of evidence revealing that Fields was a scrupulous and well-disciplined artist who liked to work out his routines in advance.

In all probability the truth lies somewhere in between. A great number of Fields' movie routines were based on stage material he had written and performed for thirty years or more, not to mention the reuse of material from earlier film appearances. Therefore, while Fields did have a keen mind and could create extemporaneous dialogue, much of his supposed "ad-libbing" was obviously a re-creation of lines or routines he'd done a hundred times before.

In fact, one can trace the ancestry of Fields material over the years. Aside from such set pieces as his golf routine (which turned up at least a half-dozen times on film) or the pool-table classic (which was the basis for his very first film, *Pool Sharks,* in 1915), such gems as "Drug Store," "Back Porch," "The Picnic," and "Stolen Bonds," which Fields performed on the stage during the 1920s, became the basis for his most beloved film sequences. In *W. C. Fields by Himself* Ronald J. Fields has assembled some of the original scripts and notes written by his grandfather to prove how closely such sequences were based on W. C.'s original sketches. Some of Fields best sound feature films, in fact, were almost scene-for-scene remakes of silent vehicles he had done for that same studio (Paramount) in the 1920s, which in turn were based on vaudeville material.

This kind of evidence removes any speculation about "the Mack Sennett touch" in Fields' shorts or the comedic contributions of such directors as Clyde Bruckman, Norman McLeod, and Erle Kenton to Fields' work. In fact, the greatest thing any director could do, from Fields' point of view, was to let him alone and present his skits as faithfully as possible. This was not merely a comedian's ego at work. Fields knew from long experience where the laughs were in a certain skit and how much each line or gesture should be "milked" for maximum results. His mortal enemies became the studio film editors who would insert a cutaway or fail to hold a shot before a laugh was sufficiently stressed.

Can it be? W. C. Fields playing with Baby LeRoy on the Paramount lot and enjoying himself? Believe it or not.

Fields as Mr. Micawber, with Frank Lawton as *David Copperfield* and Roland Young as Uriah Heep.

Until recently, Fields' silent films were all but unknown. Happily, his first short film and four of his silent features are now available for viewing, and they prove just how good a comedian Fields could be, even without the aid of sound. This should come as no surprise when one considers that he didn't speak on-stage for more than twenty years and took to billing himself at one point as "W. C. Fields, Silent Humorist."

Eddie Cantor wrote, "The first time I heard him talk on stage was in the [Ziegfeld] *Follies of 1918.* He was doing his great golf routine and was standing,

Mae West and W. C. Fields in *My Little Chickadee;*
that's Harlan Briggs in the background.

poised to putt. A gorgeous girl in a riding habit passed by, stopped, and snapped
her fingers. She went back off stage and he got all set again to putt. The girl
came in, paused, snapped her fingers and said, 'Oh, I forgot something.'

"'Must've forgot her horse,' Fields ad-libbed in his nasal drawl. The audience howled. The minute he came off, [Will] Rogers and I ran to him and
insisted he keep the line in. He protested, but he kept it and began adding
more. From then on, you couldn't shut him up."

Pantomime remained an integral part of Fields' comic performances long
after talkies made his vocal mannerisms famous. Visual bits involving his hat
and cane and his emphatic body movements when reacting to other characters
are memorable. As the earlier comment from director George Cukor reveals,
Fields was constantly working on bits of business that would enhance his dialogue. There is a wonderful scene in *David Copperfield* in which Fields delivers
a speech to Freddie Bartholomew; as the dialogue begins, he reaches for an
apple from a fruit basket. Throughout the scene, he plays with the apple and
comes close to biting into it, only to be interrupted at the last moment by the
necessity of conversation. Finally, when the topic of discussion is resolved,
Fields triumphantly tosses the uneaten apple over his shoulder and walks out
of the scene. His rendition of this sequence is brilliant.

Fields' beautifully dextrous hands were the result of his years as a juggler; he was acclaimed one of the finest in the world. To the end of his life, despite ill health, his hands remained agile and expressive.

Fortunately, his juggling expertise is captured on film (notably in *Her Majesty, Love* and *The Old-Fashioned Way*), but it's ironic to note that contemporary reviewers often complained about Fields' dragging his stage specialties into these films, as if they were unwanted hand-me-downs!

While Fields' silent features *It's the Old Army Game* and *So's Your Old Man* are precise blueprints for the later sound films *It's a Gift* and *You're Telling Me*, comparison shows that while Fields' material was just as funny in silent performance, Fields himself was not. This is no contradiction of earlier remarks about his pantomimic skill; it is simply that his characterization lacked the distinctive stamp that would make his later films so good.

While his character in the silents is roguish, antisocial, and/or henpecked, these qualities are projected without shading or subtlety. They lack Fields' mutterings and sotto voce asides to round them out. In short, his silent films present him in a more *conventional* atmosphere than one associates with Fields. William K. Everson has written of *So's Your Old Man*, "To me it seemed to be much too carefully organized a film, with much comedy potential unexploited, and with too much order for those erratic anarchists Fields and [director] Gregory La Cava."

Whatever the modern-day reaction, Fields was not a hit with the mass American public in these silent films. *Sally of the Sawdust* was warmly received, partly because the film was based on a proven Broadway hit, *Poppy,* and partly because it was directed by the still formidable D. W. Griffith. But a second Griffith-Fields collaboration, *That Royle Girl,* pleased hardly anyone, and when Fields was set on his own in a series of starring vehicles, his stock with the Paramount executives fluctuated wildly. (Years later, Fields and Griffith were in communication about a possible filming of Dickens' *Pickwick Papers.*)

It was at this time that Fields first acquired his reputation for dispensing ulcers and nervous breakdowns to motion-picture associates. He seemed to delight in upsetting continuity between scenes, disregarding instructions, and forcing upon unsuspecting directors his most distasteful gag ideas, which had already been rejected by the producers. He also took to wearing a clip-on moustache—"an object," wrote Robert Lewis Taylor, "of widespread revulsion"—and refused to appear on-screen without it!

Despite this behavior, Fields was eager to succeed in movies and expressed great disappointment when his career as a silent film star evaporated. In point of fact, Fields' film career might never have flourished if not for the enthusiastic support of producer William LeBaron. Said Mitchell Leisen, "William LeBaron thought W. C. Fields was the most fascinating person in the world." He backed up his support by repeatedly hiring the comedian and putting up with his peccadilloes, despite lukewarm response from audiences and outright hostility from other studio workers. It was he who gave Fields his first role in a feature film, Marion Davies' *Janice Meredith,* while he was director of William Randolph Hearst's Cosmopolitan Productions. It was he who brought Fields to Paramount when he became associate producer at the company's East Coast studio, and insisted that he stay. During his reign as vice president in charge

Above
Grady Sutton, Fields, and Franklin Pangborn: a memorable trio in *The Bank Dick*.

Below
Fields and fellow Ziegfeld graduate Leon Errol in a scene deleted from *Never Give a Sucker an Even Break*.

of production for RKO Radio Pictures he commissioned Fields' talkie debut in the short subject *The Golf Specialist.* When LeBaron rejoined Paramount in the early 1930s he made sure Fields was on the payroll and even produced a remake of *Sally of the Sawdust,* retaining its original stage name *Poppy.*

It was vital to Fields' screen career that he have such a powerful godfather, for the comedian's bouts with studio personnel, coupled with fluctuating popularity, would have curtailed his presence in Hollywood at an early date.

LeBaron also gave Fields the opportunity to create some of his most solid and successful films without studio tampering or interference. Such films as *You're Telling Me, The Old-Fashioned Way,* and *It's a Gift* violated practically every Hollywood rule in throwing their weight so completely on the shoulders of a misanthropic character and fashioning feature-length films on the slightest of plot hinges in order for him to perform his classic skits. But LeBaron was not alone in his appreciation of Fields. While the comedian never appealed to a wide segment of the moviegoing audience, he did have a large and faithful following who recognized in his films something fresh, different—and funny.

In reviewing *The Man on the Flying Trapeze,* the trade magazine *Motion Picture Herald* noted, "Here is W. C. Fields' distinctive type of comedy at its best. . . . He is the star, the entire firmament, of Fields' pictures. Other stars there may be—Mary Brian, as his sympathizing daughter, is the feminine lead in this film, and Kathleen Howard has considerably more to do as the nagging wife—but the comedy rests almost solely in Fields' own antics."

Fields' mid-1930s vehicles were economically produced on the Paramount lot, and while not exactly B pictures, they were considered second-echelon films in the studio's release schedule. They did not get major bookings in many cities and often played on double-feature programs when they opened.

But Fields had a loyal camp among the critics and also in many small towns. This may seem odd at first, since he poked such cruel fun at the inanities of life in small towns and small-town people. But Fields' humor was not so different from that of other great comics; he counted on audience empathy for his character and *got* it, for Fields was the ultimate American underdog. The main difference between his character and most others was that he fought back—if sometimes under his breath. He confronted the small-town gossips and bigots and unleashed verbal retorts that Harold Lloyd or Joe E. Brown would blush to even think about.

People love to recall Fields' meanness, but they rarely remember that he would seldom act unless provoked. In fact, his tolerance is enormous, and it takes a good deal to bring out the worst in Fields, who strives to present a pleasant facade to the community at large even under trying circumstances. He doesn't attack babies until they attack *him,* and even then, he tries to smile his way out of the situation if at all possible. He endures a nightlong cacophony of noises and interruptions as he tries to sleep in the famous porch scene from *It's a Gift.* He allows pressures to build up to a controlled explosion of anger that he encapsulates in one word: "Drat!"

Illness kept Fields off-screen for a year and a half before his Paramount swan song, *The Big Broadcast of 1938,* and then it was another full year before he returned in his first Universal picture, *You Can't Cheat an Honest Man.* Inspired by his now-legendary radio appearances with Edgar Bergen and

Fields in his last screen appearance, with Louise Currie in *Sensations of 1945*.

Charlie McCarthy, the film presented undiluted Fields and paved the way for his next venture, *My Little Chickadee*. Always reluctant to allow someone besides himself to fashion his comedy scenes, he was amazed to read costar Mae West's script for the film and find it so good. He wrote to a Universal executive, "During my entire experience in the entertainment world, I have never had anyone catch my character as Miss West has. In fact, she is the only author that has ever known what I was trying to do." Unfortunately, the film failed to live up to expectations, for while the individual characterizations of West and Fields were fine, the interaction between them was weak. It was not meant for two such dominant personalities to share the screen.

Fields fared much better in his next film, which ranks with *It's a Gift* as his masterpiece: *The Bank Dick*. Director Eddie Cline, who had piloted Fields once before in the nonsense classic *Million Dollar Legs*, gave him a perfect arena for his escapades—more distinctively offbeat than ever—and Fields gathered around him a priceless troupe of players to make his cockeyed conception come to life. Taking place in the town of Lompoc, with such characters as movie director A. Pismo Clam and the plot element of an investment in a Nevada Beefsteak Mine, the film is a belly-laugh bonanza from start to finish. It is also an astounding film to have come off the Hollywood assembly line—the wholly personal product of one man's imagination.

His next film was even more idiosyncratic—and also proved to be his last starring film. *Never Give a Sucker an Even Break* failed to "top" *The Bank Dick*, but that never bothered Fields. He made his final screen appearances in a trio of "revue" films, performing some of his oldest sketch material—but that didn't matter either. Because W. C. Fields himself was so unique, so original, that "fresher" comedy routines by younger performers paled in comparison.

Advanced age hurt many comedy careers, but Fields was a notable exception. He was sixty when he starred in *The Bank Dick*, but his comedy had a youthful energy and innovative quality that transcended all thoughts of age. His comedy and his spirit have not only survived him by three decades (at this writing), but his noncomformist attitudes have made his films even more popular today than they were when they first came out.

As W. C. might say, that is indeed a felicitous turn of events.

THE FILMS OF W. C. FIELDS

Pool Sharks—Gaumont/Mutual 1915 (silent short)

His Lordship's Dilemma—Gaumont/Mutual 1915 (silent short)

Janice Meredith—Cosmopolitan/Metro-Goldwyn 1924

Sally of the Sawdust—Paramount/United Artists 1925

That Royle Girl—Paramount 1926

It's the Old Army Game—Paramount 1926

So's Your Old Man—Paramount 1926

The Potters—Paramount 1927

Running Wild—Paramount 1927

Two Flaming Youths—Paramount 1927

Tillie's Punctured Romance—Paramount 1928

Fools for Luck—Paramount 1928

The Golf Specialist—RKO 1930 (short subject)

Her Majesty, Love—Warner Brothers 1931

Million Dollar Legs—Paramount 1932

If I Had a Million—Paramount 1932

The Dentist—Sennett-Paramount 1932 (short subject; Fields received screenplay credit for the first time on these four shorts)

The Fatal Glass of Beer—Sennett-Paramount 1933 (short subject)

The Pharmacist—Sennett-Paramount 1933 (short subject)

The Barber Shop—Sennett-Paramount 1933 (short subject)

International House—Paramount 1933

Tillie and Gus—Paramount 1933

Alice in Wonderland—Paramount 1933

Six of a Kind—Paramount 1934

You're Telling Me—Paramount 1934

The Old-Fashioned Way—Paramount 1934 (original story by "Charles Bogle," a.k.a. W. C. Fields)

Mrs. Wiggs of the Cabbage Patch—Paramount 1934

It's a Gift—Paramount 1934 (original story by Charles Bogle)

David Copperfield—M-G-M 1935

Mississippi—Paramount 1935

The Man on the Flying Trapeze—Paramount 1935 (original story by Charles Bogle)

Poppy—Paramount 1936

The Big Broadcast of 1938—Paramount 1938

You Can't Cheat an Honest Man—Universal 1939 (original story by Charles Bogle)

My Little Chickadee—Universal 1940 (original screenplay by Mae West and W. C. Fields)

The Bank Dick—Universal 1940 (original story and screenplay by Mahatma Kane Jeeves)

Never Give a Sucker an Even Break—Universal 1941 (original story by Otis Criblecosis)

Tales of Manhattan—Twentieth Century-Fox 1942 (Fields episode cut from final release)

Follow the Boys—Universal 1944

Song of the Open Road—Charles Rogers/United Artists 1944

Sensations of 1945—Andrew Stone/United Artists 1945

Above
Mae West as she appeared in her first film, *Night After Night*.

Below
Mae with tall, dark, and handsome Cary Grant in *She Done Him Wrong*.

15

MAE WEST

Halfway through a dreary 1932 drama called *Night After Night,* a woman rings the doorbell of George Raft's fashionable speakeasy/gambling club. Surrounded by attractive, attentive men, she announces herself to the doorman and suddenly the film comes to life. The lady is Mae West, and this is her screen debut.

Within seconds, a hatcheck girl inside the club delivers the momentous line, "Goodness, what lovely diamonds," and Mae replies offhandedly, "Goodness had nothin' to do with it, dearie."

One can well imagine the impact Mae West must have had on moviegoers who were seeing her for the first time in 1932, because her performance in *Night After Night* retains that impact today, even for viewers familiar with her unique personality.

Mae's success in *Night After Night* was due to one person only: herself. She is perhaps unique among movies' comic personalities in that she needed no time to develop her characterization or refine any rough edges and assumed full command of her film work right from the start.

A long-established stage star who also wrote and produced her own notorious plays (*Pleasure Man, Sex, Diamond Lil,* and so on), Mae West was signed by Paramount in 1932 without any strong conviction that she was "star" material. Her casting in *Night After Night* came about chiefly because George Raft requested her.

A cynical Mae with Ralf Harolde in *I'm No Angel*.

Against her better wishes, Mae signed the contract without being given a finished script to read. Like so many stage performers before and since, she was persuaded that she was in good hands. Then, as she later recalled, "I read the script. It was nothing that I had expected. My part was very unimportant and banal. The dialogue did nothing for me. I told the studio brass, 'You can get almost anyone to play the part.'" Producer William LeBaron encouraged her to work on the script herself, and Mae reluctantly obliged. "I entirely rewrote my part and gave myself my best-styled dialogue. What was good for me was good for the picture, as *Night After Night* showed."

Slightly blowsy and bra-less, Mae, with her snappy wisecracks and forthright manner, walked off with the film, accompanied by that wonderful character actress Alison Skipworth, with whom she shared her scenes.

Mae confirmed with this coup what she'd known all along: "I had to stay in command of my career." And that she did, with more control than practically any contract star in Hollywood. She had the right of approval on virtually every aspect of her films, and when she didn't have that specific right, she argued her position with directors, producers, and studio heads until she got what she wanted.

She proposed that her first starring film be an adaptation of her stage success *Diamond Lil*. The studio was wary of a period piece. She suggested that rehearsing with her cast before shooting began would make the production go quickly and smoothly. They said it was impractical. But Mae won on both counts, and *She Done Him Wrong* came in under schedule and caused a major sensation. Aside from grossing $2 million in the United States at the height of the Depression it had tremendous aftershocks: William LeBaron credited the film with saving Paramount Pictures from bankruptcy. (While the studio may have been unaware of the property's potency when Mae first suggested it, they certainly knew what they had after the film was completed. A prominent trade advertisement for the film showed a close-up of Mae's face and bust, emphasizing her cleavage and painting her lips crimson red in an otherwise black-and-white ad. The caption: "The Bull's-Eye of Lusty Entertainment.") Richard Griffith and Eileen Bowser have noted that it virtually banished from the screen the "confession tale" heroine who suffered for her sins. It sparked a controversy that led directly to the imposition of the Hollywood Production Code, which changed the face of film making. And it made Mae West a national figure beyond that of mere movie star.

"I always enjoyed my success, but this was overwhelming," she mused in her autobiography, *Goodness Had Nothing to Do With It*. "Like most, I had accepted motion pictures. But I had failed to appreciate their impact, their selling power. More people had seen me than saw Napoleon, Lincoln, and Cleopatra. I was better known than Einstein, Shaw, or Picasso. And yet I had merely done in front of a camera what I had done for years, as well, on a stage."

The enormous success of *She Done Him Wrong* was entirely deserved. It was, and remains, an outstanding film. None of her subsequent endeavors would match this one for solid construction, inventive comedy, and brilliant showcasing of her character. Told in a compact sixty-six minutes, it weaves an engaging story laced with music and melodrama against a colorful 1890s backdrop. From Mae's opening line, proclaiming herself "one of the finest women who ever walked the streets," to her scorchy encounters with tall, dark, handsome Cary Grant, she's totally in control and she wraps us, the audience, around her little finger as surely as she manipulates the various characters in the script.

The apparent cynicism embodied in Mae West's characters is nothing so much as unvarnished honesty in a world where pretension and hypocrisy often dominate. Her notoriety derived from candor regarding the enjoyment of sex, but Mae's straight-shooting attitude went far beyond that. Crooked politicians, self-serving bluenoses, wise guys, con artists, and other such unworthies come in for put-downs and showdowns in Mae's films. The triumph of her character over such adversaries represents a vicarious victory for each of us in the audience who wouldn't have the nerve to tell off people the way Mae does.

Nor would we have her wit in doing so. A Mae West script overflows with irresistible one-liners, a wisecrack for every occasion. But Mae is not a stand-up comic shoehorning gags into her dialogue in arbitrary fashion; these bon mots are an integral part of her character.

Mae's second starring film, *I'm No Angel*, is almost as good as *She Done Him Wrong*. It reunites her with Cary Grant and again casts her as an entertainer—"Tira, the girl who discovered you don't have to have feet to be a dancer." Show people are traditionally outcasts of society, and casting Mae in such roles strengthened her ability to act as an observer of human foibles. The film winds up with a classic courtroom sequence in which Mae proves that cunning and horse sense can take the place of law school any day. At the conclusion of this opus, Mae remarks, "It's not the men in your life that counts, it's the life in your men."

None of the star's subsequent films can match these first two starring

vehicles, but by the same token, there is no Mae West film devoid of interest, simply because she is there. Her personality is so compelling, her dialogue and delivery so superb, that even the weakest of West is still worthwhile.

So powerful was Mae's character, and so rigid the format in which she seemed to work best, that collaboration with the inventive comedy director Leo McCarey on *Bell of the Nineties* actually fell flat. There was no way for both figures to operate successfully, and the resulting film is meandering though certainly pleasant.

Repetition was one Hollywood habit that hurt Mae West. But the imposition of the Production Code and the sensitivity of studios to pressure from various organizations such as the Legion of Decency contributed heavily to the decline of her films' potency and popularity.

The seamy milieu of *She Done Him Wrong* is replaced by the glitter of high society in *Goin' to Town*. Nouveau-riche Mae aims her bards at snobbism and at the men who cross her path, including oily Ivan Lebedeff, who declares that

Left
Mae poses with Adolph Zukor, whose studio she saved from ruin.

Mae and Anna May Wong in *Klondike Annie*.

Margaret Hamilton gives Mae the once-over in *My Little Chickadee*.

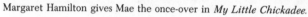

Mae works her charms on Weldon Hayburn while Walter Catlett beckons, in *Every Day's a Holiday*.

he's the backbone of his family. "Then your family'd better see a chiropractor," she snaps.

Klondike Annie is one of Mae West's most intriguing films, although it probably suffered the most from puritanical censorship. The script was watered down after the Production Code office checked it through, and then the film itself was cut by eight minutes after initial previews. Much of the impact designed by Mae and director Raoul Walsh was diluted by this tampering. But the story, of Mae taking the place of a dead missionary named Annie Alden in order to escape the police, remains unusual and worthwhile. Mae goes through the usual round of male encounters but finds herself warming to the role of "Soul Savin' Annie," commenting, "There's somethin' about liftin' up people that gets ya." Eventually she surrenders to the police to prove her innocence on a murder rap and to begin to travel the straight-and-narrow path.

The dilemma of Mae West's career at this point was the struggle between the public's appetite for more of the rowdy Mae they'd come to know and the self-appointed censors' insistence that her films be toned down.

"It was hard to fight a legend," Mae West later said, "and few people knew that I didn't *always* walk around with a hand on one hip, or pushing at my hairdress and talking low and husky." Mae's own idea was to do a film about Catherine the Great, but her producer wanted no part of that and instead convinced her to star in an adaptation of the hit play *Personal Appearance*, which was called *Go West, Young Man*.

It was Mae's most disappointing film to date, because it was just too conventional. Her role could have been played by anyone else—and that's a statement one could seldom make about a Mae West picture.

Mae hit the bull's-eye once more with her delightful *Every Day's a Holiday,* an elaborate production with a solid story line and an outstanding supporting cast—Edmund Lowe, Lloyd Nolan, Charles Butterworth, Charles Winninger, Walter Catlett, and Louis Armstrong in key roles. But ironically, this film was Mae's first box-office flop.

The public simply did not support this million-dollar-budgeted comedy, which was Mae's last for Paramount Pictures. She was off movie screens for two years, a victim of mindless censorship and Hollywood trepidation.

When she returned, it was in a Universal Picture that paired her with W. C. Fields. "I stepped off m' pedestal," Mae later remarked. "Until then I never costarred with anybody." Mae also made other concessions but maintained her most important asset, control over the script, which she wrote. Fields made embellishments, particularly his hilarious dialogue when working as bartender, but his comedy as well as hers was fashioned by West. Fields later used his clout to win equal credit with his costar on the screenplay.

"It was hard, you know," she told *Life* interviewer Richard Meryman many years later. "Fields was a comedian, depended on a lot of physical stuff, prop hats, a cane, had no romance or anything that'd make it easy to run him through the story."

Mae West and Dick Foran in *My Little Chickadee*.

Although the film has its fair share of amusing moments, it's a definite disappointment for both Fields and West, aptly described by Andrew Sarris as "more funny/peculiar than funny/ha ha."

This time there was a three-year stretch between films, and again, Mae's return to movies did not work out as well as planned. *The Heat's On* was a musical directed by Gregory Ratoff for Columbia Pictures, which fizzled for what might be termed an expected reason: Mae was not allowed to write her own script. Production problems plagued this film from the outset, and the result might be charitably called a hodgepodge.

It not only didn't revive Mae West's film career, but it convinced her to stay away from any further projects she didn't like and couldn't control.

The ensuing years were filled with successful stage revivals and nightclub tours for the ever-energetic Mae West, who became more of a legend with each passing year. Changing mores and the public's short memory helped Mae overcome much of the negative reputation she had garnered in certain circles. But ironically, a *Person to Person* television interview she taped with Charles Collingwood in 1959 was scrapped before broadcast by CBS because the network thought her remarks might be considered too suggestive!

Mae did make occasional television appearances, however, and found herself being offered a growing number of shows and movies as she entered her seventies. Federico Fellini originally wanted her to appear in his *Satyricon* as the mother of an empress. But Mae remained choosy. "My public expects certain things from me," she explained, "and I'd never do anything the Mae West character wouldn't do."

She finally said yes when Twentieth Century-Fox offered her star billing and all the accoutrements to appear in their production of Gore Vidal's *Myra Breckinridge*. The film, released in 1970, was a mess, to say the least, and its major asset—artistically and financially—was Mae herself. Despite the often sordid surroundings in which she appeared, she was the only one connected with the production to emerge with her reputation unscathed.

In the years that followed, Mae West refused to leave the limelight, surprising skeptics with delightful and vigorous performances on new record albums and occasional television appearances. As frosting on the cake, the star—well into her 80s—finally realized a longtime ambition to film her play *Sextette* in 1977. (The results were less than gratifying.)

One thing remained unchanged, however: Mae West was always good copy. During the 1970s she was profiled and interviewed in such leading magazines as *Life, Esquire, Playboy,* and *TV Guide*. Her comments regarding sex in films and sexuality in television were particularly provocative, as she seemed to contradict her "image" by denouncing these manifestations of love and passion.

What she found particularly lacking was the ingredient she knew to be the most important of all: "sex personality." And she didn't mind recounting her bouts with the censors on this score.

"Ultimately, they discovered that it didn't really matter what I said, it was the sex personality itself. It was the way I said it," she told *TV Guide's* Edith Efron. "It's the sex personality, it's not the words. The censors could never beat *that*."

Thank goodness!

Mae West remained an original right to the end. She died on November 22, 1980.

THE FILMS OF MAE WEST

Mae West received screenplay credit on all her films except *Night After Night, The Heat's On,* and *Myra Breckinridge.*

Night After Night—Paramount 1932
She Done Him Wrong—Paramount 1933
I'm No Angel—Paramount 1933
Belle of the Nineties—Paramount 1934
Goin' to Town—Paramount 1935
Klondike Annie—Paramount 1936
Go West, Young Man—Paramount 1936

Every Day's a Holiday—Paramount 1938
My Little Chickadee—Universal 1940
The Heat's On—Columbia 1943
Myra Breckinridge—Twentieth Century-Fox 1969
Sextette—Crown International 1978 (completed in 1977)

Allen Jenkins, Joan Merrill, Curly, Larry, Ann Miller, Rudy Vallee, and Moe in the feature
Time Out for Rhythm.

16

THE THREE STOOGES

The Three Stooges are an acquired taste that many people have never acquired. But during the past twenty years an interesting phenomenon has developed. In 1958, the Stooges' backlog of 190 Columbia shorts was released to television, and the slapstick trio was introduced to youngsters who had never seen their work in theaters during the 1930s and '40s. They were an immediate sensation, and while some stations have dropped the team in recent years because of parental complaints about violence, they have continued to flourish and attract a continuing turnover of young viewers.

Children have a way of growing up, however, and many youngsters of the late 1950s are now young adults who have carried with them their fondness for the Stooges. This growing body of fans doesn't care that the Three Stooges never enjoyed critical acceptance during their lifetimes. They just like them, and they aren't interested in comparisons with Chaplin and Laurel & Hardy.

After all these years the Three Stooges have become "respectable."

It isn't hard to understand why the team appeals to children. Their humor is direct and unencumbered by pretensions. Their artlessness is in fact their particular "art." There are no nuances, no layers of interpretation, no smatterings of genius in their films. They are simply hardworking clowns who will do anything for a laugh.

Their name derives from the fact that for nearly a decade they were the

163

Ted Healy and the Stooges in *Meet the Baron*.

The Three Stooges ham it up with straight man Eddie Laughton
as they return to Hollywood from a personal-appearance tour in
the late 1930s.

"stooges" or foils for Broadway and vaudeville comedian Ted Healy. It has
always been difficult to assess their work with Healy because so few of their films
with him have been available for viewing. Recently, however, several have
come to light, including their initial feature film, *Soup to Nuts,* produced in
1930. From these examples it seems clear that the Stooges found their niche
only after splitting with Healy.

In *Soup to Nuts* Healy carries the "plot," such as it is, and the Stooges—
billed then as The Racketeers and including a fourth member, Fred Sanborn
—appear in only a handful of scenes as firemen pals of kibitzer Healy. They
engage in no physical comedy whatsoever, which is somewhat startling, but
finally get to showcase their talents in a party scene in which they and Healy
do a facsimile of their vaudeville act. Again the humor is strictly verbal, with
the Stooges provoking Healy in a series of gags to which he either supplies the
punch line or reacts by slapping them. Example: Larry announces that he is
going to dance "the elevator dance." He stands stone-still while Shemp rubs
sandpaper and Moe claps hands in front of his mouth. Finally, an exasperated
Healy asks why Larry isn't moving: this is the elevator dance—it's got no steps.

Clearly, the Stooges were hampered in developing a comic style of their
own as long as they had to play off Healy and allow him to remain top banana.
When they finally split, the Stooges' individual personalities came into sharper
focus and gave them a much stronger impact.

The act had originally consisted of Moe Howard, Larry Fine, and Shemp Howard, but Shemp dropped out in the early 1930s, after making his screen debut with the team in *Soup to Nuts.* He was replaced by his younger brother, known as Curly, who quickly became the centerpiece of the group, flanked by the sourpussed bossiness of Moe and the bland idiocy of Larry.

Curly is a wonderful comic, deserving of far more praise than he has ever received. Lacking the grace or gentility of Harpo Marx, he nevertheless invites comparisons for his ability to create a totally endearing character: the over-grown child who squeals with delight or frustration and wanders through life mindless of hazards and obstacles in his path (in *Three Sappy People,* Curly is making a note to himself with a pencil; Moe grabs it away from him in a moment of anger. Curly grunts and produces a larger pencil from his coat pocket to continue his note. When Moe grabs this one he reacts even more broadly and pulls a *giant*-sized pencil from his inside pocket, which Moe uses to conk him on the head. Curly's resourcefulness in moments like this come under the heading of what Stan Laurel used to term "white magic").

Moe's character had in common with Oliver Hardy's the appearance of being smarter than his partner(s) when in reality he's just as dumb—only more arrogant about it.

Larry's is the least distinct character of the trio, but he adds a pleasing touch by siding with either Moe or Curly, depending on the situation, thereby enabling him to show moments of lucidity as well as lunacy.

Shemp Howard rejoined the team after Curly suffered a stroke in 1946, and while he was with the trio for ten years, he is the least appreciated of the team's various members, principally because he was handed the thankless task of replacing Curly. Shemp had developed into a first-rate character comedian by the 1940s, bringing his salty presence to such films as *Hellzapoppin* and *The Bank Dick.* He'd even launched his own starring series of two-reelers at Columbia, remaking such earlier shorts as Charley Chase's *The Heckler* (retitled *Mr. Noise*) and *The Grand Hooter (Open Season for Saps).*

As the "the third Stooge," Shemp offered too little contrast from Moe and Larry to really stand out. Both his facial similarity and basic gruffness linked him strongly to Moe. But he was a good, capable comic, who turned in some excellent work when the material was on his side. Stooges director-writer Edward Bernds has nothing but praise for Shemp, personally and professionally, and he recalls, "Shemp never quit when a planned scene was over, and would often surprise us with the damndest improvisations."

Improvisation is something that came naturally to the Stooges after all their years on the stage (a pursuit that continued throughout their film careers, incidentally; their yearly quota of shorts was filmed back to back to enable them to spend the rest of the year touring the country), but their tightly paced two-reelers were planned much more carefully than latter-day interviews with Moe and Larry would indicate. Columbia Pictures' careful budgets and time-tables simply wouldn't allow them the kind of freedom to experiment that they might have enjoyed some years earlier at the Sennett and Roach studios.

The volume of physical mayhem the Stooges indulged in over the years was astronomical, and like other slapstick comics, the Stooges learned to give their all for comedy. But while all of their routines were carefully laid out, and they

Moe strikes a pose in the midst of a classic pie fight in *In the Sweet Pie and Pie*. At left, Vernon Dent, John Tyrrell, a messy Dorothy Appleby; Symona Boniface over Moe's right shoulder. Sooner or later they all get plastered.

depended on timing and special rigging to carry them off, no amount of planning could eradicate the possibility of injury.

Ed Bernds recalls one incident while shooting *Brideless Groom*. "In the story line, Shemp had a few hours in which to get married if he wanted to inherit his uncle's fortune. He called on Christine McIntyre; she mistook him for her cousin and greeted him with hugs and kisses. Then the real cousin phoned, and she accused Shemp of getting kisses, as it were, under false pretenses. At that point she was supposed to slap Shemp around. Lady that she was, Chris couldn't do it right; she dabbed at him daintily, afraid of hurting him. After a couple of poor takes, Shemp pleaded with her. 'Honey,' he said, 'if you want to do me a favor, cut loose and do it right. A lot of half-good slaps hurt more than a couple of good ones. Give it to me, Chris, and let's get it over with.'

"Chris nerved herself, and on the next take she really let Shemp have it. It was a whole series of slaps—the timing was beautiful. They rang out like pistol shots. Shemp was knocked into a chair, bounced up to meet another ringing slap, fell down again, scrambled up, trying to explain—to get another crackling slap. Then Chris delivered the haymaker, a straight right that Muhammad Ali would have been proud of—and it knocked Shemp right through the door. When the take was over, Shemp was groggy, really groggy, and Chris, contrite,

Shemp Howard redoes a memorable scene of Curly's in *Vagabond Loafers*.

put her arms around him and apologized tearfully. 'It's all right, Honey,' Shemp said painfully. 'I said you should cut loose, and you did. You sure as hell did!"

Violence was, of course, a mainstay of the Stooges' comedy, and it could get out of control. Moe's constant poking and jabbing of his partners became so expected that it almost lost its sting, but other individual "gags" are not so easily dismissed. When Moe takes a pair of ice tongs, inserts them in Curly's ears and then pulls on the handle as hard as he can, the vicarious pain obliterates any possible humor except, perhaps, that of sheer outrageousness. Often a funny Stooges short is marred by this kind of startling violence.

The violence quota seemed to depend on the director who was making the two-reeler in question. Such men as Del Lord and Charley Chase were much more interested in slapstick and well-conceived sight gags than in violence. Later, Edward Bernds tried to inject some coherent story values into the films. But Jules White, who produced the Stooges' films (along with Columbia's other two-reel comedies) for twenty-five years, leaned heavily on violence and often called on it as an easy way out of a blind all out, when he directed the trio he let them go all out, with frequently painful results.

The pity of it is that the Stooges didn't need violence to create their own brand of nonsense comedy. While heavily dependent on good material and sympathetic comedy direction, they were talented comics who carried the Mack Sennett tradition of slapstick farce well into the 1960s, when pale and lumbering imitations of the same material were being presented in such films as *The Great Race* and *It's a Mad, Mad, Mad, Mad World* (in which the Stooges fleetingly appeared).

As slapstick clowns they were ideal, for they revived the silent-comedy tradition of being one step removed from reality. When sound came to the comedy short it destroyed the make-believe quality of slapstick and underlined "impossible" sight gags by making them seem too real, too tangible to be funny. The Stooges, however, existed in their own world, where, as Nora Sayre put it in her *New York Times* review of a recent compilation film, "lines essential to the action are 'Gentlemen, I demand an explanation!' and 'What's the meaning of this?' . . . The slapstick of previous periods almost always seems endearingly naïve, and that makes an audience feel worldly, even superior. While the Three Stooges weren't our leading national wits, it's a pleasure to see them bashing skulls and tweaking noses while falling about like small children unaccustomed to ice skates."

The Stooges were never credible human beings, and their shorts emphasized this almost surreal quality in many ways, not the least of which was the incredible sound-effects work contributed by Joe Henrie, who continued to work on these shorts even after he became the head of Columbia's sound department. "The Three Stooges comedies were practically all my babies," he says proudly, and recalls that the vivid sound effects that enhanced Moe's physical mayhem were achieved in a variety of ways: a bass-drum beat accompanied a sock in the stomach, while a ukulele or violin was plucked when Moe pulled a hair from Curly's head. Various ratchets were used to simulate the sound of an arm or leg being twisted, while hitting the flat side of a saw provided an especially resonant clang when someone was hit with a shovel! Of such technical wizardry was Stooges comedy born.

Dialogue was never the cornerstone of a Stooges short, but these comics were uniquely convincing in their delivery of hoary vaudeville and burlesque gags. Curly's vocal inflections were a major part of his comedy, while Moe's sarcastic asides ("Why don't you get a toupee with some brains in it?") became a trademark as well.

When Shemp Howard died in 1955, veteran comic Joe Besser was enlisted to fulfill the team's Columbia Pictures commitment. Several years later, when the act was set to go on the road, Besser demurred, and he was in turn replaced by another burlesque "pro," Joe De Rita.

So deeply rooted were the Stooges' characterizations, and so closely identified were they with the slapstick-comedy world, that even when age crept up on them they were able to function and maintain their comic prowess. Their feature films of the 1960s are surprisingly enjoyable outings, and one is never uncomfortably reminded that one is watching men in the sixties. They remain, in every sense, the Three Stooges of yore, because they don't need the violence and elaborate gags to project their by-now-familiar personalities. Clever scripting and direction places the physical burden on others but still gives the Stooges elbowroom in which to clown.

Still, there are those who cringe at the very mention of their name; to them,

Above
Larry, Moe, and Joe Besser in a posed shot from *Quiz Whiz,* one of the team's last theatrical shorts.

Below
Larry, Moe, and Curly (Joe De Rita) in their feature film *The Three Stooges in Orbit.*

the Three Stooges are an anathema. Perhaps these people like their comedy more refined. Or perhaps they've seen the Stooges at their worst; after all, they made 190 shorts and a dozen or more features, and a fair amount of clinkers is in that backlog. But when they're good, the Three Stooges are very good indeed. Snobbism has excluded them from most "respectable" surveys of screen comedy, but the time has come for at least some rudimentary recognition. The Three Stooges lasted for more than forty years because they were funny.

The Three Stooges that might have been: Moe, Joe De Rita, and longtime foil Emil Sitka filling in for Larry Fine in a publicity shot for the Independent-International feature *Blazing Stewardesses*. Moe's illness forced the group to cancel out at the last minute, and they were replaced by the Ritz Brothers. Moe died shortly thereafter.

THE FILMS OF THE THREE STOOGES

THE SHORT SUBJECTS FOR M-G-M, WITH TED HEALY

Nertsery Rhymes—1933
Beer and Pretzels—1933
Hello, Pop—1933 (in color)
Plane Nuts—1933
The Big Idea—1934
Around the World Backwards (Larry
    Fine listed this title as an
    unreleased M-G-M short)

THE SHORT SUBJECTS FOR COLUMBIA PICTURES

Woman Haters—1934
Punch Drunks—1934
Men in Black—1934
Three Little Pigskins—1935
Horses' Collars—1935
Restless Knights—1935
Pop Goes the Easel—1935
Uncivil Warriors—1935

Pardon My Scotch—1935
Hoi Polloi—1935
Three Little Beers—1935
Ants in the Pantry—1936
Movie Maniacs—1936
Half-Shot Shooters—1936
Disorder in the Court—1936
A Pain in the Pullman—1936
False Alarms—1936
Whoops I'm an Indian—1936
Slippery Silks—1936
Grips, Grunts, and Groans—1937
Dizzy Doctors—1937
Three Dumb Clucks—1937
Back to the Woods—1937
Goofs and Saddles—1937
Cash and Carry—1937
Playing the Ponies—1937
The Sitter-Downers—1937
Termites of 1938—1938
Wee Wee, Monsieur—1938
Tassels in the Air—1938
Flat Foot Stooges—1938
Healthy, Wealthy, and Dumb—1938
Violent Is the Word for Curly—1938
Three Missing Links—1938
Mutts to You—1938
Three Little Sew and Sews—1938
We Want Our Mummy—1939
A-Ducking They Did Go—1939
Yes, We Have No Bonanza—1939
Saved by the Belle—1939
Calling All Curs—1939
Oily to Bed, Oily to Rise—1939
Three Sappy People—1939
You Nazty Spy—1940
Rockin' Through the Rockies—1940
A-Plumbing We Will Go—1940
Nutty But Nice—1940
How High Is Up?—1940
From Nurse to Worse—1940
No Census, No Feeling—1940
Cuckoo Cavaliers—1940
Boobs in Arms—1940
So Long, Mr. Chumps—1941
Dutiful But Dumb—1941
All the World's a Stooge—1941
I'll Never Heil Again—1941

An Ache in Every Stake—1941
In the Sweet Pie and Pie—1941
Some More of Samoa—1941
Loco Boy Makes Good—1942
Cactus Makes Perfect—1942
What's the Matador?—1942
Matri-Phony—1942
Three Smart Saps—1942
Even as I.O.U.—1942
Sock-a-Bye Baby—1942
They Stooge to Conga—1943
Dizzy Detectives—1943
Spook Louder—1943
Back From the Front—1943
Three Little Twerps—1943
Higher Than a Kite—1943
I Can Hardly Wait—1943
Dizzy Pilots—1943
Phony Express—1943
A Gem of a Jam—1943
Crash Goes the Hash—1944
Busy Buddies—1944
The Yoke's on Me—1944
Idle Roomers—1944
Gents Without Cents—1944
No Dough, Boys—1944
Three Pests in a Mess—1945
Booby Dupes—1945
Idiots Deluxe—1945
If a Body Meets a Body—1945
Micro-Phonies—1945
Beer Barrel Polecats—1946
A Bird in the Head—1946
Uncivil Warbirds—1946
Three Troubledoers—1946
Monkey Businessmen—1946
Three Loan Wolves—1946
G.I. Wanna Go Home—1946
Rhythm and Weep—1946
Three Little Pirates—1946
Half-Wits Holiday—1947 (Curly's last
starring film with the Stooges)
Fright Night—1947 (Shemp's first
short with the Stooges)
Out West—1947
Hold That Lion—1947 (cameo
appearance by Curly)
Brideless Groom—1947

Sing a Song of Six Pants—1947
All Gummed Up—1947
Shivering Sherlocks—1948
Pardon My Clutch—1948
Squareheads of the Round Table—1948
Fiddlers Three—1948
Heavenly Daze—1948
Hot Scots—1948
I'm a Monkey's Uncle—1948
Mummy's Dummies—1948
Crime on Their Hands—1948
The Ghost Talks—1949
Who Done It?—1949
Hocus Pocus—1949
Fuelin' Around—1949
Malice in the Palace—1949
Vagabond Loafers—1949
Dunked in the Deep—1949
Punchy Cowpunchers—1950
Hugs and Mugs—1950
Dopey Dicks—1950
Love at First Bite—1950
Self-Made Maids—1950
Three Hams on Rye—1950
Studio Stoops—1950
Slap Happy Sleuths—1950
A Snitch in Time—1950
Three Arabian Nuts—1951
Baby Sitters' Jitters—1951
Don't Throw That Knife—1951
Scrambled Brains—1951
Merry Mavericks—1951
The Tooth Will Out—1951
Hula La La—1951
The Pest Man Wins—1951
A Missed Fortune—1952
Listen, Judge—1952
Corny Casanovas—1952
He Cooked His Goose—1952
Gents in a Jam—1952
Three Dark Horses—1952
Cuckoo on a Choo Choo—1952
Up in Daisy's Penthouse—1953
Booty and the Beast—1953
Loose Loot—1953
Tricky Dicks—1953

Spooks—1953 (released in 3D)
Pardon My Backfire—1953 (filmed but not released in 3D)
Rip, Sew and Stitch—1953
Bubble Trouble—1953
Goof on the Roof—1953
Income Tax Sappy—1954
Musty Musketeers—1954
Pals and Gals—1954
Knutzy Knights—1954
Shot in the Frontier—1954
Scotched in Scotland—1954
Fling in the Ring—1955
Of Cash and Hash—1955
Gypped in the Penthouse—1955
Bedlam in Paradise—1955
Stone Age Romeos—1955
Wham Bam Slam—1955
Hot Ice—1955
Blunder Boys—1955
Husbands Beware—1956
Creeps—1956
Flagpole Jitters—1956
For Crimin' Out Loud—1956
Rumpus in the Harem—1956
Hot Stuff—1956
Scheming Schemers—1956
Commotion on the Ocean—1956 (Shemp's last film with the Stooges)
Hoofs and Goofs—1957 (Joe Besser's first film with the Stooges)
Muscle Up a Little Closer—1957
A Merry Mix-Up—1957
Space Ship Sappy—1957
Guns A-Poppin—1957
Horsing Around—1957
Rusty Romeos—1957
Outer Space Jitters—1957
Quiz Whiz—1958
Fifi Blows Her Top—1958
Pies and Guys—1958
Sweet and Hot—1958
Flying Saucer Daffy—1958
Oil's Well that Ends Well—1958
Triple Crossed—1959
Sappy Bullfighters—1959 (Joe Besser's last film with the Stooges)

THE FEATURE FILMS

With Ted Healy

Soup to Nuts—Fox 1930 (with Shemp and Fred Sanborn)
Turn Back the Clock—M-G-M 1933 (this and subsequent films with Curly)
Meet the Baron—M-G-M 1933
Dancing Lady—M-G-M 1933
Fugitive Lovers—M-G-M 1934
Hollywood Party—M-G-M 1934

As the Three Stooges

The Captain Hates the Sea—Columbia 1934
Start Cheering—Columbia 1938
Time Out for Rhythm—Columbia 1941
My Sister Eileen—Columbia 1942 (gag appearance)
Rockin' in the Rockies—Columbia 1945
Swing Parade of 1946—Monogram 1946

Gold Raiders—United Artists 1951 (the Stooges' first starring film, with Shemp)
Have Rocket, Will Travel—Columbia 1959 ("Curly Joe" De Rita's first film with the Stooges; he remains with the team in all subsequent films)
Snow White and the Three Stooges—Twentieth Century-Fox 1961
The Three Stooges Meet Hercules—Columbia 1962
The Three Stooges in Orbit—Columbia 1962
The Three Stooges Go Around the World in a Daze—Columbia 1963
It's a Mad, Mad, Mad, Mad World—United Artists 1963 (guest appearance)
Four for Texas—Warner Brothers 1963
The Outlaws Is Coming—Columbia 1965
Kooks Tour—Normandie Productions (a projected television feature released posthumously in 1976 for the nontheatrical market)

Previous listings of the Stooges in two Universal features, *Gift of Gab* and *Myrt and Marge,* are erroneous; another act calling itself The Three Stooges actually appears in these films. The Stooges appeared in a 1960 featurette called *The Three Stooges Scrapbook*, and footage of their shorts with Curly was compiled into another feature called *Stop, Look and Laugh*. Moe and Curly appeared in an M-G-M short *Jail Birds of Paradise* (1934) and an M-G-M feature *Broadway to Hollywood* (1933). There is also an unconfirmed report that the Stooges appeared in the 1943 Columbia feature *Good Luck, Mr. Yates.*

Above
Bud Abbott and Lou Costello looking very natty in their screen debut, *One Night in the Tropics.*

Below
Bud and Lou in a riotous card game during *Ride 'Em Cowboy.*

17

ABBOTT & COSTELLO

If Abbott and Costello are remembered for anything, it is certainly their "Who's on First?" routine. This classic piece of dialogue, adapted from various burlesque bits, has now been reprinted in several books, reshown on television, and reissued on film.

But too many people who like the routine are willing to dismiss Abbott and Costello as patter comedians who happened to have a good piece of material. If this was the case, they never would have achieved such phenomenal popularity as movie stars in the 1940s and early '50s.

The beauty of "Who's on First?" is in the enactment by A&C. In this routine, as in all their work, the roles assumed by Bud and Lou are integral to the humor of the piece. As Jim Mulholland points out in his assessment of the underrated Bud Abbott, "In order to be a good straight man, you must be a good actor. And Bud was. He really made you believe that the first baseman's name was 'Who,' or that the refusal to buy one jar of mustard would throw the entire nation's economy out of kilter. Bud could make the most audacious statement seem sound and logical." Lou Costello's obvious comic asset was his credibility as the patsy who was engulfed by Abbott's "logic."

Each one depended on the other, and this was their formula for success as a comedy team. Costello needed a straight man just as much as Abbott needed a funnyman to work with. Their particular comedy talents were perfectly meshed.

Not that they couldn't have worked with others. In fact, one of Lou Costello's best film scenes is played with Leon Errol in *The Noose Hangs High*. Errol takes Abbott's role in the "Mudder and Fodder" sequence, while Costello enhances the natural humor of the dialogue with his vivid and hilarious performance. The scene opens as the two are discussing their bets on the next horse race.

Errol: I changed my bet from Lolly C to Lucky George because Lolly C is off her feed.
Costello: She's off her feed?
Errol: Yes.
Costello: Well, what does she eat?
Errol: Her fodder.
Costello: (*Forlorn*) Mr. Caesar—
Errol: Yes?
Costello: (*Earnestly*) She *eats* her *fodder?*
Errol: Yes.
Costello: Well, what does her mother eat?
Errol: She eats *her* fodder.
Costello: (*Hums, strolls a bit, tries desperately to be nonchalant*) Look, Mr. Caesar, suppose a little horse is born— (*now his voice is trembling*) Where's his papa?
Errol: In the pasture.
Costello: (*Regaining some control*) Now, does the little horse eat the papa?
Errol: Oh, of *course* not. His papa's in the pasture and his fodder is in the barn.
Costello: (*Now he's lost. He hesitates a moment, then flails his arms along the pool table in frustration, making a terrible commotion*) Now wait a minute. Don't make silly of me or something.
Errol: No, no, no, no—what's the matter?
Costello: Mr. Caesar (*his voice breaking with emotion*)—now—the little horse's papa, isn't that his fodder?
Erroll: Now, how can that be? The papa never saw the little horse's fodder!
Costello: (*All choked up*) Didn't he ever come home nights?
Errol: Say, wait a minute, this is no laughing matter. There's another reason why Lucky George will win. Lucky George is a mudder!
Costello: (*Lets this sink in, then strikes himself in the face and goes into convulsions. Now he's practically shrieking*) HOW CAN A HE BE A MUDDER? AIN'T A *SHE* ALWAYS A MUDDER?
Errol: Sometimes a *he* is a better mudder than a *she!*
Costello: (*Choking with confusion and frustration, pounds the table with his fist and manages to croak out one final question*) How can ya tell?
Errol: By their feet!

At this point, Costello can't stand any more and shuffles away from the pool table, exhausted and defeated in his efforts to understand.

As these descriptions have tried to illustrate, it's not the play on words that makes this sequence work, but Lou Costello's incredible reactions, which stem from his characterization as an overgrown little boy. Like a little boy, he not

Lou Costello clowns for the cameraman, while Peggy Ryan, Martha O'Driscoll, June Vincent, and Bud Abbott hold still during *Here Come the Co-eds.*

only fails to grasp the difference between similar-sounding words, but he becomes frightened and upset at the thought of a poor little horse having to eat his own father!

Lou's childlike thoughts and actions make him a most endearing character. He's a mischievous kid who often enjoys a private chuckle over a joke or piece of business that escapes the eyes of poker-faced Abbott. He's incapable of feeling hatred, but he will take a dislike to someone in a pouty, childish way. His tremendous compassion—coupled with utter naïveté—makes him an easy mark for the sharpsters and double-dealers who populate Abbott and Costello movies.

On the other hand, Bud Abbott is not a terribly likable character in the team's films. One does acquire a certain respect for his razor-sharp mind, however, which has the ability to hatch ingenious ideas that throw all the risk on the shoulders of his partner but guarantee all the returns to him.

The problem with Abbott and Costello's films is that Bud's character isn't really a character at all. He is a straight man for dialogue routines and a sobersided sounding board for Costello's antics. His relationship with Lou is an ambivalent one: He needs the little guy in order to maintain his own self-importance, yet he willingly sacrifices his pal at every turn.

The genesis of this situation is clear. Abbott and Costello came to movies with ready-made personalities established in their burlesque, Broadway, and radio routines. When they arrived at Universal studios the plan was simple: to feature them in movies that would enable them to make use of these wonderful routines. *Buck Privates* is little more than a string of burlesque sketches held together with a romantic subplot and music.

As long as the team continued to use this material (and variations provided by their longtime writer John Grant) they were safe. In these burlesque chestnuts, which no one was ever supposed to take seriously, straight man Bud was actually cast as a kind of "heavy." As Jim Mulholland explains, ". . . because he treated comics in a rough-and-tumble manner on stage—pushing and slapping them around whenever they gave a foolish answer to one of his questions . . . the audience's sympathy was then focused on the comic. . . ."

This became a problem only when Abbott and Costello became such popular stars and embarked on a feature-film schedule that saw them turning out two to three movies a year. It then became a challenge to sustain an on-screen relationship between a lovable comic and his bullying, harsh-tongued partner.

Another dilemma soon became apparent: Bud Abbott's skills stopped short of being able to handle physical comedy.

Lou Costello was the ideal movie clown for the talkie era. His flair for dialogue was great, and his infectious delivery made him a radio favorite long before audiences could see what he looked like. As it turned out, his short-statured, baby-face appearance matched his character to a tee, and his youthful experience as a Hollywood stunt man had left him with an agile body capable of taking the most incredible pratfalls. Therefore, it's common to have major comedy scenes in A&C films where Costello is carrying the ball and Abbott just seems to be along for the ride.

Where the team works best is in set pieces tailored to their particular style of comedy, and this doesn't mean just double-talk dialogue routines. The "moving candle" bit in *Hold That Ghost,* reprised with great effect in other films, is one of their classically funny scenes. Along with other hapless "guests," they are exploring an eerie, haunted house. Bud leaves Lou in one room alone while he goes to check what's outside. Lou is nervous about staying alone, so Bud tells him to keep his eye on the candle sitting on the table in front of him and concentrate on that. Lou obliges, but as soon as Bud leaves, the candle starts to move along the table! Lou is stymied with fear and calls his partner back. Naturally, as soon as Bud returns the candle stops moving. Lou cannot convince his pal that the candle budged or that anything strange is going on, but to placate Lou, Bud agrees to come right back as soon as Lou yells "Oh, Chuck!" This leads to a wonderful series of gags, the funniest coming when Lou is so totally paralyzed with fright that he cannot get his mouth to work! "Oh—Ch-Ch-Ch—," he sputters helplessly. "Oh Ch-Ch-Ch-Ch-Chu—" Then finally, "OH CHUCK!!!!!"

Two great comedians meet on the Universal lot in 1943.

Lou clowns again, with his cigar this time, for a publicity shot from *The Time of Their Lives*, with Marjorie Reynolds, Bud, John Shelton, Lynne Baggett, and Binnie Barnes.

Marjorie Main and Bud Abbott encourage Lou to act like
a man in *The Wistful Widow of Wagon Gap.*

A healthy dose of "scare comedy" worked wonders in *Hold That Ghost* and
was also responsible for another of the team's best pictures, *Abbott and Costello
Meet Frankenstein.* The secret of that film's success was that it played its horror
elements straight and let Bud and Lou's comedy arise from their entanglements
with Frankenstein, Dracula, The Wolfman, et al. The resulting film succeeds on
both levels and remains a thoroughly entertaining picture by any standards.

So does another film that qualifies as the team's most unusual effort: *The
Time of Their Lives.* Earlier in 1946 there had been an effort to split up the
team within the same film, in *Little Giant,* but the script was weak and the
outcome only fair. This time everything clicked. In a story combining comedy,

drama, and fantasy, Lou and Marjorie Reynolds play a pair of patriots from colonial times whose ghosts have inhabited a New England home for two hundred years. Bud Abbott, a psychiatrist friend of the man who plans to renovate the house and live there, is unaware that his friend is a descendant of the conspirator who framed Lou and Marjorie years ago. Clever scripting, ingenious special effects, and a light touch that aims for smiles instead of belly laughs make this film one of the team's most enjoyable, if least typical, outings.

Costello's performance is charming and calls on his natural acting instincts for scenes of pathos and sincerity as well as more typical comedy scenes. It confirms that with the proper guidance he could have tackled more ambitious and impressive roles on his own. Abbott lacks his partner's effortless charisma, but he too does a fine job in the quietly comic role of a harried psychiatrist.

Unfortunately, Abbott and Costello were at the mercy of their writers and directors. They barely participated in the making of their films, except as performers, and even then, some directors found it difficult to get the irrepressible pair to settle down long enough to shoot a scene straight through. After their first burst of success in the early 1940s, their films became wildly inconsistent, and there was no way to predict whether the next one would be dull or delightful. By the early 1950s they were turning out some downright dogs.

Left to their own devices, Abbott and Costello preferred their old standby gags and routines, and there was sound reasoning in this. While critics complained, Bud and Lou proved that some jokes with the longest whiskers got the biggest laughs, because they were still funny, and because they performed them with such vigor and enthusiasm.

Laughs were the only thing that mattered to Abbott and Costello, and this was both their strength and their failing. Blatant disregard for characterization, plot, or consistency in their work kept A&C from ever joining the ranks of great film comedians. But steadfast dedication to getting laughs put them in the front ranks of audience popularity for ten years and keeps their best films fresh and funny today, as they continue to deliver those surefire laughs. And that's no small accomplishment.

THE FILMS OF ABBOTT & COSTELLO

One Night in the Tropics—Universal 1940 (includes "Who's on First?")

Buck Privates—Universal 1941 (their first starring film)

In the Navy—Universal 1941

Hold That Ghost—Universal 1941

Keep 'Em Flying—Universal 1941

Ride 'Em Cowboy—Universal 1942

Rio Rita—M-G-M 1942

Pardon My Sarong—Universal 1942

Who Done It?—Universal 1942

It Ain't Hay—Universal 1943

Hit the Ice—Universal 1943

In Society—Universal 1944

Lost in a Harem—M-G-M 1944

The Naughty Nineties—Universal 1945 (includes "Who's on First?")

Abbott and Costello in their final film together, *Dance With Me, Henry*.

Abbott and Costello are surrounded—by Bela Lugosi and Glenn Strange—in *Abbott and Costello Meet Frankenstein*.

Universal-International 1951
Jack and the Beanstalk—Warner Brothers 1952
Lost in Alaska—Universal-International 1952
Abbott and Costello Meet Captain Kidd—Warner Brothers 1953
Abbott and Costello Go to Mars—Universal-International 1953
Abbott and Costello Meet Dr. Jekyll and Mr. Hyde—

Universal-International 1953
Abbott and Costello Meet the Keystone Kops—Universal-International 1955
Abbott and Costello Meet the Mummy—Universal-International 1955
Dance With Me, Henry—United Artists 1956

Lou Costello made one solo film before his death, *The 30-Foot Bride of Candy Rock* (Columbia 1959). In 1965 Universal produced a compilation feature called *The World of Abbott and Costello*.

Young Hope, with Jules Epailly and Johnny Berkes in
the short subject *Double Exposure*.

18

BOB HOPE

Woody Allen has said, "If I wanted to have a week-end of pure pleasure, it would be to have a half-dozen Bob Hope films and watch them, films like *Monsieur Beaucaire* and *My Favorite Brunette*. It's not for nothing that he's such a greatly accepted comedian. He is a great, great talent."

Despite this praise from the movies' current number-one funnyman, there is a tendency to take Bob Hope's films for granted. Perhaps because he was and is so popular in radio and television it is thought that his films were throwaways—or that because he is best known as a monologist he is unworthy of consideration as a film comedian.

What nonsense!

Bob Hope has starred in more than fifty feature films, as well as a handful of short subjects, spanning nearly forty years. His popularity in radio and television did not support his screen career; dozens of broadcasting stars have tried to achieve movie stardom and failed. Hope's films succeeded because they were *good* and because he adapted so well to the film medium.

He's no Charlie Chaplin, as he would be the first to admit—but he never tried to be. Hope stands alone among film comics in having created a screen character who relied so heavily on *jokes* to make his films work.

But if jokes alone were responsible for Hope's success, he would have been rivaled by such other one-liner experts as Henny Youngman and Gene Baylos.

Hope *used* jokes as part of a continuing characterization, a screen personality as solid and identifiable as any concocted by more versatile clowns of the era.

To quote Woody Allen again, "Jokes become a vehicle for the person to display a personality or attitude. Just like Bob Hope. You're not laughing at the jokes but at a guy who's vain and cowardly and says to some guy who is menacing, 'You're looking good—what do you hear from your embalmer?' You're laughing at the character all the time."

This character first developed on Hope's radio show in the late 1930s. As one of his writers recalls, "We took his essential characteristics and exaggerated them. He's woman-chasing, egotistical, somewhat stupid and somewhat smart . . . but he's enough of a comedian to see the humor in that. He couldn't put on airs because you could deflate him."

As this character evolved, Hope's films improved and soared into a ten-year winning streak. But needless to say, it took a while for Hope to hit his stride.

Hope's first appearance on-screen was in a second-rate musical-comedy short for Educational Pictures. Like many vaudeville and Broadway performers, Hope enjoyed making extra money appearing in these lightweight two-reelers, which were filmed across the East River in Astoria during the day. But when Hope saw his first film, *Going Spanish,* one night at the Rialto Theatre, he shuddered, and made his now-famous wisecrack to Walter Winchell, "When they catch John Dillinger, the current Public Enemy, they're going to make him sit through it twice."

Hope's subsequent two-reelers for Vitaphone, which were shot in Brooklyn, are a definite improvement, although they still rely on hokey comedy conventions that have little to do with individual style. In most of them Hope plays a brash wisecracking type, teamed with diminutive fall guy Johnny Berkes. *Paree, Paree,* Hope's first, was not in that mold at all, being instead a digest version of Cole Porter's show *Fifty Million Frenchmen.* And Hope's best Vitaphone short, *Shop Talk,* cast him as a straight man in the George Burns manner.

The comedian's most vivid memory of these shorts is how quickly they were filmed, under the watchful eye of Vitaphone studio head Sam Sax. "Sax could turn out a short in three days," Hope wrote in his autobiography. "If we fell behind schedule, we got a three-minute lunch period. If we really fell behind, Sam put a lunch scene in the picture, and we ate while the cameras rolled."

It was quite another matter when Hope was called to Paramount for one of the leads in *The Big Broadcast of 1938.* His role in this hodgepodge film was negligible, but his rendition of "Thanks for the Memory" with Shirley Ross marked an auspicious Hollywood debut. The song, of course, became Hope's lifelong theme.

But Bob Hope was not immediately recognized as a "hot property" at Paramount, and his subsequent assignments were merely routine. Although considered a minor release, 1939's *Never Say Die* was the comic's best to date, a sparkling and original comedy originally written by Preston Sturges and then peppered by Don Hartman and Frank Butler, who became Hope's first script specialists. Later that year came the turning point in the comic's screen career.

In reviewing *The Cat and the Canary, Motion Picture Herald* wrote, "Paramount here has solved neatly for itself, exhibitors and customers, the heretofore perplexing problem of what to do with Bob Hope, admittedly one of the funniest comedians who ever faced a camera, yet never until now the sure-fire laugh getter on the screen that his following knew him to be in fact.

"By dipping back into the yesteryears for this tried and trustworthy mystery thriller and placing Hope in it with leave to explode a full equipment of incidental gags at will, the company has achieved a film as full of laughs as chills, giggles as shrieks, an all-purpose picture appropriate for exhibition at any time and place.

"This time, too, Hope has been provided with top quality support and polished production, the latter by gifted Arthur Hornblow Jr. He is beneficiary likewise of the knowing direction of Elliott Nugent, who acted the play when it was a stage hit and knows its points accordingly."

Here, in one film, all the elements of an ideal Bob Hope vehicle crystallized perfectly: first, a solid story peg; second, a glamorous leading lady (Paulette Goddard); third, ample opportunity for Hope to run the gamut of his comic emotions—bravado backed by sheer cowardice, baseless egotism, an eye for pretty girls; and finally, plenty of room for wisecracks (forced to spend the night in a creepy mansion, Nydia Westman asks Hope, "Don't big, empty houses scare you?" "Not me," says Bob. "I used to be in vaudeville").

The Cat and the Canary was such a hit that Paramount tried to make lightning strike not twice but three times, with surprising success. In 1940 Hope and Goddard were reunited in *The Ghost Breakers.* Like *Canary,* it had been filmed before (in 1915 and 1922) and was an airtight "spook story," with Bob as Larry L. Lawrence (the "L." stands for Lawrence, too—"my folks had no imagination"), a radio star who becomes involved with murder and a "haunted" house. One-liners were abundant, but they never interfered with the progression of a solid script, making *Ghost Breakers* top entertainment. Paramount brought Hope and Goddard together one more time, in 1941, for a non-ghost story that nevertheless had proud lineage: *Nothing But the Truth* was a hit play, which had been filmed before, in 1920 and 1929, with a foolproof premise: A man bets that he can tell the absolute, unvarnished truth for twenty-four hours, no matter what provocation there may be to lie. Willie Best encored his role from *Ghost Breakers* as Bob's comic valet, and director Elliott Nugent, who'd started the ball rolling with *The Cat and the Canary,* spirited George Marshall away from *Ghost Breakers.*

Nugent had directed Hope in *Give Me a Sailor* and remained in the comedian's stable of directors for many years. He became accustomed to a definite procedure in the creation of a Hope vehicle after the comic scored his initial screen successes. "When the producer and I were satisfied with the writers' script, then Hope's writers would take over and they would submit to us various gags to be spotted here and there. He would take maybe half of them, and reject the other half. But he had two writers on the set at all times, and every once in a while they would come up with an idea, sometimes for a gag and sometimes

Bob and Paulette Goddard in *The Ghost Breakers*.

Walter Slezak and Bob make a big splash in *The Princess and the Pirate*.

Anthony Quinn has his doubts about these two, in *The Road to Morocco*.

a little directorial suggestion. Quite often they were good."

When Hope made *The Princess and the Pirate* for perfectionist producer Samuel Goldwyn in 1943, the script went through no less than fifteen writers, all adding gags and embellishments to satisfy Goldwyn as well as Hope and director David Butler. When all was said and done, the result was a lavish and funny film, but its finale provided the biggest laugh: leading lady Virginia Mayo abandons Hope to run to the arms of—Bing Crosby! "How do you like that?" Hope complains to us in the audience. "I knock myself out for nine reels and some bit player from Paramount comes over and gets the girl! Boy, that's the last picture I do for Goldwyn." (P.S. it was.)

By this time, Hope and Crosby were established as a team in their wonderful *Road* pictures. The first, *Road to Singapore,* was in production as *Cat and the Canary* was released to theaters, and its success caught almost everyone unawares. Hope and Crosby were reteamed a year later in *The Road to Zanzibar* and the unofficial "series" was launched—each one seeming to top the one before in zaniness and spontaneity.

That spontaneity was genuine. David Butler, who directed *The Road to Morocco,* says, "We did very little rehearsing. We'd go over the scene probably a couple of times, and then we'd start. I'd say 'Roll 'em.' Bob would say 'You going to play golf this morning?' Bing would say, 'Yes.' 'Tomorrow?' 'Yes.' 'Are you going to meet me or should I meet you?' And I'd say 'We're rolling.' And Bob would say, 'Well, I'd better come over and get you, because ...' 'We're rolling!' Then they'd go ahead and talk about a lot of things like that and finally zing right into the scene. They were perfectly at ease.

"If anything happened that was out of the ordinary, I'd always let the camera run, and we got some of the funniest stuff after the scene was over. We'd

Hope and Lucille Ball in *Fancy Pants*.

do the scene, and then if there was any ad-libbing, I'd always let the camera run until they got off the set, or walked out, or whatever happened."

Says Butler, "I had a lot of fun with those pictures, because it wasn't like work." That happy feeling came through to audiences and accounts for much of the success of this series.

Because they were so unpretentious and popular, the *Road* pictures never got much serious attention from critics, but in fact they utilized the motion-picture medium for comedy effects with a freedom and flexibility that few film makers have ever achieved.

Everybody got into the act—including Robert Benchley, who patiently tried to "explain" certain confusing scenes in *Road to Utopia;* producer Jerry Fairbanks, whose "Speaking of Animals" techniques were used to allow bears, camels, and fish to make wisecracks; and songwriters Johnny Burke and James Van Heusen, who beautifully captured the spirit of the films in their theme song, which had Bob and Bing declare, "Just like Webster's dictionary, we're Morocco-bound."

Jane Russell comes to the rescue of Bob and Roy Rogers in *Son of Paleface*.

Writer Don Hartman always maintained that the formula for a *Road* picture was pitting comedy against a background of menace, and the same ingredients continued to serve Hope in his solo efforts, such as *My Favorite Blonde*, *Monsieur Beaucaire*, *My Favorite Brunette*, *The Great Lover*, and *My Favorite Spy*, all of which were fast, funny, well-constructed comedies—and all of which boasted beautiful leading ladies (Madeleine Carroll, Joan Caulfield, Dorothy Lamour, Rhonda Fleming, and Hedy Lamarr, respectively).

Hope also carried over from his *Road* pictures the facility for talking directly to the camera, making "in-joke" references that were beyond the boundary lines of the story, and continuing to kid Crosby.

In 1948 Hope starred in his biggest solo success, *The Paleface*. In truth, it is not his funniest film, but it's extremely entertaining and well mounted (in Technicolor), and it scores points by weaving Hope's humor into the fabric of a first-rate script. By this time Hope had also developed a sharp sense of visual comedy and knew how to make the most of a slapstick scene or broad facial reaction.

The only person who wasn't pleased with *Paleface* was its writer, Frank Tashlin, who later complained to Peter Bogdanovich, "I'd written it as a satire on *The Virginian*, and it was completely botched. After seeing the preview of it, I could've shot Norman McLeod. . . . And I realized then that I must direct my own stuff." Three years later, Tashlin co-wrote and directed *Son of Paleface*, a sequel that was in some ways even better than the original, brimming with wild slapstick gags that Hope carried out in fine fashion.

Like any star making two to three pictures a year, Hope ran the risk of falling into a rut, and around this time he began to experiment, first with a pair of Damon Runyon stories that seemed unlikely vehicles for his humor, *Sorrowful Jones* (a remake of *Little Miss Marker*) and *The Lemon Drop Kid*. The results were uneven, and Hope returned to his proven formula.

Then in 1955 he took a bold plunge by starring in *The Seven Little Foys*, a serious look at a funnyman, Eddie Foy Sr. The script was written by two men who had been on his radio staff in the 1930s and '40s and were part of the Goldwyn comedy team as well, Mel Shavelson and Jack Rose. Shavelson persuaded Hope to let him direct the film ("That's no big deal," Hope said to him, "my last three pictures have been so bad I can't sink any lower").

"He was very good at it," Shavelson says today, "but he was always embarrassed about being any good in a dramatic scene. He would always break up, or try to break up the crew after the shot was over . . . but he was a pretty good actor."

The role was designed to show off Hope's many talents to best advantage: his natural instincts for acting, his proven comedy sense, and his often-forgotten skills as a hoofer.

He followed this success with an attempt at sophisticated comedy, *That Certain Feeling*, that wound up a disaster. Then Hope went to England to film another offbeat picture, *The Iron Petticoat*, which costarred Katharine Hepburn in a thinly disguised update of *Ninotchka*. Although considered a turkey in its day, and the cause of considerable flack between Hope and screenwriter Ben Hecht, it's not nearly as bad as one might think. Hope and Hepburn may seem an unlikely pair, but they work quite well together as he (a brash Air Force man) tries to thaw a cold Russian defector (Hepburn). It was ponderously directed by Ralph Thomas, and its good intentions and good scenes got lost, as *Time* indicated in a perceptive review: "For a couple of reels the leading comedian plays it, not for guffaws, but for the quiet snickers he is really better at getting; yet in the last half of the picture he goes right back to the cheap tricks that in recent years have made many moviegoers give up Hope."

Back in Hollywood, Hope again submitted to the growing expertise of Mel Shavelson and Jack Rose for one final shot at a serious role, without "guffaws," in *Beau James*. He turned in a first-class job as Jimmy Walker, the celebrated mayor of New York City during the 1920s, in a film that deftly worked lighter moments into its basically serious story.

Unfortunately, after this film Hope's annual screen endeavors became increasingly erratic, with more bad than good. *Alias Jesse James* was a highly entertaining reprise of *Paleface* ingredients, and *The Facts of Life* was an excellent adult comedy, which proved that Hope and Lucille Ball could handle more than gag lines and TV sit-com scripts. But such films as *Bachelor in*

Bob goes straight—as Mayor Jimmy Walker in *Beau James*, with Paul Douglas.

Older but no wiser: Bob and Jill St. John in *Eight on the Lam*.

Paradise, Call Me Bwana, and *A Global Affair* buried Hope's onetime reputation as a reliable movie laugh maker. By the time he made *Boy, Did I Get a Wrong Number* in 1966 the tide seemed too strong to turn backward. His later films have been, for the most part, embarrassing.

Why should this be? Bob Hope remains one of the kings of the entertainment industry. His television specials are among the most popular on the air, and his monologues are as topical and as funny as ever.

The answers lie in several areas. First, by the 1960s movies were no longer Hope's major endeavor. They commanded less of his attention with each passing year, and the lack of commitment showed. Second, he stopped using the best writers for his films as he continued to do in television. What's more, he used the same writers repeatedly, allowing them to compound their first flop with a second, and then a third, fourth, and fifth.

Another veteran Hope staffer says, "I think the years and the success and the money have changed a lot of people—there are very few who keep their equilibrium. Even twenty-five years ago I can remember Frank Freeman, who was head of Paramount at the time, trying to tell Bob that he couldn't chase girls any more, because he was too old, people wouldn't accept it. Twenty-five years later Bob was still chasing girls, and he doesn't realize that he has changed, you don't get the laughs the way you used to."

Bob Hope is still going strong, on TV and in personal appearances. But it seems a shame that he couldn't find a way to continue making quality film comedies as well, for in his prime, he was unbeatable, and Bob Hope pictures were as good as any being made in Hollywood.

THE FILMS OF BOB HOPE

THE SHORT SUBJECTS

Going Spanish—Educational Pictures 1934

Paree, Paree—Vitaphone-Warner Brothers 1934

The Old Gray Mayor—Vitaphone-Warner Brothers 1935

Watch the Birdie—Vitaphone-Warner Brothers 1935

Double Exposure—Vitaphone-Warner Brothers 1935

Calling All Tars—Vitaphone-Warner Brothers 1936

Shop Talk—Vitaphone-Warner Brothers 1936

THE FEATURE FILMS

The Big Broadcast of 1938—Paramount 1938

College Swing—Paramount 1938

Give Me a Sailor—Paramount 1938

Thanks for the Memory—Paramount 1938

Never Say Die—Paramount 1939

Some Like It Hot—Paramount 1939

The Cat and the Canary—Paramount 1939

Road to Singapore—Paramount 1940

The Ghost Breakers—Paramount 1940

Caught in the Draft—Paramount 1941

Nothing But the Truth—Paramount 1941

The Road to Zanzibar—Paramount 1941

Louisiana Purchase—Paramount 1941

My Favorite Blonde—Paramount 1942

The Road to Morocco—Paramount 1942

Star Spangled Rhythm—Paramount 1942
They Got Me Covered—Goldwyn-RKO 1943
Let's Face It—Paramount 1943
The Princess and the Pirate—Goldwyn-RKO 1944
Road to Utopia—Paramount 1945
Monsieur Beaucaire—Paramount 1946
My Favorite Brunette—Paramount 1947
Where There's Life—Paramount 1947
Variety Girl—Paramount 1947 (guest appearance)
Road to Rio—Paramount 1948
The Paleface—Paramount 1948
Sorrowful Jones—Paramount 1949
The Great Lover—Paramount 1949
Fancy Pants—Paramount 1950
The Lemon Drop Kid—Paramount 1951
My Favorite Spy—Paramount 1951
The Greatest Show on Earth—Paramount 1952 (guest appearance)
Son of Paleface—Paramount 1952
Road to Bali—Paramount 1953
Off Limits—Paramount 1953
Here Come the Girls—Paramount 1953
Scared Stiff—Paramount 1953 (guest appearance)
Casanova's Big Night—Paramount 1954

The Seven Little Foys—Paramount 1955
That Certain Feeling—Paramount 1956
The Iron Petticoat—M-G-M 1956
Beau James—Paramount 1957
Paris Holiday—United Artists 1958
The Five Pennies—Paramount 1959 (guest appearance)
Alias Jesse James—United Artists 1959
The Facts of Life—United Artists 1960
Bachelor in Paradise—M-G-M 1961
The Road to Hong Kong—United Artists 1962
Critic's Choice—Warner Brothers 1963
Call Me Bwana—United Artists 1963
A Global Affair—United Artists 1964
I'll Take Sweden—United Artists 1965
The Oscar—Embassy 1966 (guest appearance)
Boy, Did I Get a Wrong Number—United Artists 1966
Eight on the Lam—United Artists 1967
The Private Navy of Sergeant O'Farrell—United Artists 1968
How to Commit Marriage—Cinerama 1969
Cancel My Reservation—Warner Brothers 1972

Hope has produced or co-owned most of his films since the late 1940s. He also appeared in a number of promotional, wartime, and industry-oriented short subjects over the years.

Danny Kaye does "The Lobby Number" in his first feature film, *Up in Arms*.

19

DANNY KAYE

An energetic young "toomler" from that well-trod comedy training ground the Catskill Mountains scored his first major success on Broadway in 1940 singing a high-speed novelty number called "Tchaikovsky" in *Lady in the Dark,* which starred Gertrude Lawrence. Danny Kaye stopped the show with his verbal acrobatics (naming fifty-four Russian composers in thirty-nine seconds) and rubber-faced delivery.

Within a few short years, he was in Hollywood under contract to Samuel Goldwyn. But Kaye had appeared in films long before his Broadway success. In 1937 he found occasional work in two-reel comedies produced by Educational Pictures in Astoria, on Long Island. With his gift for dialects, he created some highly amusing characterizations in middlingly funny shorts like *Getting an Eyeful, Cupid Takes a Holiday,* and *Dime a Dance,* which also featured Imogene Coca, June Allyson, and Hank Henry.

Goldwyn had no knowledge of Kaye's earlier film work. He saw Kaye during a nightclub engagement in New York and decided to bring him to Hollywood and make him a star. He tried to get the performer (born David Daniel Kaminsky in Brooklyn) to have his nose fixed, but Kaye refused. When Goldwyn had a screen test made in Hollywood, he agonized further over Danny's appearance and decided that lighter hair might brighten his features. This time he offered no alternatives, and Danny Kaye became a blond.

Goldwyn also signed Kaye's wife, Sylvia Fine, whose special-material songs and behind-the-scenes encouragement were the backbone of her husband's career. Her first contribution was a show-stopping number devised for his initial Goldwyn film, *Up in Arms.* A flimsily plotted Technicolor musical, this wartime hit had little to recommend it except Kaye himself, seen at his best in "The Lobby Number." Sylvia Fine and Max Liebman concocted the song, spoofing the long wait customers had before getting to see a film (first standing in line in the lobby, then wading through an endless parade of meaningless credits on screen). Danny auditioned it for Goldwyn, who uncharacteristically soared into peals of laughter. Mrs. Kaye recently recalled that no other number she and Danny ever did pleased the producer so much. Nodding reluctant approval to later ideas, he would sigh, "Well, they can't *all* be 'The Lobby Number.' "

Nevertheless, Goldwyn believed in Danny Kaye and produced a series of lavish vehicles: *Wonder Man, The Kid From Brooklyn, A Song Is Born,* and *The Secret Life of Walter Mitty,* all four pairing him with beautiful Virginia Mayo. Kaye's character was usually patterned after Harold Lloyd—the shy schnook who triumphs in the end and gets the girl—and, in fact, Goldwyn purchased Lloyd's talkie film *The Milky Way* in order to reshape it for Kaye as *The Kid From Brooklyn.*

Logic went out the window as he was allowed to perform a number called "Pavlova" that was completely at odds with the character he was playing. But Goldwyn never let logic stand in the way of making a musical comedy—as witness the sudden appearance of Goldwyn Girls at the unlikeliest times throughout his films.

Nearly everyone agreed that these films' only true worth was as a showcase for Danny Kaye, utilizing his great gift for musical spoofery (as in the double-talk opera at the end of *Wonder Man*) and the surefire device of placing wide-eyed Danny in an incongruous setting and letting him fend for himself. But in terms of plotting and characterization, the films failed to create any real audience empathy for Kaye. He remained an entertainer and not a screen performer.

Being a movie star was never Danny Kaye's top priority, however. He'd turned down an offer from M-G-M back in 1941 for $3,000 a week. "I would work for much less, believe me," he explained, "almost for nothing, if they would give me character roles and let me learn how to act. But I know they would just put me into a specialty spot here and there and one bum picture would put me back two or three years. I'm very young. I've got lots of time. My wife doesn't want me to go into pictures for at least a year, and then as an actor and not as a specialty performer."

Even after his Goldwyn success, Kaye made no more than one film a year, leaving ample time to perform on radio, make records, and appear onstage. Seeing Danny Kaye in person was a much more vibrant experience than watching him on film—because in concert there were no excuses or explanations needed for him to perform an unconnected series of songs and comedy routines. What's more, his rapport with audiences was extraordinary. His enormous success in London stage appearances, including a Royal Command performance, prompted Bob Hope to remark, "Danny has been practically adopted by the British. I used his dressing room when I was over there. It was a modest affair; just two mirrors and a throne."

Later in the 1950s he began his now-famous tours for UNICEF, the United Nations Children's Emergency Fund, and captivated youngsters in countries around the world who had no understanding of English. Kaye communicated with mime, music, gibberish, and a unique understanding of childhood's sublime foolishness. He was one of the few adult entertainers who could imitate children's mannerisms without seeming childish himself. There was always a marvelous warmth and openness about Danny Kaye when he performed in this setting that has never diminished, as witness his recent cultural outings on television. His first UNICEF tour was delightfully captured in a short subject called *Assignment Children,* which is still distributed through 16mm. libraries. He also recorded a captivating album called "Mommy, Gimme a Drink of Water," expressing children's poignant and humorous feelings.

Meanwhile, his film career remained erratic. *The Inspector General* was a very mild adaptation of the story by Gogol, with a few good songs; *On the Riviera* was a splashy remake of two films, *Folies-Bergère* (Maurice Chevalier) and *That Night in Rio* (Don Ameche), which cast him in his second dual-role endeavor, after *Wonder Man;* and *Hans Christian Andersen* was a well-intentioned Goldwyn production with a melodious Frank Loesser score that simply didn't come together.

Then Danny and Sylvia Fine formed their own production company, named after daughter Dena, and decided to engineer their own films, for Paramount release. Their first wise decision was to hire Norman Panama and Melvin Frank.

The writing/directing/producing team of Panama and Frank—both of whom had worked for Goldwyn as comedy writers—brought something new to Danny's screen repertoire: believability. Just because he was supposed to get laughs didn't mean that he had to play a fool, as he nearly always did in the plastic Goldwyn vehicles. Panama and Frank enabled him to play comedy but develop a reasonably realistic character as well, a character who could act a love scene and be hero as well as clown.

Their efforts bore delicious fruit in *Knock on Wood* and *The Court Jester.* In *Knock on Wood* he's a ventriloquist who becomes involved with international espionage and winds up ducking his pursuers onstage in the midst of a ballet. The complicated proceedings enable Danny to practice his dialects as an Irish roisterer in a rousing pub sequence and as a British sportscar customer—then salesman—with a classic broad-A accent. *Knock on Wood* remains Kaye's favorite film. Loath to discuss his old movies in any detail, he did remark to Tom Burke of *The New York Times* in 1970, "Things like the ballet, the bit under the table—I hate to use the word, but those are *classic* routines."

The Court Jester is perfection in every way. Billed at the time as the most expensive screen comedy ($4 million) to date, every dollar showed on the screen in this lavish costume production. Danny is part of an underground movement to restore a rightful infant king to power; scorned by his hero the

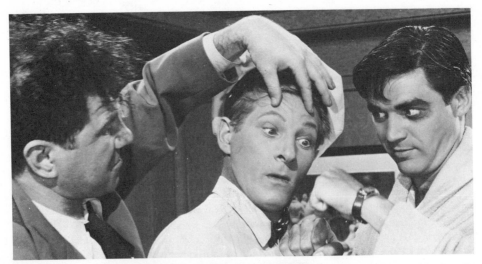

Danny is roughhoused by Lionel
Stander and Steve Cochran in *The
Kid From Brooklyn*.

Danny has eyes only for Virginia
Mayo in *The Secret Life of Walter
Mitty*.

Mai Zetterling and Danny in
Knock on Wood.

Danny becomes a dashing
swordsman to fight with Basil
Rathbone at the snap of a finger in
The Court Jester.

Black Fox, he sees his chance to make good by impersonating a traveling jester
(Giacomo—King of Jesters and Jester of Kings) who has been commissioned to
join the royal court.

The film is full of memorable scenes, tuneful songs, and bright bits of
comedy business, including the deathless warning to Danny as he enters into
combat with swarthy Robert Middleton: "The pellet with the poison's in the
vessel with the pestle; the chalice from the palace has the brew that is true!"
The film also boasts Sylvia Fine's clever soliloquy "The Jester's Lament," which
concludes with the observation that "an unemployed jester is nobody's fool."

But most important, the film gives Danny Kaye a role no one else could
have played. For the first time, a Kaye vehicle wasn't warmed-over Harold
Lloyd or imitation anybody. Panama and Frank were able to capture in a
screenplay what Sylvia Fine had been able to capsulize in her comedy songs for
Danny over the years: his gifts for comedy, music, mimicry, pantomime, and
fast-paced patter. They also created for him a completely likable and empathic
character who was worth caring about and laughing with. In *The Court Jester*
Kaye's clowning never interferes with the story line, and one never has the
feeling that his comedy is merely an excuse to counterpoint a romantic subplot
or to pad out an elementary story.

In many ways, this was the zenith of Danny Kaye's film career. As ambitious
as *The Court Jester* was, *Merry Andrew* was not. It was and remains an extremely pleasant film with Danny as an unconventional teacher at a British
boarding school who becomes involved with a traveling circus troupe and falls

in love with its young aerialist (Pier Angeli). The score is undistinguished, and there are no specialty songs by Sylvia Fine.

His next film strayed even further off the beaten path, as Kaye played it straight for the first time on-screen in *Me and the Colonel,* a rather placid adaptation of Franz Werfel's *Jacobowsky and the Colonel,* about a quiet but forthright Jew who flees from the Nazis during World War II with an autocratic colonel (Curt Jurgens) who happens to be anti-Semitic. The humor in this film was low key and cerebral.

In 1959 Kaye returned to Hollywood surroundings but again opted for something unusual: a biographical film that would combine elements of music, comedy, and drama. The result was *The Five Pennies,* directed and co-written by Mel Shavelson, who'd been a contract writer on most of the Goldwyn comedies of the 1940s and who would also create Kaye's next successful comedy, *On the Double.*

Says Shavelson, "Kaye was really different. He was never a stand-up comic. He never depended on words as much as the other comics did. He depended on visual comedy, facial expressions, and vocal tricks, rather than just the content of a joke. (Sylvia Fine's jokes are Danny Kaye jokes in the sense that they're onomatopoeic—they're sound jokes. She likes a sound, a funny word, and she loves puns.) But the thing is, even as Red Nichols in *The Five Pennies,* you had to write Danny Kaye routines into the story line, so what happened is that everybody thinks that Red Nichols was really Danny Kaye, instead of the other way around."

In fact, the most memorable scene of *The Five Pennies* has nothing to do with Kaye's comedy or Shavelson's script: It's a dynamic duet with Danny and Louis Armstrong.

Comedy—pure and unadulterated—was the aim of his next film, *On the Double,* and it happily hit the bull's-eye to become the last really good Danny Kaye vehicle. In this one, as an American GI stationed in England, he is asked to impersonate a British commanding officer whose life has been threatened. The situations are hilarious, but much of the film's comic energy derives from the fact that Danny's peril is convincingly real. His love scenes with Dana Wynter—as the unhappy wife of the real officer—are equally credible. But the comic highlights (aside from some startling double-exposure scenes) come during a frantic chase through a Berlin opera house where Danny disguises first as Adolf Hitler and then as a Dietrich-inspired chanteuse named Fräulein Lily.

Kaye made only one more starring film after *On the Double:* 1963's *The Man From the Diners' Club,* an anachronistically simple slapstick comedy directed by a master of that genre, Frank Tashlin. The problem was a silly script that was particularly ill-suited to Danny's talents.

His only film appearance since that time was as the Ragpicker in Bryan Forbes' unsuccessful adaptation of Jean Giraudoux's allegory *The Madwoman of Chaillot,* with Katharine Hepburn in the title role. As a scruffy-but-wise Greek chorus for the all-star cast, Kaye had little to do and, like the rest of the film, came across much too mild to make a vivid impression.

After limiting himself to occasional special programs, Danny Kaye plunged into television in 1963 with a weekly hour-long variety program, which lasted four years. While it brought him to a wide and appreciative audience, the

Above
Louis Armstrong and Danny do a memorable duet in *The Five Pennies.*

Below
Danny does a dual role for the third time in *On the Double;* Wilfrid Hyde-White
looks on at right.

Danny Kaye as the philosophical Ragpicker in *The Madwoman of Chaillot*.

pressure of creating an hour of new material every week naturally diluted some of the "special" qualities of this gifted artist. He also decided to abandon some of his timeworn specialties and told special-material writer Billy Barnes, "I don't want any fast numbers or double-talk. I don't do that anymore."

Since that time he has drifted in and out of show-business activity, pursuing various hobbies with great intensity and occasionally surfacing for a major enterprise, such as Richard Rodgers' Broadway show *Two By Two* in 1970 and a pair of elaborate television specials in 1976, *Pinocchio* and *Peter Pan,* which confirmed rather ironically the inevitable passage of time. Twenty or thirty years ago, who would have lent more charm and distinction to those leading roles than Danny Kaye, but now he has outgrown them and played, instead, the character roles of Geppetto and Captain Hook.

Because his screen career was so brief, and so sporadic, one could say that he never achieved the status of a great movie clown. But while the quantity of Kaye's film work was small, the impact was great and his achievements were too special to dismiss so summarily.

Some comic artists embrace the camera and create their own universe on-screen—this was true of many great clowns of the silent era. But other comic artists perform for the camera and do not exercise the same kind of total control. This does not diminish the value of their work—it only makes the viewer regret that others could not find a better showcase for their talent. Danny Kaye falls into that category.

He never gave less than one hundred percent, and when the films were his equal, the results were simply glorious.

THE FILMS OF DANNY KAYE

Dime a Dance—Educational Pictures 1937 (two-reel short subject)

Getting an Eyeful—Educational 1938 (short subject)

Cupid Takes a Holiday—Educational 1938 (short subject)

Up in Arms—Goldwyn/RKO 1944

Wonder Man—Goldwyn/RKO 1945

The Kid From Brooklyn—Goldwyn/RKO 1946

The Secret Life of Walter Mitty—Goldwyn/RKO 1947

A Song Is Born—Goldwyn/RKO 1948

The Inspector General—Warner Brothers 1949

On the Riviera—Twentieth Century-Fox 1951

Hans Christian Andersen—Goldwyn/RKO 1952

Knock on Wood—Paramount 1954

White Christmas—Paramount 1954

Assignment Children—Paramount 1955 (UNICEF short subject)

The Court Jester—Paramount 1956

Merry Andrew—M-G-M 1958

Me and the Colonel—Columbia 1958

The Five Pennies—Paramount 1959

On the Double—Paramount 1961

The Man From the Diners' Club—Columbia 1963

The Madwoman of Chaillot—Warner Brothers-7 Arts 1969

Kaye also appeared as a cameo guest in the Warner Brothers film *It's a Great Feeling* (1949).

Red and John Regan in the short
subject *Seeing Red*.

Red sounds off as "The Fox," while
Ann Rutherford stands by in
Whistling in Dixie.

20
RED SKELTON

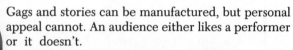

Gags and stories can be manufactured, but personal appeal cannot. An audience either likes a performer or it doesn't.

Red Skelton is one of the most *likable* comedians of all time, and this is an asset far more valuable than any script or piece of material.

There is something instantly appealing about the man. His smile, an almost permanent fixture, seems genuine and sincere, while his eyes add a wistful tinge of melancholy, as if to confirm his role in life as a clown by placing a mask over feelings of sadness and hurt in order to make us laugh. Red seems eager to please, in his live performances just as in his typical movie roles. He wants you to have fun, and when performing live he laughs along with you, reasoning, "Why should the comic be the only guy who's not allowed to laugh?"

When Skelton arrived on the Hollywood scene he seemed destined to carry on the great traditions of screen comedy. He brought a rare combination of visual and verbal agility to his work that would soon put him in a class by himself. Unfortunately, he wound up at M-G-M, a studio that offered everything money could buy except respect for individual comic genius.

Writer Ross Wetzsteon feels that Skelton's entire career has been one of contradiction: "A mime whose greatest success was on the radio. A folk humorist in the years when American entertainment was becoming urban. A vulgar knockabout at a time when American comedy was becoming sophisticated and verbal. A naïve ne'er-do-well in the age of the self-conscious schlemiel. Red Skelton's career is a study in how to miss every trend that comes down the pike."

No amount of obstacles or frustrations could get in the way of Red's enormous talent, however. Whatever feelings one may have of untapped potential in discussing his career, the fact remains that Red Skelton has been a star for nearly forty years—on the stage, in nightclubs, in radio, television, and movies.

His first contact with audiences was at age ten when he joined a medicine show. To young Richard Skelton, it seemed that performing was in his blood (his father, who died before he was born, had been a clown with the Haggenback and Wallace Circus), and he got his training in stock companies, tent shows, burlesque, and vaudeville. He learned how to play an audience.

Then, working in vaudeville during the 1930s, he started to develop material—individual routines that were distinctively his own. When he scored a hit doing a treatise on the different ways people dunked their doughnuts, he realized he was on to something special and followed up with other routines about people's idiosyncrasies. They showed off his pantomimic skill and wiry frame and gave him the kind of material that any audience could identify with. (He developed much of this material with his first wife, Edna, who was his foil, manager, and writer for many years).

It was Red performing these routines that brought him to the big time, first with major vaudeville bookings, then on radio, and then in films. He made his motion-picture debut in RKO's *Having Wonderful Time,* the much laundered version of Arthur Kober's Broadway hit about a resort camp in the Catskill Mountains. In the role of Itchy Faulkner, entertainment director of the camp, he was able to incorporate some of his vaudeville routines verbatim, such as showing the way different people walk up a flight of stairs. But Skelton, billed as Richard, did not make a good impression on the critics or the public, and RKO made no further bid for his services. When Red returned East he starred in a pair of two-reel shorts for Vitaphone in which he performed still more of his own material (in *Seeing Red* he shows different people sitting down, and how people eat corn on the cob; in *The Broadway Buckaroo* he does the classic doughnut bit and shows how people walk, as well as singing "Never Be Rude to a Dude").

When he was signed by M-G-M in 1940, the studio's immediate thought was to assign him "comedy relief" roles in their aviation picture *Flight Command* and in two of the Dr. Kildare films. But Red's first major break came in a grade-B remake of a 1933 film that had starred Ernest Truex, *Whistling in the Dark.* Ace comedy writer Nat Perrin stuck to the original story line but enhanced and updated it with some new twists and a truckload of snappy gag lines for Skelton. More than one observer noted its family resemblance to the "scare comedies" Bob Hope had been making, and doubtless it was those films' success that inspired this one.

Whistling in the Dark is no gem, but it's a very pleasant film, and it served a dual purpose: to lay the groundwork for a pair of even better sequels and to introduce its star to the moviegoing audience in a hand-tailored vehicle. Bosley

Crowther of *The New York Times* responded most favorably: "To the cheerfully swelling list of bright new film comedians you may add the rosy name of one Richard (Red) Skelton. For Metro has really turned up an impressive Bob Hopeful in the person of this jaunty chap.... Mr. Skelton is another of those blithe and easy gag-busters whose careless way with a line is a thing to be greatly enjoyed and whose use of the double-take is a studied accomplishment. When his mind snaps his muscles taut in a moment of dire emergency, when the impact of a threat sinks in after slight delay, he stiffens like a man grabbing hold of a highly charged wire. And his face becomes a mask of comic horror. Mr. Skelton shocks beautifully and often.... To (Mr. Skelton) it is a pleasure to extend a warm welcome.... The screen needs smooth comics like this one."

In retrospect, the *Whistling* films are among Skelton's best screen endeavors, not only because they showcase him so well, but because they are such unpretentious and spirited outings. They benefit from M-G-M gloss but they are not drowned in M-G-M overproduction, and Skelton is not obliged to share his screen time with musical stars or production numbers.

He plays Wally Benton, better known to millions of radio listeners as The Fox, who broadcasts over station WHN for the benefit of Grape-O Mix ("The Tonic for the Chronic"). His radio sleuthing spills over into private life as Wally gets mixed up in real-life murders and mysteries along with his girl-Friday and perennial fiancée, Ann Rutherford. The suspense angle allows for plenty of atmosphere and dangerous elements; *Whistling in Brooklyn* even goes in for Harold Lloyd-ish thrill comedy with Red, Ann, Jean Rogers, and Rags Ragland caught in a freight elevator shaft.

And, courtesy Nat Perrin, the scripts keep Red supplied with an overabundance of one-liners (in *Whistling in the Dark* he's said to be "following in his father's fingerprints," and when he and Ann get a marriage license from Mr. Panky in *Whistling in Dixie,* Red cannot resist asking, "Got a hanky, Panky?").

The *Whistling* films are no classics, but they're consistently diverting and often quite funny. This contrasts with Red's more ambitious M-G-M assignments of the next few years, where he was elevated to star billing with other established studio luminaries but fell back to the task of "comedy relief." *Maisie Gets Her Man* even shoehorned him into an uncomfortable role as a good-natured but doggedly unfunny young comic who teams up with Ann Sothern in vaudeville but can't get over his paralyzing stage fright.

The role had a curious parallel in real life, as director Vincente Minnelli recalls in his autobiography. Minnelli was assigned to pull together a hodge-podge film called *I Dood It,* which was somewhat based on Buster Keaton's M-G-M silent *Spite Marriage.* "It marginally gave me a look at the comedian's psyche, Hollywood style. It wasn't much different from the Broadway version. Red's humor revolved around one-liners and he was unsure of his effectiveness in comedy of the situation. 'I'm not funny,' he complained to Edna, then his wife and manager. She and Red's agent came to look at the rushes. 'You're crazy,' she told him. 'You've never been funnier.' Red proceeded to agonize over all his previous performances. It was a wonder to him that he'd ever gotten this far."

Red Skelton performs his classic "Guzzler's Gin" routine in *Ziegfeld Follies*.

Red is caught by Bill Hall and Jake Harrison in *A Southern Yankee*.

Red had some memorable routines in *Bathing Beauty* (originally titled *Mr. Co-Ed* but rechristened to spotlight Esther Williams), including his now-famous pantomime of a woman getting up in the morning and applying her makeup, plus a ballet class with Red and a host of M-G-M chorines (later reprised as a flashback in *The Clown*). But it was further evidence that M-G-M thought Red was better suited to splashy musicals than his own carefully prepared comedy vehicles. He later appeared in such well-mounted productions as *Neptune's Daughter, Three Little Words, Texas Carnival,* and *Lovely to Look At.*

Filmed before he joined the army but released in 1946, Red's classic "Guzzler's Gin" routine was one of the comic highlights of M-G-M's all-star *Ziegfeld Follies* and happily preserves this great comedy piece on film for all time. Filmed without scenery or "production" in one day and featuring Red with a handful of props, it showed how little he needed in order to get big laughs, and how silly Metro's elephantine productions really were in contrast. Cinematographer George Folsey recalls that when they shot this routine his camera operator laughed so hard he fell on the floor and almost missed getting the end of the skit on film! Retitled "When Television Comes" for this picture, the comic portrait of a commercial pitchman who gets drunk on his own product remains a key part of Skelton's repertoire today.

When Red returned from army service, the studio decided to try a different approach for their comedy star and put him into remakes of two well-worn properties: *The Show-Off* and *Merton of the Movies.* Both had been filmed before and were considered surefire, but they misfired instead. The hero of *The Show-Off* is an obnoxious character, and this didn't serve Red terribly well, while all the possibilities of *Merton* were thrown out the window by a shoddy script that discarded every comic opportunity inherent in the story. The direction of Robert Alton was flat and lifeless, as well.

What Skelton needed was someone who knew comedy, who knew how to make the best use of his talents. The man who volunteered was Buster Keaton, then employed as a gagman at the studio where he had once been a major star. Keaton knew firsthand about M-G-M's insensitivity to comedy crafting, but he couldn't resist giving this a shot. According to Rudi Blesh in *Keaton,* he went to studio chief Louis B. Mayer and said, "Let me take Skelton and work as a small company within Metro—do our stories, our gags, our production, our directing. Use your resources but do it our way—the way I did my best pictures. I'll guarantee you hits. I won't take a cent of salary until they have proved themselves at the box office."

Sadly, Mayer said no, but Keaton did get to work with Skelton on his next M-G-M features, and the results were heartening. The screen credit for directing *A Southern Yankee* and for "comedy consultant" on *The Yellow Cab Man* went to Edward Sedgwick, but Sedgwick was a Keaton colleague and crony, and there was no doubt about who Sedgwick's "consultant" was.

A Southern Yankee is superior Skelton all the way. In fact, its main weakness was spotted right off the bat by Keaton when he was called in to watch a rough cut by producer Jack Cummings. "I told Cummings he had a whale of a story but, in my opinion, they had made a couple of mistakes," Keaton recalled. "One was having Red behave like an imbecile in the opening scenes. As the comedian and leading man, Red lost the audience's sympathy by behaving too stupidly. If you act as screwy as he was doing, the people out front would not care what happened to the character you were playing. They reshot those scenes, toning down Red's nutty behavior and also eliminating some of the noise that marred the opening scene.

"I also contributed the gag in which Red was shown walking between the Union Army and the Confederate Army, with both armies cheering him madly. The reason was that Red was wearing half of a Union Army hat and uniform on the side facing the Northern soldiers and a Southern hat and uniform on the other. In addition he had sewed together the flags of the two opposing sides so that the boys in blue saw a Union flag and the Southerners only the flag of the Confederacy.

"Both sides cheer him wildly until a sudden gust of wind reverses the flag, showing both sides the game he is playing. As Red turns around to straighten the flag they discover his half-and-half uniform."

The Yellow Cab Man is a much more cumbersome and complicated comedy—more than it need have been—but it's first-rate in gags and plotting and includes some of Red's funniest screen moments, as an accident-prone young goof who devotes his life to inventing wacky "safety" devices. Aside from some sight gags, gimmicks, and a chase sequence, the film features a hilarious set piece of Red's first day at driving a cab that builds one laugh on top of another to a memorable climax.

Around this time Red was loaned to Columbia Pictures for another pure-gag comedy, *The Fuller Brush Man,* which reunited him with his *Whistling* director, S. Sylvan Simon, and gave him an action-filled script by Frank Tashlin and Devery Freeman. The film's problem is that there's too much action and silliness and too little Skelton, but it does have some pearly moments: Red pantomiming a typical lady customer for his brushes and getting caught in a wave of atomizers when he tries to sneak through a garden that's being tended.

Skelton's final brush with Buster Keaton was in *Watch the Birdie,* a remake of Keaton's *The Cameraman,* which unfortunately fell flat. His remaining comedies for M-G-M failed to hit the bull's-eye, and Red seemed to find more comfortable surroundings in the lavish musicals instead.

Two of his last pictures for the studio are worth noting because they were so offbeat. *The Clown* is certainly the better of the two, a remake of King Vidor's sentimental drama *The Champ,* which had starred Wallace Beery as a down-and-out prizefighter and Jackie Cooper as his adoring son. Frances Marion's original script was updated and Red was cast as a second-rate comedian whose time has passed and whose irresponsibility makes him his own worst enemy—except in the eyes of his loving son, played by Tim Considine.

Although the story stretches credibility, Skelton's performance is excellent and calls for a wide range of emotions. A crucial scene in which he strikes Considine and then smashes his fist into a glass-framed photo on the wall, crying "I hit my son!," is extremely well played.

This marked the first time that Skelton really let his comic mask drop, and his efforts were well received, even if the film was far from perfect.

For his next picture, M-G-M decided to give Skelton yet another unusual task: playing low-key situation comedy. *Half a Hero* was written by Max Shulman and directed by Don Weis, the team that had recently enjoyed success

Dick Wessel, Red, and Janet Blair in *The Fuller Brush Man*.

Musical-comedy Red with Howard Keel, Kathryn Grayson, and Marge Champion in *Lovely to Look At*.

Red and Janet Blair in his last starring feature, *Public Pigeon No. 1*.

Red Skelton takes flight in *Those Magnificent Men in Their Flying Machines.*

with *The Affairs of Dobie Gillis.* But *Half a Hero* has none of that film's cleverness or buoyancy. A poor man's *Mr. Blandings Builds His Dream House,* it recounts Red's adventures in suburbia with more cynicism and frustration than humor.

Yet here as in all of Skelton's misfires, one cannot place the blame on his shoulders. He gives his all in every film and turns in a creditable performance. But Skelton did not participate behind the scenes as he later did in television, and consequently he was left in the hands of constantly shifting studio personnel. There was no Skelton "unit," as Keaton had proposed, and the result was chaos.

One is tempted to say that perhaps live performance (on radio, stage, and TV) was better suited to Skelton's talents and temperament; he certainly enjoyed more consistent success in these media than he did in films. But one cannot dismiss his film career so casually.

Even his brief pantomimes in *Those Magnificent Men in Their Flying*

Machines rank as outstanding screen comedy and put not only the rest of that film but much of the competition of the 1960s to shame.

Perhaps some of Skelton's checkered film career can be attributed to his own indifference or insecurities. He is a quixotically complex man who admits "I'm even an enigma to myself," and after years of praise for his pantomimes remarked, "You know, if I gave up television and worked on the things I do best —as Marcel [Marceau] told me to do—I'd be remembered."

But Red Skelton will be remembered for his films as well, because film can freeze moments in time and capture the magic of an inspired clown at work, if only in fleeting moments. The talent is what counts, and Red Skelton has always had so much to give.

THE FILMS OF RED SKELTON

Having Wonderful Time—RKO 1938

The Broadway Buckaroo— Vitaphone-Warner Brothers 1939 (short subject)

Seeing Red—Vitaphone-Warner Brothers 1939 (short subject)

Flight Command—M-G-M 1940

The People vs. Dr. Kildare—M-G-M 1941

Whistling in the Dark—M-G-M 1941 (his first starring role)

Dr. Kildare's Wedding Day—M-G-M 1941

Lady Be Good—M-G-M 1941

Ship Ahoy—M-G-M 1942

Maisie Gets Her Man—M-G-M 1942

Panama Hattie—M-G-M 1942

Whistling in Dixie—M-G-M 1942

Du Barry Was a Lady—M-G-M 1943

Thousands Cheer—M-G-M 1943

I Dood It—M-G-M 1943

Whistling in Brooklyn—M-G-M 1944

Bathing Beauty—M-G-M 1944

Ziegfeld Follies—M-G-M 1946

The Show-Off—M-G-M 1947

Merton of the Movies—M-G-M 1947

The Fuller Brush Man—Columbia 1948

A Southern Yankee—M-G-M *1948*

Neptune's Daughter—M-G-M 1949

The Yellow Cab Man—M-G-M 1950

Duchess of Idaho—M-G-M 1950 (guest appearance)

Three Little Words—M-G-M 1950

The Fuller Brush Girl—Columbia 1950 (guest appearance)

Watch the Birdie—M-G-M 1950

Excuse My Dust—M-G-M 1951

Texas Carnival—M-G-M 1951

Lovely to Look At—M-G-M 1952

The Clown—M-G-M 1953

Half a Hero—M-G-M 1953

The Great Diamond Robbery— M-G-M 1953

Susan Slept Here—RKO 1954 (guest appearance)

Around the World in Eighty Days— United Artists 1956

Public Pigeon No. 1—RKO 1957

Ocean's Eleven—Warner Brothers 1960 (guest appearance)

Those Magnificent Men in Their Flying Machines—Twentieth Century-Fox 1965

As they were: Dean Martin and Jerry Lewis.

Jerry and Eddie Mayehoff in *That's My Boy*.

21
JERRY LEWIS

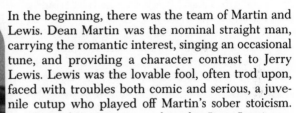

In the beginning, there was the team of Martin and Lewis. Dean Martin was the nominal straight man, carrying the romantic interest, singing an occasional tune, and providing a character contrast to Jerry Lewis. Lewis was the lovable fool, often trod upon, faced with troubles both comic and serious, a juvenile cutup who played off Martin's sober stoicism.

From the outset it was clear that Jerry Lewis was the comedy star of this comedy team, although Dean Martin's low-key participation was also important. Lewis' antics in such films as *At War With the Army, Sailor Beware, Living It Up, You're Never Too Young,* and *Artists and Models* were memorable. His comedy was, and is, gut-funny. He is not afraid to be silly, to appeal to the child in all of us. In point of fact, director Norman Taurog, who worked with Jerry many times, has said that directing him was tantamount to directing a child!

As the years passed, Lewis became more ambitious. Tempers and egos flared, bringing an end to the Martin and Lewis team. Jerry immediately scored a hit on his own, in such films as *The Delicate Delinquent, The Sad Sack, Rock-a-Bye Baby,* and *Don't Give Up the Ship.* His directors included such comedy pros as Taurog and Frank Tashlin.

Then Jerry Lewis decided that he wanted to write and direct his own films, to become "the total film maker." The difference in his films was obvious: they were ponderous where once they were light and airy, pretentious where once they had been so unassuming. Although Lewis was concerned with his characterization, he no longer supported it with a strong story line, preferring blackout gags instead. Worst of all, especially to a young and nonanalytical viewer, his films were simply not as funny as those that others had written and directed for him.

Not so, say Lewis buffs and auteurists. His earlier films were conventional Hollywood comedies, while the Lewis-made projects are complex, brilliant. But even Andrew Sarris, who agrees with that basic thesis, says that Lewis "has never put one brilliant comedy together from fade-in to fade-out." The French, who remain Lewis' biggest supporters, apparently don't care about the sloppy construction of his films or the arid stretches between funny scenes or the banal, sentimental, self-indulgent moments of "pathos" or sentiment that Lewis includes in most of his works. They also don't seem to care that so many of his films are not funny. But as Sarris points out, "The argument about laughs is irrelevant because laughter is less decisive in this instance than love. The French critics love Jerry Lewis. Many Americans do not."

This wasn't always the case. When Martin and Lewis burst on the scene (and the term is used advisedly) in the late 1940s, they took the country by storm. Films and television brought them to a national audience, and by the early 1950s they were the hottest act in show business, bar none.

Jerry was the ultimate schnook, the lovable little guy who rose to moments of glory when indulging in childhood prankishness. This in fact was the basis of his act with Dean Martin, in which he would cavort around the stage while Dean tried to sing a straight rendition of some song. This direct and spontaneous clowning was nicely captured in some of their earliest films: in the nightclub sequence of *My Friend Irma,* their first movie, in which Dean recruits Jerry to provide accompaniment for his rendition of "The Donkey Serenade," and in *Sailor Beware,* in which Jerry fools around with a group of singers who are supposed to provide the backup vocals for Dean's version of "Today, Tomorrow, Forever."

The secret of Jerry's appeal at this time was pinpointed by Steve Allen in his book *The Funny Men:* "Lewis' advantage over most of his competitors lies in his exceptionally comic appearance. With his close-cropped, monkeyish hairdo, his limber, impish face and his thin, angular body, he is equipped with a vital plus that makes his success as a clown seem to have been predestined. . . .

"Another of Jerry's assets is his youthful, almost childish appearance. It allows him to indulge completely in the physical lunacies that have become his stock in trade. Milton Berle or Red Skelton may also take a pie in the face or a fall into an orchestra pit, but somehow these older men have a certain touch of stature and dignity under their clown's clothes. . . . When Jerry Lewis performs these same actions he does so with no dignity whatsoever. He is a *complete* buffoon, the hundred-per-cent fool, of whom insanity is expected and hoped for. There is still much of the child in Jerry; on stage he does not *revert* to idiocy, he sometimes seems to *be* an idiot, and the effect is wonderfully, heart-warmingly hilarious."

Allen's book was writtten in 1956, the fateful year that Martin and Lewis split up and went their separate ways. The ensuing years have only served to underscore how right Allen was in his assessment of Lewis' appeal . . . because year by year, Lewis has alienated his once-enormous audience by straying from that path.

In one respect Lewis was powerless: He got older. Even by the mid-1950s his face filled out and he was no longer an angular juvenile.

Then Jerry became concerned with showing audiences the serious side of his personality, the wistfulness and pathos underneath the goofy facade. What's more, he injured his movie credibility as the lovable kid by appearing on television "au naturel" as Jerry Lewis, savvy show-biz comic with serious aspirations. It became difficult to reconcile this man with the screen personality he continued to project, a problem earlier generations of comics never had to worry about. Perhaps if Chaplin and Keaton had appeared on TV talk shows, it would have been tough to believe in *their* characters so completely.

Thus, by the mid-1960s, Jerry Lewis was neither youthful, funny looking, nor believable as the "hundred-per-cent fool" Steve Allen described so well.

Not that this destroyed his ability to get laughs. Jerry's most surefire shtick was the creation of chaos, and its frequent use accounted for the funniest moments in his films. In fact, it was chosen to herald his entrance in the first solo Jerry Lewis film, *The Delicate Delinquent,* where the electric tension of an imminent rumble between two gangs is suddenly interrupted by Jerry barging through an alley door and tripping into a mountain of clanging garbage cans.

Because such blunders were his stock-in-trade, with Dean Martin gone, someone else had to represent order and authority in Jerry's films, and this task fell to a succession of stalwart character actors. When Lewis made his own films he used a "stock company" of players, including Milton Frome, Del Moore, Buddy Lester, and Kathleen Freeman, to act as foils for his disruptive humor.

One of the most felicitous collaborations was that of Lewis and director-writer Frank Tashlin. A former cartoonist and animation director, Tashlin used Lewis as a living cartoon and devised incredible sight gags and slapstick sequences for him in such films as *Rock-a-Bye Baby, The Geisha Boy, It's Only Money,* and *The Disorderly Orderly* (there's a wild gag in the last film where Jerry, bound in a straitjacket and crawling along the ground as fast as he can, is passed by an animated-cartoon snail!).

Lewis refers to Tashlin as "my teacher," but whatever he may have learned in terms of technical matters and the engineering of gags, he assimilated into his own very personal and distinctive style. As a former full-time scenarist, Tashlin knew the importance of film construction, which Jerry never seemed to care that much about. Tashlin also knew how to build a comedy sequence and pile one laugh on top of another, while Jerry preferred isolated, individual gags.

There's another quality lacking in Lewis' films that especially stands out to Norman Taurog, who directed him six times: "Taste. If you have taste that covers everything. He tried to prove a gag to me three times and each time it never worked. And I told him the first time, second time, third time. That is, a little old lady comes up to him; he looks at her and says, 'You're beautiful,' takes her and bends over away from the camera, and looks like he's kissing her

Jerry in *Living It Up*.

With Dean Martin and Barbara Bates in *The Caddy*.

the greatest soul kiss in the world, and straightens her up. I said, 'Jerry, it's distasteful, it's rotten, nobody will laugh at it.' He tried it three times and the third time he said, 'You're right, they ain't gonna laugh at it.' It had to take three times to tell that. And yet, he has magnificent taste in things about himself—but not about pictures."

Taurog's anecdote indicates exactly what happened to Jerry Lewis' films once he took hold of the reins as director, writer, and often producer as well: There was no longer anyone to veto an idea, so Jerry indulged his every whim, allowed Jerry the comedian to milk gags far beyond endurance, and discarded conventional notions of good taste, modesty, continuity, and—oddly enough—humor.

Lewis seems more interested in acting out his emotional problems than in getting a laugh. Even his gags are set up in such a way that they vitiate laughter, while calling attention to their cleverness or intricacy. It's ironic that these qualities are precisely what attract so many French and American film buffs to Lewis, while turning off so many people who just want to enjoy a funny film.

Most observers regard *The Nutty Professor* as Lewis' masterpiece, so it is worth examining in detail. Jerry plays a clumsy, chipmunk-faced science professor, Julius Kelp, who inadvertently prepares a potion that transforms him into a suave, swinging performer (in a Sy Devore suit) named Buddy Love who has everything Kelp lacks—confidence, sex appeal, and nerve.

Of its creation, Lewis told Axel Madsen, "The truth is that I had written the story synopsis ten years before, but I was afraid of the subject. I was too young to go near it. You might say I lacked maturity. If I have matured at all since then it is because I now realize that everyone is two people, but I loved the film because I thought it was everybody's story, only done in a glamorous Hollywood fashion."

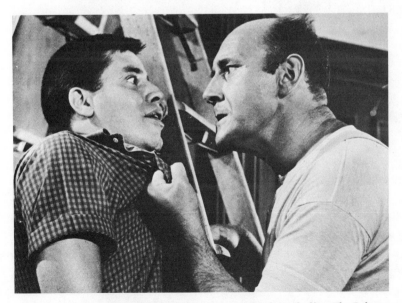

Jerry is threatened by Milton Frome in his first solo film, *The Delicate Delinquent*.

Many people believed that the character of Buddy Love was based on Dean Martin, and that the film, in Charles Michener's words, was "an exorcism ... of his feelings about [his] ex-partner." In an interview for *Focus*, Lewis replied, "I wasn't portraying the role of any one person; I was portraying about six people. It's interesting that (friends picked it up first) they thought I was doing something on Dean. So ludicrous. That was very, very close to the time we broke, at least closer than it is now; and that was kind of unfair because if that's what I was doing, I'd *say* that's what I did. But I was writing about five

Director Jerry Lewis rides the camera crane to make a shot for *The Errand Boy;* notice that the name of his studio has been altered for the occasion.

Jerry Lewis as *The Nutty Professor*.

Jerry in one of his seven roles in *The Family Jewels,* with Sebastian Cabot.

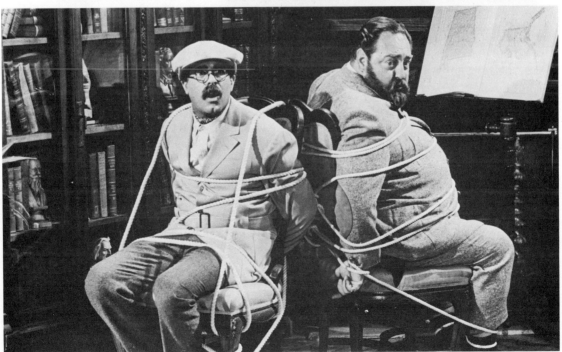

or six people that are like that. A small portion of Dean's arrogance might have been there—subconscious, again, I was not aware of it. . . . It was the one time that I had trouble directing Jerry—that was the only time—when the objectivity and all of the science and everything I had expounded upon earlier really didn't work for him."

The Nutty Professor is a fascinating film because it reveals so many facets of Lewis' ego. It contains a fair amount of funny and inventive gags, but in typical Lewis fashion they are spotlighted and accentuated in such a way as to undermine their natural humor. Lewis does not recognize the value of a "throwaway." It is not enough to do the gag, he must call our attention to it lest we miss the point. (Seeing ten men unintentionally standing in a formation like bowling pins, Jerry obligingly "bowls" them down, with appropriate sound effects. There is no purpose, no context, no follow-up for the gag. He just felt like doing it, and he did.)

More importantly, Lewis somehow feels that his contorted professor character (who turns up again in other films) is sympathetic, a Chaplinesque outcast of society who wins our hearts. As he delivers his final speech about the foolishness of trying to be something you're not, he brings tears to Stella Stevens' eyes and obviously expects us to feel the same way. But Lewis' professor is not an empathic character; he is a grotesque, performing an unreal charade in artificial surroundings.

The single funniest moment in *The Nutty Professor*—which, after all, is supposed to be a comedy—is the final shot of the film, which in its lunatic way crystallizes the kind of humor Jerry Lewis does best. It uses the film medium more imaginatively than all the self-conscious sequences that have preceded it, yet it harks back to Jerry's most tried-and-true performing shtick: Taking a final bow with the rest of the film's cast, Jerry walks toward the camera, trips, and, flailing wildly, falls into the camera lens, "breaking" the film and bringing the picture to an abrupt end.

Here, for one moment, Jerry the comedian and Jerry the filmmaker produce a perfect collaboration—and a perfect laugh. It's too bad someone with such comic ability can't harness that talent more often.

The Nutty Professor was based on the idea that everyone is two people, and Jerry Lewis is a perfect example. Never was this duality more apparent than in his "comeback" movie, *Hardly Working*, which finally saw U.S. release in 1981 after sitting on a shelf for more than a year. Here, an older Jerry than we're accustomed to seeing reveals the terrible conflict that brews inside him: at one moment, he'll do his time-worn *schlemeil* routines, as if he were "that kid" again (though he no longer looks it), then he'll abruptly change masks and ask us to deal with him as a serious human being. Even while playing an unemployed circus clown in this film, he wears his Cartier watch and gold jewelry on-screen, as if to say, "Look, folks, I may be *playing* a jerk, but I'm really Jerry Lewis, wealthy and successful entertainer/filmmaker."

True, this makes Lewis' work more intriguing, from a psychological standpoint, than the films of a less challenging performer. But it doesn't do anything for the comedy quotient; *Hardly Working* has hardly any laughs.

The French people don't care; but then, as they say, *chacun à son goût.*

THE FILMS OF JERRY LEWIS

WITH DEAN MARTIN

My Friend Irma—Paramount 1949
My Friend Irma Goes West—
   Paramount 1950
At War With the Army—Paramount
   1951
That's My Boy—Paramount 1951
Sailor Beware—Paramount 1952
Jumping Jacks—Paramount 1952
Road to Bali—Paramount 1952 (guest
   appearance)
The Stooge—Paramount 1953
Scared Stiff—Paramount 1953
The Caddy—Paramount 1953
Money From Home—Paramount 1954
Living It Up—Paramount 1954
Three Ring Circus—Paramount 1954
You're Never Too Young—Paramount
   1955
Artists and Models—Paramount 1955
Pardners—Paramount 1956
Hollywood or Bust—Paramount 1956

SOLO STARRING FILMS

The Delicate Delinquent—Paramount
   1957
The Sad Sack—Paramount 1958
Rock-a-Bye Baby—Paramount 1958
The Geisha Boy—Paramount 1958
Don't Give Up the Ship—Paramount
   1959
Li'l Abner—Paramount 1959 (guest
   appearance)
Visit to a Small Planet—Paramount
   1960
The Bellboy—Paramount 1960
   (directed and written by Lewis)

Cinderfella—Paramount 1960
The Ladies' Man—Paramount 1961
   (directed and written by Lewis)
The Errand Boy—Paramount 1961
   (directed and written by Lewis)
It's Only Money—Paramount 1962
It's a Mad, Mad, Mad, Mad World—
   United Artists 1963 (guest
   appearance)
The Nutty Professor—Paramount
   1963 (directed and written by
   Lewis)
Who's Minding the Store?—
   Paramount 1963
The Patsy—Paramount 1964 (directed
   and written by Lewis)
The Disorderly Orderly—Paramount
   1964
The Family Jewels—Paramount 1965
   (directed and written by Lewis)
Boeing-Boeing—Paramount 1965
Three on a Couch—Columbia 1966
   (directed by Lewis)
Way, Way Out!—Twentieth
   Century-Fox 1966
The Big Mouth—Columbia 1967
   (directed and written by Lewis)
*Don't Raise the Bridge, Lower the
   River*—Columbia 1968
Hook, Line and Sinker—Columbia
   1969
Which Way to the Front?—Warner
   Brothers 1970 (directed by Lewis)
The Day the Clown Cried—
   unreleased (directed and written by
   Lewis)
Hardly Working—Twentieth
   Century-Fox 1981 (completed 1979)
King of Comedy—Twentieth Century-
   Fox 1981

Most of Lewis' screenplays in the 1960s were co-written by Bill Richmond.
Jerry Lewis also appeared with Dean Martin in a 1952 Columbia "Screen Snapshots" short, *Hollywood Fun Festival*, which was comprised of informal footage
taken over several years' time in Hollywood.

Woody and China Lee in one of the saner interludes during *What's Up, Tiger Lily?*

22

WOODY ALLEN

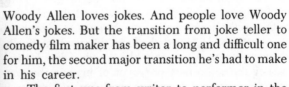 Woody Allen loves jokes. And people love Woody Allen's jokes. But the transition from joke teller to comedy film maker has been a long and difficult one for him, the second major transition he's had to make in his career.

The first was from writer to performer in the early 1960s. Having earned a successful living as a comedy writer for such television stars as Sid Caesar, Garry Moore, and Art Carney since his late teens, he was comfortable in that niche and desperately uncertain of himself as a potential nightclub comedian. Manager Charles Joffe recalled of his nightclub debut, "Woody was just terrible. Crippled with fear, he'd come on the floor in a cold sweat, trying to hide his face."

One early lesson that Woody learned was the difference between written comedy and spoken comedy. "I thought that if S. J. Perelman went out and read, say, 'No Starch in the dhoti, s'il vous plaît,' they're going to howl. But that's not what it is at all; it's that the jokes become a vehicle for the person to display a personality or an attitude, just like Bob Hope. You're laughing not at the jokes but at a guy who's looking at Arnold Palmer and saying, 'He's one of my best pupils.' You're laughing at character all the time. I had it backwards. I was totally oriented as a writer."

Gradually, Woody developed confidence at the microphone and with it came a comic personality that made his word portraits uniquely hilarious. As

227

funny as his jokes and stories were, they could not be told by anyone else; they sprang from his individual character, and this character propelled him to success.

His first brush with the movie world came in 1964 when he was signed to write and appear in *What's New, Pussycat?* But so much tampering was done with his script that Woody has always disavowed the picture.

His next experience was even more unusual: He was approached to dub a comedy sound track onto a slick, silly Japanese James Bond-type feature. Woody gleefully accepted, and set to work with a group of friends to create dialogue as incongruous as possible to match the actions on-screen. The Japanese hero was renamed Phil Moskowitz, and his secret-agent capers were said to be in pursuit of a stolen egg-salad recipe! There is absolutely no reason why *What's Up, Tiger Lily?* should be so good. It's a one-joke idea, and a rather sophomoric joke at that. But logic aside, it's uproariously funny, and its contagious silliness defies you not to laugh.

It would be another three years before Woody got a chance to make his first full-fledged film as director, writer, and star, *Take the Money and Run.* Enjoyed by critics and audiences alike, it illustrates Allen's problem in translating jokes to film. One suspects that this must have been an excruciatingly funny script to *read*, but too many of the gags just don't play on the screen. Thus, one is *impressed* with the brilliance of a gag during the prison-camp sequence, in which for punishment Allen is cruelly sentenced to three days in a sweatbox with an insurance salesman, but one *laughs* when his mother and father, to avoid disgrace while being interviewed about their son, don Halloween glasses with nose and moustache attachments to obscure their faces.

Fortunately, Woody had one thing automatically going in his favor: No one delivers Woody Allen jokes like Woody Allen. He is, like Robert Benchley in an earlier time, the best purveyor of his own humor, and as soon as he walks on-screen, the audience is ready to laugh. This can make up for an awful lot of flat punch lines.

From the outset, Woody was unfazed by the mechanics of making movies. "It's what you say, not how you say it," he maintained. "If you have an unfunny line, it doesn't matter how it looks; it won't make any difference." And from the start, he brought a lifetime of passionate moviegoing to bear on his comedy ideas; *Take the Money and Run* incorporates a fair share of movie parody, particularly in the prison-camp sequences.

But there's no doubt that a bigger budget gave Woody the opportunity to create handsomer, better-crafted films, and his work has improved cinematically from one project to the next. "I've gotten more confidence in my film making," he recently told Bernard Drew, "in my knowledge of the technical end of it. If I look at *Take the Money and Run,* and then *Annie Hall,* even I can feel I've become much more skilled, technically."

And, of course, technical confidence has gone hand in hand with a better understanding of what constitutes film comedy, as opposed to a joke committed to film.

Bananas has a firmer grip on screen technique, although it has its share of "clever" gags that don't pay off, as when Miss America, testifying at a trial,

Woody attempts a holdup in *Take the Money and Run.*

bursts into a rendition of "Caro Home" as if she were back at the talent trails of a beauty contest. Compare this with the belly laugh of a gag that works entirely because of the way it's filmed: The camera follows Woody along a New York sidewalk in a continuous, unbroken tracking shot as he "guides" a car into a parking space so enthusiastically that the car crashes into the one behind it. As Moe Howard once said, "People want to laugh with their mouths, not their minds."

Nowhere is the contrast between Woody in control and Woody out of control greater than in his two films of 1972, *Play It Again, Sam* (which he wrote and starred in but did not direct) and *Everything You Always Wanted to Know About Sex,* for which he was completely responsible.

Sex, a multi-episode film, is brilliantly directed, with each segment treated in a different style, enhanced by fluid photography and ingenious art direction. The period flavor of the opening segment, laid in medieval England, is much more vivid and authentic than that of many a "serious" film. The segment spoofing Italian movies crystallizes Allen's almost unique penchant for cinematic satire (he calls it "the most fun I've had . . . because I could just come in and not think about anything except what is the fanciest, the best shot I can make with the camera"). In short, *Sex* is the work of a talent laced with genius.

Yet it is not nearly so funny as *Play It Again, Sam.*

Based on his own Broadway play, *Sam* is a neatly contrived set piece about

When visiting a foreign dictator, don't forget to bring a cake: Woody and Carlos Montalban in *Bananas*.

Diane Keaton and Woody reenact the final scene of *Casablanca* in *Play It Again, Sam*.

Woody battles with mad scientist John Carradine in *Everything You Always Wanted to Know About Sex But Were Afraid to Ask.*

Woody Allen in *Sleeper.*

a movie-mad neurotic (played, inevitably, by Woody), abandoned by his wife who, in his desperate attempt to pull himself together, falls in love with the wife of his best friend. His counselor in these amorous pursuits is his idol Humphrey Bogart, whom he tries to emulate with catastrophic results.

Allen has explained that the major difference with Sam is that "with a play you write characters. *Sam* was a play made into a film that will always be a good story." And he admits, "It's a more popular taste" than his usual work. But this goes beyond appealing to the masses. *Play It Again, Sam* is a clever, original, and consistently funny film, even though it is more conventional than the innovative but hit-or-miss *Sex* opus.

The problem is one of credibility. *Play It Again, Sam* teeters on the edge of truth, managing to be poignantly real when it wants to be and outrageously unreal when the situation calls for it. One can readily identify with Woody's character—particularly in the hilarious scene in which he makes a shambles of a blind date by tripping over, spilling, or breaking practically everything in his apartment while trying to act nonchalant.

In *Sex,* Allen tosses off all conventions and lets his imagination run wild, straying so far from reality that there is nothing tangible for the audience to grab on to. For example, there is an elaborate mad-scientist spoof, in which Woody and a girl reporter go to visit an eminent sex researcher, played by John Carradine. There is some obvious humor at the outset (the doctor mutters, "They called me mad at Masters and Johnson's") before going into Carradine's bizarre basement laboratory, where he proudly displays some of his current experiments, such as a man trying to have sexual relations with a six-foot rye bread. Then, in a burst of activity, Carradine tries to trap the girl reporter into becoming his next victim. Allen tries to ward him off and sets off a fire. He and the girl flee from the house, which explodes behind them, revealing the most fiendish of Carradine's projects: a giant breast, the size of a building. Slowly, it lumbers forward and starts a rampage over the countryside, destroying everything in its path. Allen goes to work with the State Police, assuring them, "Believe me, I know how to handle tits." He finally lures the giant mammary onto a huge open field, where it is captured with an elephantine brassiere.

One cannot help but admire the mind that conceives such inspired nonsense, and it is reassuring to know that there is someone willing to let this kind of comic mind run free. But this whole sequence draws few laughs, because it isn't really all that funny; in fact, like many of Allen's film gags, it is funnier when described than when seen firsthand. There is nothing inherently funny about the idea of a man having relations with a rye bread, except in the absurdity of *saying* it. Actually watching it on the screen is taking the joke one step too far, making what may be funny in abstract terms unfunny in three dimensions; it is too real to be amusing.

Woody's next film, *Sleeper,* is even more elaborate in its trappings but simpler in its goals: "It's exactly the kind of picture that I used to see as a kid and love," he explained, a broad, fast-moving comedy based on visual gags and jokes. It bears all the virtues and faults of Allen's earlier films. There are some wonderful visual ideas, many of them pleasing echoes of silent comedy, with Woody dangling out a window at the end of a long reel of tape, smashing a plate of gooey food into an adversary's face, contending with a cake batter that grows to monstrous proportions, trying to operate a flying machine, pretending to be a robot, and engaging in various chase scenes. But in many ways the apotheosis of this homage to an earlier style of laugh making is a sequence involving a field of giant vegetables. Woody tries to steal an eight-foot banana and has just finished unpeeling the mammoth specimen when a supervisor comes after him. What happens then is so obvious that one doesn't even consider the possibility of its occurring: Both Woody and his pursuer slip on the giant banana peel!

In our comedy-starved times, Woody Allen's films have been greeted with critical huzzahs from the very beginning, and these writers seem to find more to praise in each successive release. *Love and Death* was hailed as a brilliant step toward Woody's maturity as a film humorist, probably because of its Bergman-inspired spoofery and intellectual references. But more than one comedy buff looked twice and perceived underneath a vague resemblance to such Bob Hope comedies of the 1940s as *Monsieur Beaucaire!*

While Woody hasn't commented directly on that point, he did tell his chronicler Eric Lax about his devotion to Hope. "It's everything I can do at certain times not to actually do him. It's hard to tell when I do, because I'm so unlike him physically and in tone of voice, but once you know I do it, it's absolutely unmistakable. You've got to go by his older movies. He had those sort of snotty one-liners that I always liked." Of course, Woody *did* do his Hope impression in the opening segment of *Sex,* as a Court Jester, and it is unmistakable when he calls on the Hope personality again in *Love and Death* to make coward jokes, talk directly to the audience, and make fun of his supposed sexual prowess.

Woody's personality, as the neurotic with a sense of humor, had become so well known by the 1970s that casting him as the main character in *The Front,* a script by Walter Bernstein about the 1950s witch-hunt era, seemed a natural. *New York Times* critic Vincent Canby called the idea "an inspiration," as Woody's likable nebbish character served to illustrate the comedy and tragedy of this blacklist period better than any dramatic actor could hope to do.

It remained to see what Woody Allen would turn to next. *The Front* had been a worthwhile venture that didn't require his writing or directing talents. But what about his growth in those areas? Would each new film be another uneven mixture of highs and lows—inventive comedy scenes interspersed with stale jokes?

Woody Allen responded in 1977 with *Annie Hall.* A critic has called it his "breakthrough film" and that is the best way to describe it. It is tantamount to a butterfly emerging from its cocoon, for *Annie Hall* presents Woody the actor, Woody the writer, Woody the film maker at the peak of his powers. The film has purpose; it has heart; its gags make sense and have a place in the context of the narrative. As for Woody the performer, he has never been more human or likable—and behold, being more credible doesn't make him any less funny. He can still toss off a line like "I've been seeing an analyst just fifteen years— one more year and I go to Lourdes," but he isn't shoving it into a scene where it's superfluous and spoken just for the sake of a laugh. He can tell a story and set a mood but still infuse the film with ingenious visual gags from *Strange*

Interlude-like subtitles during a conversation to sneezing into a friend's precious container of cocaine.

Woody Allen has always been funny...but the film comedians we cherish and remember are those who deal in something more than jokes. With *Annie Hall*, Woody Allen showed us that he had something more to offer. His efforts were rewarded with no less than *four* Academy Awards—Best Picture, Best Direction, Best Original Screenplay (with Marshall Brickman), and Best Actress (Diane Keaton—incredible recognition for *any* screen comedy).

Obviously, this would be a tough act to follow. The three films that did follow *Annie Hall* took Woody Allen into new and often unexpected directions.

Interiors was his first attempt at a completely serious film—in some eyes, deadly serious. A story of torment, anguish, and frustration in a wasp-y family, it resembles nothing so much as an Ingmar Bergman film. Bergman being one of Woody's heroes, the resemblance was not coincidental.

Manhattan marked a return to *Annie Hall* turf, with the emphasis on milieu and characterization instead of comic situations. Strikingly photographed in black and white, it once again plumbed semi-autobiographical ideas and attitudes in a funny way—with Woody's involvement with teenaged Mariel Hemingway providing a memorable and bittersweet finale.

One observer criticized Allen at this juncture for narrowing his focus with each successive film, leading to speculation that his next work might take place exclusively inside his apartment.

While that wasn't the case, *Stardust Memories* did turn its attention to a facet of Woody Allen that a majority of critics and customers rejected: the ungrateful celebrity. As a successful filmmaker coerced into attending a weekend seminar, Woody spends most of his time in the film having to contend with sycophants, would-be advisors, cloying fans, groupies, former acquaintances, and obnoxious opportunists who want something from him.

Sardonic and accurate in his portrayals, Allen nonetheless offended a great many people with this film. Cries of "how dare he turn on the fans who made him a success" could be heard (and read) across the country. Apparently, these people simply didn't like the way they were depicted on-screen. The film's real concern was Allen's inability to deal with his success—and not just from a standpoint of fan relations. In fact, he is almost unfailingly patient with the people who press against him in the film. He even spoofs the studio executives who want to change his moody, symbolic screen drama (a reference, one presumes, to *Interiors*.)

But most viewers received *Stardust Memories* with unbridled hostility, and echoed the sentiments of one fan in the film who tells Woody how much she likes his movies—especially the early, funny ones.

The truth is, Woody Allen could probably make hilarious films with one eye shut and one hand tied behind his back. But he doesn't want to do that kind of film right now, and he has earned the artistic freedom to do as he pleases. We are witnessing the evolution of an artist who is growing and changing with each passing year.

Surely his enormous comic gifts are not put aside forever. When Woody Allen finds a way of using them—without feeling that he's merely repeating himself—he will probably scale new heights of comedy. It's just possible that the best is yet to come.

Woody Allen and Diane Keaton in *Annie Hall*.

THE FILMS OF WOODY ALLEN

What's New, Pussycat?—United Artists 1965 (written by Allen)

What's Up, Tiger Lily?—American International 1966 (written by Allen)

Take the Money and Run—Cinerama 1969 (directed and written by Allen)

Bananas—United Artists 1971 (directed and written by Allen)

Everything You Always Wanted to Know About Sex But Were Afraid to Ask— United Artists 1972 (directed and written by Allen)

Play It Again, Sam—Paramount 1972 (written by Allen)

Sleeper—United Artists 1973 (directed and written by Allen)

Love and Death—United Artists 1975 (directed and written by Allen)

The Front—Columbia 1976

Annie Hall—United Artists 1977 (directed and written by Allen)

Interiors—United Artists 1977

Manhattan—United Artists 1979

Stardust Memories—United Artists 1980

Most of Allen's screenplays have been written in collaboration with either Mickey Rose or Marshall Brickman.

INDEX

Page numbers in italics refer to photographs.